Routledge Revivals

The Theory and Practice of Neutrality in the Twentieth Century

Originally published in 1970 *The Theory and Practice of Neutrality in the Twentieth Century* documents the various shapes and forms that neutrality has taken. The most important are neutralization, traditional neutrality, ad hoc neutrality and non-alignment. Each of these terms is carefully defined and illustrated by documents running from the beginning of this century to the late 1960s. This enables students to judge for themselves whether neutrality can again become, as it was in the past, an honourable convenience, or whether, except in so far as it contributes to mediation and peacekeeping, it is an anachronism.

The Theory and Practice of Neutrality in the Twentieth Century

Roderick Ogley

Routledge
Taylor & Francis Group

First published in 1970
by Routledge & Kegan Paul Ltd

This edition first published in 2022 by Routledge
4 Park Square, Milton Park, Abingdon, Oxon, OX14 4RN
and by Routledge
605 Third Avenue, New York, NY 10158

Routledge is an imprint of the Taylor & Francis Group, an informa business

ISBN 13: 978-1-032-32309-1 (hbk)
ISBN 13: 978-1-003-31439-4 (ebk)
ISBN 13: 978-1-032-32348-0 (pbk)
Book DOI 10.4324/978-1-032-32309-1

The Theory and Practice of Neutrality in the Twentieth Century

Roderick Ogley

Lecturer in International Relations
the University of Sussex

LONDON
ROUTLEDGE & KEGAN PAUL

First published 1970
by Routledge & Kegan Paul Limited
Broadway House, 68–74, Carter Lane
London, E.C.4.

Printed in Great Britain
by C. Tinling & Co. Ltd
London and Prescot

ISBN 0 7100 6828 X

Contents

General Editor's Preface

The World Studies Series is designed to make a new and important contribution to the study of modern history. Each volume in the Series will provide students in sixth forms, Colleges of Education and Universities with a range of contemporary material drawn from many sources, not only from official and semi-official records, but also from contemporary historical writing from reliable journals. The material is selected and introduced by a scholar who establishes the context of his subject and suggests possible lines of discussion and inquiry that can accompany a study of the documents.

Through these volumes the student can learn how to read and assess historical documents. He will see how the contemporary historian works and how historical judgments are formed. He will learn to discriminate among a number of sources and to weigh evidence. He is confronted with recent instances of what Professor Butterfield has called 'the human predicament' revealed by history; evidence concerning the national, racial and ideological factors which at present hinder or advance man's progress towards some form of world society.

Human strife has always been laced with examples of neutrality—attempts of particular groups or nations to remain aloof from the conflict of warring parties. Mr. Ogley points out that in the twentieth century these have taken four different shapes, Neutralization, Traditional Neutrality, Ad Hoc Neutrality and Nonalignment. Each of these terms is carefully defined and appropriately documented in such a way that this volume makes a unique contribution to the World Studies Series.

As a result the reader is enabled to decide whether neutrality can again become, as it was once in the past, an honourable convenience, or whether, except insofar as it contributes to mediation and peacekeeping, it now constitutes an anachronism.

JAMES HENDERSON

Volume Editor's Preface

Neutrality in the twentieth century is an enormous subject, almost coterminous with world politics as a whole. The material for its study could not possibly be compressed into a book of this size. What I have tried to do is, first, to illustrate, by means of speeches, articles, memoranda, and treaties, what neutrality was *meant* to entail; secondly, to show some of the attitudes that neutrality has evoked: the contrast, for instance, between the philosophy of Woodrow Wilson at the outbreak of the First World War (Document 2 (i)), and that of the poet Louis MacNeice during the Second World War (quoted at the head of Part IV); and thirdly, and most importantly, to trace what happened in selected cases to states that were, or tried to be, neutral in conflicts between their neighbours. I have included examples both of neutrals that were summarily overwhelmed by one or both belligerents, and of those that survived to face a succession of taxing policy choices, in which they had constantly to ask themselves whether, how, and at what cost they could stay neutral.

Since this volume was completed, Prince Sihanouk has fallen, and American and South Vietnamese troops have entered Cambodia. Document 32 now looks somewhat out of date. True, the first part of it emphasizing the fragility of Cambodian neutrality has been underlined; but the second, explaining Sihanouk's ideas of how the Vietnam War would end, and how he would then seek to maintain Cambodia's neutral status, has lost much of its interest; and my confident assertion that his was a popular and effective régime now looks dubious. This should teach us always to expect the unexpected.

One thing Document 32 shows clearly is that this is not the first time that South Vietnam, at any rate, has violated Cambodian neutrality. Now as in 1965, the reason given is the alleged use of that territory, as base, sanctuary, or transit route by the National Liberation Front (Viet Cong) and North Vietnamese. In 1965 the general consensus was that this allegation was largely false; today, its truth seems equally widely conceded, even, before his fall, by Sihanouk himself (who tried to stop it). Against such unneutral use of neutral territory, it is not entirely surprising that the United States should have retaliated, with or without the Cambodian Government's consent.

That is not to say that this foray into Cambodia will shorten rather than lengthen the war; or that the American involvement in Vietnam itself is morally right, either in its conception or its execution; or that it has any chance of ultimate success; or that even if it could in the end succeed, it would justify the cost already paid in Vietnamese and American lives. Overwhelmingly important though these questions are, they do not belong to a book about neutrality. What *is* relevant is that, between the Vietnamese Communists, and the Americans, Cambodian neutrality now seems to have totally perished.

I should like to thank the secretaries of the University of Sussex School of Social Sciences, especially Mrs Kathy Kirby, for their valuable help in typing and assembling the manuscript.

Acknowledgments

The author and publishers wish to thank the following for kind permission to print in this volume extracts from the works cited:

The Carnegie Endowment for International Peace for *On the Law of War and Peace* by Hugo Grotius; *The Reports to the Hague Conferences of 1899 and 1907*, edited by James Brown Scott; and *Outbreak of the World War: German Documents collected by Karl Kautsky*

Frank Cass and Co. Ltd. for *The Decline of Neutrality 1914–41* by Nils Ørvik

The Clarendon Press, Oxford for *The Great European Treaties of the Nineteenth Century* by Sir Augustus Oakes and R. B. Mowat

The Controller of Her Majesty's Stationery Office for *British Documents on the Origins of the War* edited by G. P. Gooch and H. V. Temperly; and *Collected Diplomatic Documents relating to the Outbreak of the European War*

Curtis Brown Ltd. for *Gustav Stresemann; His Diaries, Letters and Papers* edited by Eric Sutton

Faber and Faber and Oxford University Press Inc. (New York) for 'Neutrality' by Louis MacNeice, from *The Collected Poems of Louis MacNeice*, edited by E. R. Dodds. Copyright © The Estate of Louis MacNeice 1966

H. E. Gunnar Hägglöf, former Swedish Ambassador to Britain; and *International Affairs* for 'A Test of Neutrality: Sweden in the Second World War'

Leicester University Press for *Neutralism* by Peter Lyon

Longmans, Green & Co. Ltd. for *International Law and the World War* by J. W. Garner

Macmillan & Co. Ltd. for *Undeclared War* by Elizabeth Wiskemann

The Neue Helvetische Gesellschaft for *Switzerland, Present and Future*

Oxford University Press for the R.I.I.A. for *A History of the League of Nations* by F. P. Walters; Survey of International

Affairs 1939–46, *The War and the Neutrals*, and *The Initial Triumph of the Axis*, edited by Arnold Toynbee and Veronica M. Toynbee

Oxford University Press for *The New States of Asia* by Michael Brecher

Pall Mall Press Ltd. and Frederick A. Praeger, Inc. for *Cambodia* by Michael Leifer

Franklin D. Roosevelt Library of New York for *The Public Papers and Addresses of Franklin D. Roosevelt* edited by S. I. Rosenman

Yale University Press for *Neutrality for the United States* by E. Borchard and W. P. Lage (Copyright 1937, 1940, by Yale University Press)

The editor has not been able to trace the present holder of copyright, if any, in *Albert of Belgium* by Emile Cammaerts, or in the Report of the Belgrade Conference of Heads of States and Government of Nonaligned Countries, 1–6 September 1961.

Introduction

Neutrality is rather like virginity. Everybody starts off with it, but some lose it quicker than others, and some do not lose it at all. Unlike virginity, however, neutrality once lost can sometimes be recovered, albeit with difficulty.

The idea of neutrality is simple enough. It means, obviously, not taking part in others' quarrels: that is, for states, keeping out of other states' wars. Strictly speaking, therefore, the question of neutrality can only arise in time of war, and it is here that the paradox of neutrality appears. War is not a game: certainly not in the twentieth century. It is an agonizing and desperate struggle in which each side is likely to feel that its whole existence, or at any rate its conception of justice and humanity, is at stake. In such a struggle, neither side is going to deny itself any advantages that might come from fighting in a third country, transporting its own troops through that country's territory or monopolizing its trade, simply because that country has declared its neutrality. Thus while a country can only be neutral if there is a war going on, it is precisely in time of war that a neutral state is in greatest danger of losing its neutrality. To put it another way: keeping out of other states' wars is, or can be, a difficult and hazardous enterprise.

This is particularly true of world wars. The First World War began with a dramatic violation of the neutrality of Belgium, whose status as a neutral had been recognized and supposedly guaranteed by all the powers of Europe; and in the next four years neutral rights were repeatedly infringed by both sides. The Second World War bore even more hardly on neutrals. Only five European states remained neutral throughout and some of them behaved at times in very unneutral ways. But if there is ever a third world war, fought with the full array of weapons available to today's superpowers, the neutrals might stand a scarcely better chance of surviving than the belligerents.

I

The latter might hit only each other with their missiles, but they could kill the rest of us with the fallout.

There has never been an environment in which neutrals were automatically safe, in which wars could, so to speak, be fought only between consenting parties. But nineteenth-century Europe, from 1815 onwards, was a more congenial setting for the practice of neutrality. The politics of this time were free from the rigid bloc structure which had developed by 1914. Today's ally might be tomorrow's enemy, and vice versa. The wars were limited; there were always at least two major powers on the sidelines. Thus a small neutral could be guaranteed by a great neutral, as Belgium was by Britain in the Franco-Prussian war. In this climate, where war was an accepted, and limited, instrument of policy for all states, the option of neutrality was a clear-cut one which was normally respected by the belligerents. It was a legal status, with its own rights and obligations. There was certainly a good deal of dispute about such questions as how far a belligerent, in imposing a blockade on its enemy, could interfere with neutral shipping. Britain, the world's ruling naval power, and a relatively frequent belligerent, stood for wide powers to 'seize contraband'; other states, notably the U.S.A., who simply wanted to remain neutral and trade with both sides, contested Britain's claims. But a law of neutrality had developed, and was still developing. It was later to be embodied in the Hague Conventions (see Chapter 1), although these were never ratified by Britain.

Four kinds of neutrality can be distinguished: first, *neutralization*, where neutrality is imposed upon a state by international agreement. Thus Belgium was neutralized from its inception by the Treaty of 1839, by which Britain, Austria, France, Prussia and Russia each guaranteed Belgian neutrality and Belgium herself was made a 'perpetually Neutral State' and charged with observing and defending its neutrality at all times. Other states to be neutralized were Luxembourg (1867), and, more recently, Austria (1955) and Laos (1962). The arrangements and commitments of the neutralizing powers vary from case to case, but the distinctive characteristic of a neutralized state is that it is not neutral by choice (though it may be perfectly content with its status) and does not have the legal right to abandon its neutrality when it wishes.

Most akin to the 'neutralized' state is the 'traditional neutral', of which Switzerland and Sweden are the obvious examples. (Technically, Switzerland might be said to be 'neutralized', since its neutrality was officially recognized under the Treaty of Vienna in 1815; but its subsequent history has been that of a state neutral by tradition and choice, attempting by its own efforts to uphold its neutrality, rather than that of a neutralized state, whose neutrality is imposed and in certain circumstances guaranteed by others.) Originally neutral by choice, it retains the right, in theory, to participate in any war. Yet its neutrality is so much a matter of principle and tradition, rather than of policy, that in practice it can be relied on not to fight, except when it is itself attacked. Part of the security of 'traditional neutrals' (but only part) derives from this reliability. They can be entrusted with delicate commissions, with the inspection of prisoner-of-war camps, and with the holding of conferences between the belligerents, because they are not suspected of covertly helping one side, or of planning to enter the war openly at a suitable moment. As such they have value for the belligerents, and are that much the less likely to be molested. A 'traditional neutral' that decided to enter a war would no longer be reliable. It would lose all the advantages that flow from its status. It therefore has some commitment to maintain its neutrality at all costs; it cannot lightly abandon its position.

'Traditional' neutrals and even neutralized states, despite enjoying some prior recognition of their neutrality by other states, can be very insecure in time of war. The position of an *ad hoc* neutral—one that simply wishes to keep out of a particular war, or that has not yet established its own tradition of neutrality, may be even more hazardous. Of course a major power can usually maintain its neutrality if it wishes, since it can obviously retaliate effectively against infringements by either side: and even a minor neutral is unlikely to be seriously affected by a limited war from its own territory; but the position of a small weak power, such as Cambodia, that is territorially adjacent to a major ideological conflict, is precarious indeed. It is for these *ad hoc* neutrals that the question of neutrality is important. The Cambodias of this world do not choose their political environment; but in that environment they do have a limited choice. To a much greater extent than neutralized states and traditional neutrals, they can choose whether to be neutral or not, as well as how to preserve their neutrality.

The fourth and final category of neutral states is that of the nonaligned. Nonalignment, or 'neutralism' as it is sometimes called, is a recent concept, a response to those two conspicuous landmarks of the post-1945 world, the atomic bomb and the cold war.

The atomic bomb compelled states to ally in advance, if they were to ally at all; when war comes, it is too late to choose between alliance and neutrality. The cold war expressed the fact that the two greatest powers in the world, after 1945, had radically different social and political systems, and each regarded its own system as the only proper pattern for the rest of the world to follow, and as menaced by the existence of the other. As a result there grew up, in the late 'forties, two closely-integrated blocs; the communist bloc, consisting of the Soviet Union, China, North Korea, Mongolia, and the communist régimes imposed by the Soviet Union on Eastern Europe; and the anti-communist bloc made up of the United States and her allies in Europe, America, the Middle East, and the Pacific.

In this situation, the few states who were concerned not so much with who should win the conflict as with toning it down and creating bridges between the two sides, called themselves 'nonaligned'. India under its first Prime Minister, Pandit Nehru, set the pattern for this kind of foreign policy; a pattern that has now been followed, in name at least, by almost all the new states of Africa and Asia.

Nonalignment thus differs from other forms of neutrality. Whereas neutrals are concerned with keeping out of war when it comes, nonalignment is an active policy, primarily aimed at averting a major war, and settling minor ones, between two contesting sides so well-armed that if they fought with all their strength they would destroy human life itself; it is a specific kind of neutrality in a war that has not yet begun, and one hopes never will. Moreover, a nonaligned state, unlike a neutral, can fight its own wars and still be nonaligned, as India has done with Pakistan and Portugal. Its nonalignment is imperilled only if it is drawn into conflict with one side in the cold war, and has to rely on help from the other. That was why, during the Sino-Indian conflict of 1962, India was so anxious to secure some—even if only token—help from the Soviet Union against China, and therefore not have to rely solely on Western support.

2. NEUTRALITY AND WORLD ORDER

In the twentieth century the right to be neutral has been assailed, not only by the breadth and intensity of the two world wars, but also by the principles underlying the international political organizations that followed them. Both the League of Nations and the United Nations were set up by the victors in the preceding war; and both were built on the premises that 'peace is indivisible', that war cannot be tolerated by international society as simply one more, perfectly legitimate, instrument of policy, and that when war occurs, one side must be in the wrong. Both organizations provided means by which disputes could be settled, and in the League's case, to go to war without using these procedures, or abiding by their decisions, was, by the Covenant, to commit an act of war against the whole League; to which all members agreed to respond with, at least, total economic sanctions. The United Nations Charter, on the other hand, envisaging apparently a more centralized structure, empowers the Security Council, in the case of a Threat to the Peace, Breach of a Peace, or Act of Aggression, to instruct all members to apply diplomatic, economic, or even military sanctions. In either case, no loyal member of the organization can insist on remaining neutral.

The idea that neutrality was obsolete already appears in the First World War—for instance, in the speech of Woodrow Wilson recommending Congress to declare war on Germany on 2 April 1917 (see Document 12(b)). As enthusiasm for world organization gained ground, neutrality began to be thought of as a betrayal of the common interest; neutrals were seen as indifferent to the mortal dangers in which others were placed, too timid to fight for the cause of world order, heedless of latent threats to themselves, and perhaps as prospering unjustly by selling the sinews of war to the belligerents. Louis MacNeice's lines about Ireland, quoted at the beginning of Chapter 5, express this view at its bitterest. John Foster Dulles's strictures on those non-communist states that did not want to accept an American alliance seem almost mild in comparison.

This is a highly simplified view of the morality of being neutral. There is, it is true, a contradiction between the idea of world order and that of neutrality. If war were to be abolished, there would be no more neutrals. When we look at the elaborate Conventions on the Rights and Duties of Neutrals drafted by the Hague Conferences (see Document 2), their ingenuity seems misapplied. If the states of the world can genuinely agree on, and stick to, such detailed rules about how neutrals should be treated in war, can they not agree to abolish war itself? And would they not have done better to try to integrate the world, by whatever means was open to them, so as to reduce the chances of war, rather than to ensure that when war does come, the neutrals can go unmolested?

This kind of argument is not very fair to the Hague Conferences. They did concern themselves with averting war, and produced some significant conventions on the Pacific Settlement of Disputes; and we see their deliberations with hindsight; the unprecedented carnage of the First World War took everybody by surprise. But even accepting the argument that it is better to abolish war than to provide for the neutrality of states in it, does that mean that neutrality, or nonalignment, is necessarily a betrayal of world order?

The answer to the question 'Is neutrality antisocial?' must be 'It all depends.' It depends, largely, on the nature of the situation. If one party to the conflict is seen as an aggressor, and a threat to the peace of the world, the obvious need is to organize the strongest possible coalition with which to deter, or defeat, the common threat; and those who excuse themselves as neutrals or 'nonaligned' will seem traitors to the common cause. If the conflict is seen as between two equally frightened or menacing powers or blocs, third parties will seem to be serving the common good better by building bridges than by choosing sides. But that is not the whole story. Even if justice and humanity are all on one side, states that remain neutral may render greater service to the international community than if they fought on the 'right' side. In the Second World War, for instance, the Swiss and the Swedes, though neutral in diplomatic posture, were solidly pro-allied in sentiment. Had either fought the Axis they would certainly have been defeated and occupied, although they might, for a time at least, have drawn German troops away from other fronts, and relieved some of their hard-pressed opponents. As neutrals, however, the Swedes were able to take up with the Nazis the treatment of occupied Norway and Denmark. These appeals were not entirely ineffective, especially after 1942. They were also able to prepare relief and rehabilitation schemes for the war-afflicted countries (see Document 27).

Neutral Switzerland's major contribution was to house the Red Cross, which looked after the welfare of prisoners-of-war on both sides: she was sometimes able to secure the exchange of sick or wounded prisoners (see Document 28). Both these neutrals were able to admit refugees from Axis rule who might otherwise have suffered death or imprisonment. Then there is mediation. Mediation did not play much part in the Second World War—the Axis powers were made to surrender unconditionally; but clearly, if there is to be successful mediation in a conflict, it must come from neutrals—which accounts for the failure of Harold Wilson's attempts to mediate in Vietnam and over Biafra.

It is always useful, then, to have some neutrals on any dimension of conflict, unless it is to be settled by brute force. The usefulness of neutrality (and of that peculiar, some would say bastard, form of neutrality known as nonalignment), in the post-1945 period is greater than ever. When two powers dominate the world, in military terms, to the extent to which the U.S.A. and the U.S.S.R. do today, allies matter much less. No accretion of allies will enable one of these two powers to force the other to surrender. The choice, for the foreseeable future, is not between co-existence and victory for one side, but between co-existence and catastrophe. Neutrals, as mediators, have an important role to play in averting that catastrophe; so, too, has the United Nations, though it has not always played it, since for long it was under Western domination.

The cold war has not been the only arena of international conflict since 1945, and of recent years it has rather faded into the background: today Rhodesia, the Nigeria-Biafran war, the Arab-Israeli conflict, and the fighting between the Soviet Union and China, are as prominent in the headlines as the war in Vietnam. Each of these situations, including that of Vietnam, represents a different dimension of conflict; and in each conflict, the neutrals, if any, and therefore the potential mediators, are a different set of states. The neutral in one case may be an active partisan in another. Theoretically, the experience of neutrality should give a state some understanding of the position of others that are neutral where it is partisan. It must be admitted that this does not seem to happen very often. States—politicians that is—see questions of neutrality and partisanship not in terms of a theory of neutrality, but in terms of the merits (as they see them) of the issue in question; or more cynically, in terms of their interests. But that admission does not prevent neutrality, both in the cold war and elsewhere, from having its uses for the international community as a whole and even for the two sides concerned; still less does it prove that neutrality is necessarily antisocial.

3. THE BELLIGERENT'S VIEW OF NEUTRALITY

A country can only remain neutral if both, or all, belligerents respect its neutrality. But why should they? No state in the twentieth century goes to war lightly; generally speaking it fights either because it sees its national survival or integrity at stake; or because it judges that it can now settle in its favour once and for all an issue vital to its plans. In either case, it is not likely to be ready to lose the war out of respect for neutrals. If there are advantages to be gained out of infringing another state's neutrality, it is logical to assume that it will take them.

The extreme form the infringement of a neutral's rights might take is that of direct attack on its territory leading to occupation. Whether one or other belligerent will find it advantageous to attack a neutral depends on several factors. The most obvious is probably the strategic. A neutral is most liable to be involved if it lies between the belligerents, such as Belgium in both world wars, or if it allows for the possibility of outflanking the enemy, as Norway and Denmark did in the second. Any neutral whose geographical location impedes the most effective form of military operations for either belligerent, or whose territory could be used to advantage by either, is likely to be under pressure.

Economic resources are another important factor affecting the attitude of belligerents to a neutral. Generally speaking, the richer the neutral is economically, the more tempting a target it is for attack. Valuable resources can, of course, be secured by trade as well as conquest; but only in rivalry with others, and by offering something in return. In both world wars, Britain was adept at economic warfare, part of the tactics of which was to persuade neutrals to limit their trade with her enemies. The dominance of the Royal Navy, and the resulting capacity to blockade other states almost at will, gave her a powerful weapon with which to dictate to neutrals how much trade they should do with Germany; but every curtailment in Germany's share of a neutral's trade gave Germany that much greater incentive to attack and occupy it. Britain was aware of this, and usually moderated her demands accordingly.

But there are cases in which a neutral's possession of some valuable economic resource or facility can cause a belligerent to hesitate before attacking it. If the neutral can only, in practice, be attacked from one side, and that side already buys most of the resource in question, or makes most use of the facilities, and if the neutral can at a moment's notice destroy its own usefulness to the belligerent, the belligerent may have a strong incentive not to attack. Sweden and Switzerland, for instance, who for a large part of the Second World War were virtually entirely surrounded by the Axis powers and their allies, both had resources of this kind. The German war economy fed greedily on Swedish iron ore, and the Swedes could easily destroy the power stations without which the mines could not be run; the Axis powers also used the Swiss tunnels through the Alps for transport of supplies between Germany and Italy; and the Swiss had plans to blow them up if invaded. In each case, invasion of the neutral would have brought the Axis economy disadvantages, at least in the short term.

The belligerent will also ask himself how reliable a neutral's neutrality is. He will be quick to suspect the neutral of covertly helping the enemy; or of yielding to enemy pressures; maybe even of preparing to enter the war later on the enemy's side. A 'traditional' neutral will have some advantage here, but even they are liable to bend, if not break, under overwhelming pressure, as we shall see, and in the belligerent's eyes such unneutral tendencies are magnified. For instance, in the later stages of the Second World War, the Nazis contemplated invading Switzerland for fear she might allow free passage to

9

allied armies, which the Swiss government had no intention of doing.

A strong neutral may be attacked because its neutral intentions are doubted; a weak neutral, because it seems incapable of defending its neutrality against an enemy. A belligerent will be less likely to attack a state with both an established tradition of neutrality, and the capacity for sufficiently protracted resistance to enable help from the non-attacking side to be significant. And even when a belligerent has a strong reason to invade a neutral, it still has to assess the costs of such a decision. Economic and military resources will have to be spent on defeating the neutral's forces and occupying it. The belligerent may pride itself on its respect for international law and for the rights of small nations, to a greater or lesser degree. It may or may not wish to incorporate the neutral into its own state; and if not, it may consider what effect invasion will have on its post-war relations with the neutral so invaded. Even if it does annex and occupy the neutral it may find the population hostile and uncooperative. Sabotage, terrorist attacks and even guerrilla warfare, may persist long after the regular army has been defeated and the official government has surrendered. Much will depend on the unity of the country. Ideally the belligerent will want to be able to install a government that is both favourable to itself and is accepted as legitimate by the population. It can achieve this by occupation and invasion only if the population was, initially, divided. Thus the acute political divisions in France in the late 'thirties gave the Vichy government, that had come to terms with Nazi Germany, what legitimacy it had in 'unoccupied' France. Normally, an imposed régime will be alien to the population, and will require considerate military force, or economic concessions, or both, to maintain itself in power.

Of these costs, the military ones, depending on the resistance anticipated, will probably weigh the heaviest, for they are the most immediately felt. Whether they will be weighed accurately is another question. Optimism is such a virtue for nations at war that even the politicians are liable to catch it. A belligerent state may therefore attack a neutral with a totally erroneous estimate of its capacity for resistance, as Germany attacked Russia in 1941.

There are two other, minor, elements that might come into such a decision. On occasion, a belligerent might refrain from attacking a neutral out of recognition of the indispensability of the services provided for both sides, like the Red Cross activities of the Swiss. Secondly, a belligerent might be irritated into action against a neutral by the tone of its newspapers and broadcasts. An otherwise tolerated neutral might be invaded because of the hostility of its public opinion to the belligerent concerned. It is not easy to see why such expressions of opinion should worry the belligerent, except where they can reach the belligerent's own population and perhaps puncture the illusions created by its own propaganda, but they do. Allied to this, but more serious, is the question of subversion. If a state is having difficulty with its own nationals, and their cause is supported by an adjacent state, the first state will find it easy to believe that the trouble arises from outside subversion, from people who use the other side as a base and infiltrate into the belligerents' territory to arouse opposition and perhaps commit acts of violence. Even if the state acknowledges that there is a basic internal conflict, it will suspect an adjacent state, where opinion is sympathetic to the rebels, of offering sanctuary and assistance. It may be right or wrong in its suspicions; but if it does suspect the neutral of affording comfort to its enemies, internal or external, it will be strongly tempted to attack.

Belligerents may also infringe neutral rights in less drastic ways than those of invasion and occupation. Germany did not initially declare war on Belgium in 1914, for instance; she merely demanded the right of her armies to pass through Belgian territory on their way to attack France. Conceivably, Belgium could have conceded these demands and remained at peace with Germany; but she would have gravely compromised her neutral status under the 1839 Treaty (see Chapters 1 and 2). Britain and France made similar demands of Norway and Sweden in 1939–40, in an effort to assist Finland against the U.S.S.R.; and later in planning to send forces in Norway to forestall a German invasion; in the latter case, unlike the first, they did not propose to take no for an answer. Germany also successfully demanded from Sweden the right to send a whole division of German troops through Sweden to the Finnish front against Russia. There are of course important differences between these cases and that of Belgium in 1914—none of the other states were neutralized—but they do suggest that transit of troops through a neutral's territory does not automatically make that state either an ally, or a satellite.

Both sides in the two world wars made economic demands upon neutrals; this was especially true of the Second World War; in addition, the Germans demanded of Switzerland that she impose a black-out, to ensure that allied planes sent to bomb Italy would not be helped to navigate by the lights of Swiss cities. The Swiss gave way on this; and also accepted some curb on the freedom of their press and radio. Even more drastic action may on occasion be taken against neutrals without terminating their neutrality. In the First World War, German submarines sank nearly half the Norwegian merchant shipping fleet; in the second, Britain mined the 'Leads' (the channel between the north-west Norwegian coast and the chain of off-shore islands, which was part of Norway's national waters), through which Swedish iron ore came down to Germany from Narvik. In each case Norway protested, but in neither did she abandon her neutrality as a result.

Belligerents are far less likely to tolerate the neutrality of a former ally that makes a separate peace with the enemy in the course of war, than that of a state that has been neutral from the start. Thus when Russia after the Bolshevist Revolution, sought to make peace with Germany in the First World War, the Allies, notably Britain and France, intervened by force to attempt to install a government that would continue to fight; and in 1943 the Italian surrender led only to the take-over of the Italian position by their German allies.

Finally, it is always possible for a belligerent to attack a neutral, not for any reason arising from the war in which it is already engaged, but out of a direct quarrel with the neutral state. It may want to annex the neutral, or parts of it; to determine what régime it shall have; or to exploit it economically. Theoretically, that is another story; but in practice it is just one more consideration which may enter into the belligerent's policy; and thus into the neutral's strategy for maintaining his neutrality.

4. THE ART OF BEING NEUTRAL

Before we consider how a state can preserve its neutrality against the pressures of twentieth-century war, let us ask why, when war breaks out, a state would choose—if it had a choice—to remain neutral rather than to intervene on one side or other.

There are three main reasons why a state might decide to join in a war. First, it might be keenly interested in securing the victory of one side; or at least in ensuring that it was not defeated. The more powerful the state, the more likely it would be to intervene, since the more confident it would be that its own decision would shape the outcome of the war. Secondly, it might regard its own participation in the war, not as militarily crucial, but as diplomatically advantageous. Cavour took Piedmont into the Crimean War to win British and French sympathies for his claims against Austria in northern Italy; many of the sixteen United Nations members who fought in Korea did so to ensure American support if they were attacked. Finally, it might fear it could not preserve its neutrality at all, or at any rate only at such military, economic or political cost as would be far outweighed by the costs of participation; and so might prefer to commit itself at the beginning, and incorporate itself in the defence system of one side, rather than be dragged into the war in the end.

For the state that chooses neutrality, none of these reasons, presumably, hold good. Either it has no vital stake in one outcome of the war rather than another, or else it cannot see itself as tipping the scales; it sees no diplomatic gains to be got from participation; and it believes it can preserve its neutrality at a cost that would, at worst, be less than the cost of fighting the war.

Not all neutrals base their decisions on such calculations, of course. Neutralized states have neutrality legally imposed on them, although in practice there is little to prevent them repudiating their obligations; pacifist states, if any, can hardly take sides in a war; and for some states, like Switzerland, and Norway until 1940, the policy of neutrality is almost automatic, a matter of principle rather than considered choice.

Having chosen a policy of neutrality, how does a state maintain that policy throughout a war? Basically, the strategy for preserving neutrality depends on the policy of the belligerents. We saw in the last section of the various circumstances in which belligerents might be tempted to invade neutrals or otherwise infringe their neutrality; clearly, the strategy of a state that wants to remain neutral must be to minimize those temptations and give each potential attacker the greatest possible incentive to respect its neutrality. It must convince him that he gains by leaving the neutral in peace and will lose by molesting it. In this, the neutral's cards are largely dealt to him by circumstances: the extent to which he can deal his own hand is very limited, but he can play it with lesser or greater skill. Some neutrals show impressive diplomatic skill in defence of their neutrality, for instance Sweden, Switzerland and Turkey in the Second World War. (The first two of these are dealt with in Chapter 4.) To appreciate the cards a neutral may have, consider the case of a neutral state set between two belligerents. Now imagine that instead of this there was simply an unoccupied piece of territory, in the same position, with no particular legal or religious status. Clearly in the latter case one side will occupy the empty land insofar as it offers any strategic advantage. This is what happens with the High Seas, an area which cannot, as yet, be settled by humans and is therefore occupied only intermittently in war. The neutral state, however, has a population and a government—and, usually, an army. All three, and especially the last, can be used to make it more difficult for a belligerent to use the neutral's territory as if it were its own. Thus each belligerent has the maximum incentive to respect the neutrality of a given state if he knows that, if he violates it, these resources will be used against him; if neither side violates it, they will not be used at all; and if the other side violates it, they will be used against the other side.

A neutral must first of all, therefore, convince each belligerent that, if left alone, it will not go over to the enemy, nor help the enemy in any unneutral way. Secondly, it may have to assure each belligerent that it will continue to trade with it. Belligerents are apt to put intense pressure on neutrals, not merely to maintain, but to increase their share of its trade particularly in militarily significant commodities like iron ore. Clearly as between the two (or more) belligerents, the neutral cannot increase both sides' share in its trade simultaneously. Thirdly, it may need to convince one belligerent, or each in turn, that it can and will stop encroachments and attack from the other. A militarily weak state may be unable to do this; a pacifist state, still less so, even though it is well organized for 'civilian defence'; even a strongly defended neutral may have to fight a war because one belligerent did not believe it capable of resisting the other: this is perhaps why the U.S.S.R. (anticipating the German invasion that was to come) attacked Finland in 1939.

The strongest military incentive a neutral can offer a belligerent not to attack is a guarantee by a major power that is also, otherwise, neutral in the war, such as Belgium had from Britain in 1870, but not in 1914 (see Chapter 1). Failing that, a neutral must rely on its own military forces. These forces do not have to be equal to the belligerent's to exercise some influence over the latter's policies. They do have to be strong enough either to inflict substantial—or in current jargon 'unacceptable' —losses on the enemy, or to hold him up long enough to allow help from the other side to come in, and gain strategic and other advantages from the fact that the first side has attacked.

Some economic deterrents to attack have already been mentioned (see above p. 9). They rely on the 'scorched earth' principle. If you can destroy or seriously damage your own assets, you will not be so valuable a prize; but they have to be assets that the side contemplating attack makes more use of than the other. If Swedish iron ore exports had mattered as much to Britain as they did to Germany, Germany could hardly have been deterred by a Swedish threat to incapacitate the iron mines, since she would have had the satisfaction of knowing that any difficulties she had through shortage of iron ore were matched by similar difficulties for the Allies. Thus Sweden could only use this kind of threat because her iron exports were already making a net contribution towards Germany's war effort.

The analysis so far suggests that a pacifist policy would not help a state to stay neutral; but pacifists might well argue that the argument is not so simple as that. A pacifist state, for instance—assuming one were possible—might perform valuable services for the international community, which would render belligerents unwilling to attack it; by having no axe to grind, and no interests of its own, it might be able to mediate between the belligerents; it might have influence of a non-military kind, such as that wielded by the Vatican; or it might be able to organize non-violent resistance—or civilian defence as it is now called—which would discourage attack and frustrate its objects if it occurred. These are not negligible considerations; but only the last of them directly springs from pacifism. A state can perform services for the international community, can mediate between belligerents, and can exert non-military influence—all without being pacifist; only civilian defence is intrinsically pacifist, and it has recently been suggested that even that could be combined with more conventional military operations. The techniques of civilian defence, which include strikes, demonstrations, go-slows, and various other ways of resisting the order of an occupying power, were not entirely unsuccessful when used by the Danes and the Norwegians against the Nazis in the Second World War; more recently, the Czechs' response to Soviet invasion seemed at least to have achieved something by these means. But these are at best techniques for mitigating the severity of an occupation. They do not show that the prospect of civilian defence would be likely to deter an invader nor—with the possible exception of Gandhi's campaign against British rule in India—is there any evidence that its practice can induce an occupying power to withdraw. Nor, for a neutral exposed to attack from both sides, does the traditional pacifist answer make much sense, that by having no military forces one would obviously pose no threat to a potential attacker, and would thus remove the motive for attack. For, if the motive for one belligerent to attack a neutral is to make sure the other doesn't get there first, the lesser-armed the neutral, the greater the incentive to attack. Pacifism can, of course, be defended on principle; and it can plausibly be argued that in a nuclear age it is better—morally and materially—to be occupied than actually to fight the invaders. But it might be conceded that armed neutrals like Sweden and Switzerland seem to survive better in war than unarmed or lightly-armed neutrals like Norway and Denmark. (Liechtenstein, which somehow maintained its independence against Germany in the Second World War, seems to be an exception.)

Survival, for neutrals, is not merely a question of dissuading any belligerent from invading; it is also a question of resisting demands that are not compatible with neutrality. How far a neutral can resist such demands varies with circumstances. Sweden and Switzerland, who for much of the war were virtually surrounded by the Axis powers and their allies, had to make substantial concessions. The Swedish transit facilities for German troops; the Swiss blackout; the restraints both states accepted on their free expression of opinion—these were hardly compatible with neutrality in the strict legal sense. But even after making these concessions Sweden and Switzerland remained independent states—far freer than they would have been under Nazi occupation. A Danish Jew who reached Sweden, or a refugee from Nazi Germany who was admitted into Switzerland—though not all were admitted—would certainly find a political and intellectual atmosphere far different from that which he had just left.

Gunnar Hägglöf argues in Document 27 that the basic condition of neutrality is the existence of a balance of power. The First World War seems to bear this out, but not the Second. In the latter, of the five surviving European neutrals, two (Sweden and Switzerland) were oases of neutrality in the vast desert of Nazi-occupied Europe; one (Ireland) was behind Allied lines, and only Spain and Portugal, and perhaps Turkey, could be said to be situated where the power of the two sides was balanced. Five of the neutrals to be overrun, Belgium, the Netherlands, Luxembourg, Norway and Denmark, lay more or less between the two sides; and were being pressed by the allies economically before they were occupied by the Nazis. Against this, and in support of Hägglöf, no neutrals survived in the Balkans, where Axis influence was supreme. On the whole, states that could be occupied by both sides were at least as exposed to attack in that war as states that could only be attacked by one; but of the latter, those survived best that could offer the dominant side the most adequate incentives to respect their neutrality; and in some cases this meant making concessions to the dominant side that compromised their rights as neutrals.

But the fact that Sweden and Switzerland survived at all as neutrals in the Second World War says much for their diplomatic skill. Their problem, essentially, was to concede what had to be conceded to the Axis powers and no more, while making clear that they would fight against any wholesale assault on their independence; at the same time, they had to avoid provoking the Allies, who if they could not invade, nor protect them against Axis invasion, could usually control valuable rights of access to trade outside Europe. In such diplomatic manoeuvres timing and foresight are important. The neutral must be able to see further ahead than the belligerent; it must be discreet yet not unfriendly in its relations with both—or all—sides; and at the same time keep its eyes open for omens of impending attack from any quarter.

5. CONTEMPORARY NEUTRALITY AND NONALIGNMENT

Since 1945 the nature of neutrality has been changed, not only by the atomic bomb and the cold war, but also by new and more sophisticated forms of international organization. Switzerland, for instance, is now almost entirely surrounded by members of NATO. Her chief neighbours, as well as joining forces militarily, have formed with the Benelux countries the Coal and Steel Community, the E.E.C. and Euratom. Wider groupings of European states have been created, such as the Council of Europe and O.E.C.D. (formerly the O.E.E.C.), with commitment to political and economic liberalism in the abstract rather than to specifically pro-Western alignment in the cold war. Swiss neutrality has meant saying no, so far, to membership in any of these organizations, even in time of peace. Just as alliances have to be made in advance in the atomic age, so neutrality has had to be demonstrated in advance. Yet Switzerland remains a 'traditional neutral'; she is far from being 'nonaligned', for her ideological sympathies are all with the West against communism and she has made little attempt to mediate between the two blocs.

The pioneer of 'nonalignment' was Pandit Nehru, India's first Prime Minister. Under Nehru, India's attempts to build bridges between East and West were courageous, skilful, and on occasion strikingly successful. They were courageous because, at the height of the cold war, neither superpower accepted that states could be 'nonaligned'. The Soviet Union regarded all non-communist countries as bourgeois and capitalist-dominated; the United States, particularly under Dulles, saw the fact that India neither fought in the Korean War, nor joined the South East Asia Treaty Organisation (SEATO), as a betrayal of democracy. The skill of Indian diplomacy was shown in the early 1950s when, despite the initial suspicion of both sides, India played an indispensable role in the negotiations leading up to the armistice in Korea in 1953 and in those preceding the Geneva Accords on Indo-China in 1954, and in each case was entrusted with the pivotal position in the machinery set up to administer the terms of the agreement— the Neutral Nations Repatriation Commission in Korea, and the International Control Commission in Vietnam.

Indian acceptance of, and friendship with, the new communist régime of China, under the slogan of 'Panch Sheel'—the five principles—was an outstanding feature of her nonaligned policy. Her warnings about the danger of Chinese intervention in the Korea war, if the United Nations force, predominantly American, and led by the American General MacArthur who was directly responsible to President Truman, went on to unify the country after expelling the communist invaders from South Korea, were ignored. Had they been listened to, the Korean war might have been over in three months instead of three years, China might have been admitted to the United Nations, and South East Asia might have experienced, in the years that followed, at least that degree of cold war co-existence that Europe now enjoys, since much of China's recent xenophobic behaviour may well be due to her exclusion from the United Nations and other world forums during the last twenty years.

India set the fashion for most of the many new states that were created by decolonization. Prince Sihanouk of Cambodia, for instance, admitted that his foreign policy was modelled on Nehru's. Nonalignment became a way for these newly independent states to show that they intended to establish relations with, and seek aid from, the East as well as the West. Some did not go as far as this. Nigeria, for instance, after declaring herself nonaligned, kept her relations with communist states to a minimum for several years. Here it seems that her object in proclaiming herself nonaligned was to establish herself as a respectable African state, rather than to mediate in, or on the contrary profit from, the cold war.

As the cold war receded from its predominant position in

world politics, and as states further and further from the geographic boundaries of the communist world, less and less in demand as allies of the West, became independent, so the emphasis of the nonaligned platform was less on mediation in the cold war, and more on remedying the deficiencies of the colonial powers, and the injustice of European rule, wherever it still persisted in Africa and Asia. This can be seen in the Declaration of the Belgrade Conference of Nonaligned countries in 1961 (Document 30). It is significant that the organizers of this Conference rejected an Indian suggestion that invitations to it should be extended to a number of other states, including European neutrals like Sweden and Finland. These two countries would have had much in common with the original conception of nonalignment, with its emphasis on attempts to soften cold war acerbities; they had much less to offer a conference dedicated to making a final assault on the last outposts of European colonialism.

The active conception of neutrality, focussed primarily on the cold war, which was the essence of nonalignment, eventually found its central expression not in a state, but in the United Nations. Originally, as we have seen, the United Nations seemed to go even further than the League in abolishing neutrality. The Charter made it look—to the unsophisticated—easier for a camel to pass through the eye of a needle than for a member state to stay neutral. Chapter 7 gives the Security Council the power to direct members to apply diplomatic, economic, or military sanctions on other states, members or not, at its discretion, and by Article 25 members oblige themselves to obey such Security Council directives.

These provisions have been enough to deter Switzerland from ever applying for United Nations membership. In practice, however, the risk a state runs of becoming involved in the conflicts of others through its membership of the United Nations is far smaller than these provisions of the Charter might suggest. All permanent members of the Security Council (China, France, the United Kingdom, the United States of America and the U.S.S.R.) have to concur in all Security Council decisions, except those solely concerned with procedure. It is true that 'China' in this context means *nationalist* China'—the régime of Chiang-kai-shek on the island of Taiwan (Formosa)—since communist China is still not represented in the United Nations. This no doubt makes a Security Council decision somewhat less difficult to arrive at; but it is still highly unlikely that *both* the Soviet Union *and* the three Western powers would agree to make some drastic demand of the remaining members, such as might seriously compromise the position of any would-be neutral. Moreover, the plans envisaged in Article 43 by which all members would make military agreements with the Security Council specifying the forces they would place at the Council's disposal, have never materialized since the Council has never agreed on what forces to ask members to make available.

So long as the Council takes no decision in an international crisis, the United Nations Charter imposes fewer obligations on would-be neutrals in a conflict than did the League Covenant. It contains no direct obligation to outlaw 'aggressors' or take sanctions against them, as did Article 16 of the Covenant, and in practice, neutrals other than Switzerland have felt able to apply to join the United Nations without any of the fuss that characterized the position of neutrals in the League (see Chapter 3), and have generally been admitted without difficulty. It is the partisans of one side or other that have been delayed or excluded.

Where the United Nations has affected the idea of neutrality significantly has been in the realm of peacekeeping. The use of forces directly under United Nations command, though composed of contingents offered voluntarily by member states, as in the Congo and Cyprus, has created a new role for smaller, and generally nonaligned, states. The essential qualification here is not so much general nonalignment, as neutrality in the particular situation into which the force is being inserted, and many Western allies have contributed contingents to one or other of these forces. Such operations bring into acute controversy the position of the Secretary-General; it was of his handling of the Congo operation that Mr. Khrushchev, then Soviet Prime Minister, said 'There can be neutral nations but there can be no neutral men', and called for a replacement of the office of Secretary-General by a troika of three people, one of whom would represent the nonaligned states and all three of whom would need to agree to all decisions. This radical demand gained little support and the U.S.S.R. agreed without much difficulty to the election of U Thant as (originally Acting) Secretary-General on Hammarskjöld's death in 1961, and even to further peacekeeping operations under his direction, such as that in Cyprus, although with greater safeguards against his arbitrary action. The opposition of most nonaligned states to the troika proposals was remarkable. They identified so closely with the United Nations in general, and the Secretary-General in particular, that they preferred a situation in which the United Nations could act independently to one which, for the first time, would have given them an institutionalized veto over its activities.

The United Nations is not yet completely controllable by the nonaligned, however; if it had been, the resolution which has been before the General Assembly annually since 1961, calling for the representation of China by Peking rather than Tai-wan, a resolution supported even by some of America's allies—would have gained at least a simple majority before now. Conor Cruise O'Brien described it as 'neutral between the Americans and the Afro-Asians'; nevertheless, it has changed a lot since 1950, when the United States fought with fifteen of its allies against communist North Korea under the banner of the United Nations, and the Assembly condemned as aggression the intervention of the Chinese to save North Korea from extinction. Today it is extremely unlikely that such a war could be fought under U.N. auspices; the war in Vietnam has been entirely outside the U.N.'s jurisdiction, and the organization's chief contribution has been the patient attempt at mediation by the Burmese Secretary-General U Thant, on his own initiative.

Contemporary neutralism or nonalignment is, then, a peculiar form of neutrality. It is neutral solely with respect to the cold war. The cold war has now receded. The superpowers now seem to have learnt how to avoid a third world war. This fact may be, at least in part, a consequence of nonalignment. If there had been no nonaligned states, if the world of the late 'forties and the early 'fifties had been totally bipolar, the chances that world war would have been unleashed between the two military giants then confronting each other, would have been significantly greater. We may owe more than we acknowledge to the nonaligned states, and above all to Nehru's India.

As nonalignment becomes less urgent, the nominally nonaligned states have become more preoccupied with other issues; anticolonial causes, as the Belgrade Declaration illustrates; frontier disputes with one another; internal conflicts and civil wars. The fact that a state is 'nonaligned' tells us nothing about its attitude towards a border dispute between two other non-aligned states, or an internal war in one of them; and being nonaligned is certainly no guarantee that a state will not attack, or be attacked by, its neighbour, nor that it will not fall victim to internal conflict or secession. As world politics become more multidimensional, neutrality becomes more relative, and non-alignment begins to seem something of an anachronism; but still the superpowers spend enormous sums of money on arms directed at each other; they may have learnt to coexist, but they certainly need to learn to coexist more cheaply, and in this nonalignment may still have a role to play.

6. NEUTRALITY FOR BRITAIN?

Neutrality in the cold war, or nonalignment, has often been advocated as a policy for Britain. The Campaign for Nuclear Disarmament, for instance, has stood not only for British renunciation of her own nuclear weapons, but also for British withdrawal from NATO. In the early years of the Campaign, when its aims gained substantial, though always minority, public support, it would have been a breach of international law to have withdrawn from NATO; the North Atlantic Treaty, signed in 1949, committed its members initially for twenty years. The twenty years were up in April 1969. Since then any member has been legally free to leave NATO by giving a year's notice. However, under the 1954 Amendments to the Brussels Treaty of 1947, which established the Western European Union, Britain committed herself to a collective alliance with the six Common Market countries, which was to last for fifty years. So even now, she cannot be neutral in any conflict in which these six countries are involved, before 2005, without repudiating her obligations under this treaty.

This little-known commitment is a remarkable example of the way in which our political system allows the government of the day to impose obligations which will be legally binding on their successors long after they have left office, and even after they are dead. This, of course, is only a legal obligation. Where there is enough political support for a change in policy, legal obstacles to that policy are liable to be swept aside without much compunction. Still, breaches of international law are distasteful in themselves and often have disagreeable consequences. Supporters of a neutral Britain may well complain of the difficulties that these commitments have put in the path of their policy, even if a solid electoral majority thought it the right policy, and voted for a party that proposed to make Britain neutral.

The question 'Is neutrality for Britain legal?' is simpler, and less important than the question 'Is such neutrality wise?' The latter question involves a whole range of vast and inconclusive subordinate enquiries. The experience of neutrals in the two world wars of this century is one, but not the most crucial, of these; because the case for British neutrality is not that, if the cold war became a hot war, Britain would be safer neutral than belligerent, but that Britain has an overriding interest—which is also that of the other states affected—in the cold war not becoming a hot war, and that British neutrality would reduce the likelihood that such a disaster would occur, by promoting the relaxation of tension between the blocs. In other words, the case for neutrality in the cold war, for Britain as for other states, is basically a case for nonalignment.

To examine this case, four main questions must be asked. First, what is the nature of the cold war? Second, what does the present constellation of military power amount to in terms of proneness to war, or potential domination by one side? Thirdly, if Britain were neutral in the cold war, would she be more or less vulnerable to pressure from one side or other, than if she were, as she is now, aligned with the West. Fourthly, and this is where the experience of neutrals in the two world wars becomes relevant, if war came, would it make any difference, for good or ill, for herself or for others, whether or not Britain was neutral?

It is probably the answer to the first of these questions that lies at the core of the debate between NATO supporters and neutralists. The former see communism as a menace, liable to expand by force, under the leadership of the Soviet Union, from Eastern into Western Europe, if not checked by the united resistance of the democratic states with America at their head.

Seen in this light neutrality seems both treacherous and short-sighted.

Neutralists, on the other hand, see Soviet policies as essentially defensive. They may blame the cold war on American, or West German, aggressiveness; or concede that it was the unplanned consequence of fears on both sides. In either case, they believe that the greater the military strength of the West, the more the Soviet Union will be alarmed, and the more likely it will be to be provoked into retaliation.

It would take a full-length study of Soviet policy since 1945—perhaps even since 1917—to decide which of these views of it was nearer to the truth. Probably both are wrong if taken to extremes. The Soviet Union might well dominate Europe as the United States dominates the Americas, if the states of Western Europe were entirely defenceless, and might well use their dominant position to settle some questions—like that of Berlin's future—to their liking; just as, if the Soviet Union were weak, the West might try to unify Germany, or have gone to the defence of Czechoslovakia in 1968. Neither bloc trusts the other; each will use force, when it can do so with impunity, to get what it can from the other. This is an argument for the states of Western Europe to have defences of some kind; but it is not by itself a conclusive argument for NATO, still less for Britain's remaining a member of it. For although the Soviet Union might be 'aggressive' if the states of Western Europe were impotent, it does not follow that every increase of Western strength necessarily makes the Soviet Union less aggressive. There could come a point where the accumulation of military power in NATO is seen not as a curb on Soviet expansions and ambitions, but as a threat to what she now has—and worse to what she considered vital to her security.

If that point were reached, the West, by its very strength, could provoke a war with the Soviet Union. This would not be a war over any specific issue; it would be one which the West would have been able to avoid, without making concessions, simply by not frightening the Russians.

Ten years ago, that kind of war looked a serious possibility; today it seems much less likely. So, despite the Soviet occupation of Czechoslovakia in 1968, does an invasion of Western Europe. Russia can have little to gain from the forcible establishment of

new communist régimes in European countries. British withdrawal from NATO would hardly tempt her into such hazardous adventures.

How far a neutral Britain could play the role of mediator is
difficult to determine. Certainly for the foreseeable future there
can hardly be any shortage of issues, between Western and
communist states, on which mediation would be desirable. New
weapons, or new internal developments in Germany, may
provoke new dangers of war; moreover, even the present arms
confrontation is enormously costly, yet all proposals for mutual
reductions in the arms level are likely to be viewed suspiciously,
by at least one side. Suggestions from a manifestly neutral
source are at least more likely to be listened to; and in other
parts of the world, the confrontation between communist states
and others is as strident as it ever was. Even if the Soviet Union
and the United States, together with their European allies,
came to an understanding because of their shared fear of China,
there would be need for mediation between them and China.
It is now twenty years since the communists won the civil war
in China and established the People's Republic of China; the
new régime remains unrecognized by the United States, and
unrepresented in the United Nations. One of the few major
agreements to which China and the Western powers were both
parties, the Geneva Accords of 1954, was in effect disowned by
the West. There is plenty of room for bridge-building here. It is
true that a war between the U.S.A., or the U.S.S.R., and China
alone, would probably not as things now stand be the final
catastrophe for the rest of the world, that a Soviet-American
all-out war would certainly be; and that therefore for Britain to
try to avert such a war would be a matter of humanity, almost,
rather than vital interest. But even those for whom vital interests
are the only respectable motives for foreign policy might reflect
that, in the long run, China may also become a superpower, and
today's voice of humanity may become tomorrow's voice of
prudence.

What might be doubted is whether Britain would be acceptable as a mediator. Legal considerations apart, she is highly
vulnerable economically to United States pressure, and Washington could easily generate a new sterling crisis, all the more so
if the other major capitalist countries which are mostly America's

allies acted with her. Even without such pressure, those former allies might resent her 'defection'; while on the other hand neither the communist states, nor even the other nonaligned states, might take her professions of neutrality or nonalignment at face value.

These are not so much arguments against neutrality as arguments against expecting too much of it. Britain's present economic dependence on America may inhibit her from anything but a position of close alliance; but if that is true she has virtually ceased to be an independent state. The economic success of neutrals like Sweden and Switzerland shows that it is not necessary to be allied with America to be prosperous.

One thing is clear. Being neutral in the cold war, even though it was conceived of as a withdrawal from power politics, would not exempt Britain from the need for diplomacy. The government of a neutral Britain would need to bargain, threaten and negotiate with the resources at its disposal in order to preserve existing British interests; perhaps even in order to keep out of the cold war. This would not mean that she would have to retain nuclear weapons; these may have some bargaining power in the day-to-day issues of international life, though this is speculative; but certainly states with neither alliances nor nuclear weapons, like India and Sweden, manage to bargain fairly effectively. But it would be a mistake to think that the foreign policy of a neutral or nonaligned state is single-mindedly dedicated to cold war mediation. Nonalignment, for a state, is at best an orientation, a way of looking at the major issues of world politics, which would come into play when her government was not wholly preoccupied with national concerns; it is far different from the neutrality of the United Nations Secretary-General, for whom mediation is close to being the core of his function.

To speculate how a neutral Britain might fare in the event of an actual war breaking out between the superpowers is even more hazardous. If nuclear weapons were used, there would be little reason to use them against neutrals; that means that Britain would probably escape the direct effects of their use; but she could easily be affected by fall-out. It hardly seems likely that a future world war would be one of territorial advance and retreat; or that the belligerents would be sufficiently interested in wartime trade, territory, or public opinion in neutral states to intervene forcibly in them. If such a war ever came, Britain would almost certainly stand a better chance of survival if she had established her neutrality in advance, than if she remained in NATO with American bases on her soil and at least a part of her armed forces under NATO command.

What is unpredictable is how great the chance of survival would be, bearing in mind not only the side-effects of nuclear attack, but the disruption of the trade on which Britain would still need to rely even to feed herself.

The case against neutrality is largely implicit in the preceding argument. Perhaps the most powerful influence against British neutrality is that of inertia—'better the devil we know than the devil we don't'; apart from that, it is said that a neutral Britain could be directly subjected to blackmail, even nuclear blackmail. Hedley Bull, for instance, in *The Control of the Arms Race*, equates the policy of C.N.D. (that is, renouncing nuclear weapons as well as leaving NATO), with 'surrender'.

Whether a neutral Britain could be blackmailed more easily than it can now, depends on how likely she is to come into conflict on her own account with Communist states. This is, of course, a matter of political judgment. War between a neutral Britain and the Soviet Union seems a very remote possibility. The position of Hong Kong might suggest that even a neutral Britain could be drawn into conflict with China; certainly Britain could not defend Hong Kong without American help if China decided to absorb it; indeed even with American help she could hardly do so. Western ally or neutral, she would almost certainly have to abandon Hong Kong in such a case just as Portugal had to abandon Goa when India attacked it in 1961.

Staying in NATO is also a matter of political judgment. It implies that perpetuating the division of Europe into two military blocs is safer than fragmenting one of the blocs in the hope of reducing the tensions between them. There is nothing self-evident about this. Those who believe it is true need to show why their answers to the four questions raised above (page 24) are more plausible than those of the neutralists. And whatever judgment one makes is provisional; the relevant circumstances may change, and it will need to be revised.

Can one escape from such inconclusiveness? One way is that of the pacifist, who must be neutral because alliances imply readiness to fight wars, and war, for him, is wrong under all circumstances. The absolute pacifist position became peculiarly difficult to defend in the Second World War. How could one seriously argue that Britain should never fight, come what may, when what did come, and would have spread further and lasted longer if Britain had not fought, was Nazi rule, with its enslavement of entire nations and its wholesale elimination of what it considered the inferior races? But if Hitler made pacifism morally untenable, the lesson of the atomic bomb used against Japan in the year of Hitler's defeat pointed in exactly the opposite direction. As nuclear weapons were developed with ever-increasing destructive power, many felt that no future war in which they might be used could be justified. For these 'nuclear pacifists', again, membership of NATO, since it relied on nuclear weapons, was unconditionally wrong. They support British neutrality, and British renunciation of nuclear weapons, regardless of the consequences, though some of them would concede that a neutral Britain might need to arm in its own defence, with 'conventional' weapons.

We seem to be left with a choice between saying that any decision by Britain as to whether not to be neutral depends on the circumstances of the time; and accepting the absolutes of the pacifist and the nuclear pacifist. There is perhaps another way of looking at it. We can ask, what is the future of neutrality? What trend can we see in history which might show the general tendency of the policies of States like Britain? As early as 1917, President Wilson of America declared that there was no longer any room for neutrality in the modern world; and in one sense his words are even truer of 1970 than they were of 1917. To survive a world war as a neutral state is not an ambition that makes very much sense; we are all of us involved in the general pattern of the world's future. In another sense, though, this is false. For any given great power, at the end of its day of military glory, may mature into neutrality, by ceasing to have military ambitions of its own. Sweden, once the dominant power of northern Europe, is one such example. Austria, although still concerned about the fate of the German-speaking population of Italian-ruled South Tyrol, is another. This maturing may take the form of merging into an alliance. The Netherlands, the greatest power of seventeenth-century western Europe, had withdrawn into neutrality by the nineteenth century, survived the First World War as one, but after being occupied by the Nazis in the Second, has been a member, first of the Brussels Pact, and then ever since its foundation, of NATO. In fact, of all the countries overrun by Germany in the last war, only Yugoslavia is not aligned with either East or West today. This is a natural response to a shattering historical experience; it does not necessarily represent learning the lessons of history, for the lessons of the Second World War may not be applicable to any future situation.

What does seem of general historical application is this tendency of once militant states to abdicate from high politics; and neutrality is perhaps the natural form in which to do this. That Britain, whose role in the Second World War only thirty years ago was so significant for its outcome, should now accept a future in which her military influence ceases to be felt outside her borders may seem to be both unnecessary and calamitous. Yet in an age of superpowers and guerrilla warfare, Britain is no longer a major force to be reckoned with militarily. And now that so many organizations and channels exist for international activities outside the military sphere, neutrality no longer need mean isolation. In the long run, whatever influence Britain may have on world events (and not merely on the cold war) will arise not from her military strength but from the degree of wisdom, generosity or understanding she can show; and this is likely to be more effective if she is not militarily committed to one particular grouping, but instead is unattached, and therefore capable of objectivity. In the short run, circumstances may or may not seem to require that Britain should remain within the Western alliance; but in a longer perspective such alliances are likely to prove temporary and abnormal, and the trend is likely to be towards neutrality; not the self-contained neutrality of the early twentieth century, but the positive and constructive neutrality for which the late twentieth century, whatever its other shortcomings, offers virtually unlimited scope.

1. Does there have to be a set of rules governing neutral rights and duties before a state can be neutral in a war involving any of its neighbours? Who should determine what the rules are, at any given time, and on what basis?

2. Has there been a decline in neutrality in the last seventy years? If so, to what should it be attributed?

3. Were Germany's violations of neutral rights in the First World War more serious than those of the Allies? Could either side plausibly claim that such violations as they committed were dictated by 'strategic necessity'?

4. What obstacles did membership of the League of Nations put,
   (a) in theory
   (b) in practice
   in the way of remaining neutral in wartime?

5. How far can Hitler's success up to 1941 be explained by a tendency of other states to 'retreat into neutrality'? Can we learn anything of general application about neutrality from the history of this period, or was Hitler an exceptional and misleading case?

6. Were the Swedish and Swiss experiences in the Second World War typical of those of neutrals as a whole? (Consider, for example, Ireland, Portugal, Turkey and Latin America.) Why did some states succeed in staying neutral while others were invaded or otherwise drawn into the war?

7. In what sense, if at all, are nonaligned states 'neutral'? Is nonalignment an intelligent response to the unique predicament the world has been in since 1945?

8. Compare the present position of Austria, as a neutralized state, with that of Belgium before 1914. Is there any current international situation to which neutralization could be applied?

9. What are the advantages and disadvantages for Britain, of leaving NATO and becoming neutral? What impact, if any, would such a decision be likely to have on East-West relations generally?

10. What role do neutral states play in contemporary international organizations?

PART I

Traditional Neutrality

As we saw in the introduction, the nineteenth century, from 1815 onwards, was a good time for a European state to be neutral. There were no general wars after the defeat of Napoleon, and no wars at all in Europe for the last twenty years; and when war had occurred, states that did not want to involve themselves in the quarrels of others could usually declare their neutrality with some confidence that it would be respected, even if they bordered on the belligerents.

In the early years of this century, two contrary processes were at work. On the one hand, the legal basis of neutrality was clarified and formalized. At the Hague Conferences of 1899 and 1907, attended by representatives of almost all states of political significance in the world, conventions were accepted which specified in considerable detail the legal duties of belligerents to neutrals, and of neutrals to belligerents, in time of war. On the other, the political basis on which neutrality rested was being eroded. For neutrality to thrive, it must be possible to localize war, or at least confine it within some geographical limits. But in the last quarter of the nineteenth century a system of alliances had grown up which made it likely that any war between European states would be a general war. Germany and Austria were joined in the Dual Alliance of 1879, which was extended, less convincingly, to include Italy and become a Triple Alliance in 1882. France was allied to Russia from 1894 onward. This trend continued into the twentieth century. By *ententes* first with France in 1904, and then with Russia in 1907, Britain, without committing herself to a legal alliance in either case, made it highly probable that her weight would be thrown on the side of those two countries in any conflict with the Dual, or Triple, Alliance.

The first two documents illustrate the elaboration that had taken place in the legal concept of neutrality from Grotius to the Hague Conferences. Grotius, writing in 1625, is often called 'the father of international law'. Yet in his three-volume work on the law of war and peace this brief extract is virtually all he has to say about neutrality. By contrast, the Hague Conference of 1907 took the question of neutrality seriously enough to draft two separate conventions (that is, multilateral treaties), one for naval and one for land warfare, and each ran to more than twenty articles.

DOCUMENT 1. Extracts from *On the Law of War and Peace* by Hugo Grotius, translated by Francis W. Kelsey (Oceana, 1964).

What the duty of those at peace is towards belligerents

1. On the other hand it is the duty of those who keep out of a war to do nothing whereby he who supports a wicked cause may be rendered more powerful, or whereby the movements of him who wages a just war may be hampered, according to what we have said above. In a doubtful matter, however, those at peace should show themselves impartial to either side in permitting transit, in furnishing supplies to troops, and in not assisting those under siege. In Thucydides the Corcyreans say that it is the duty of the Athenians, if they wish to be impartial, either to prevent the Corinthians from hiring troops on Attic soil, or to allow them the same privilege. Philip, king of Macedon, was charged by the Romans with having violated his treaty in two ways, both in having done injury to the allies of the Roman people, and in having aided the enemy with soldiers and money.

The same points are stressed by Titus Quintius in a conference with Nabis:

'Still', you say, 'I have not, strictly speaking, done violence to you and your friendship and alliance.' How many times do you wish me to prove that you have done this? I do not wish to do so at greater length, and I shall sum up the gist of the matter. By what things, then, is friendship violated? In very truth by these two things, by treating my allies as enemies, and by allying yourself with the enemy.

34

2. In Agathias we read that an enemy is one who does what the enemy wishes; and in Procopius, that he is counted in the ranks of the enemy who supplies a hostile army with what is directly useful for war. Demosthenes long ago said: 'He who creates and devises the means whereby I may be captured is my enemy, even if he does not strike me nor hurl a javelin at me.' Marcus Acilius told the Epirotes, who had not supported Antiochus with troops, but were accused of having sent him money, that he did not know whether he should class them as enemies or those at peace. The praetor Lucius Aemilius censured the people of Teos for having aided the fleet of the enemy with supplies, and for having promised them wine; adding, that he would treat them as enemies unless they gave the same to the Roman fleet. And there is recorded a saying of Caesar Augustus: 'A state, which receives an enemy, loses the right of peace.'

3. It will even be of advantage to make a treaty with either party that is waging war, in order that it may be permissible to abstain from war while retaining the goodwill of either, and to render to each the common duties of humanity. We read in Livy: 'Let them desire peace with either side, as befits impartial friends; let them not intervene in the war.' Archidamus, king of Sparta, when he saw that the Eleans were leaning to the side of the Arcadians, wrote a letter containing only this: 'It is a good thing to remain quiet.'

Editor's Note to Document I

Corcyra became an ally of Athens in 433 B.C., the year before the Peloponnesian War broke out. She had appealed for Athenian support, or at least neutrality, in her conflict with Corinth, an ally of Sparta. By agreeing to a defensive alliance with Corcyra, Athens increased the tension between her alliance system and that of Sparta and thus contributed to the outbreak of the war.

Titus Quintius, Marcus Acilius, and Lucius Aemilius were Roman commanders in the Greek wars at the beginning of the second century B.C., first against Philip of Macedon, and later against Antiochus of Syria. Nabis was king of Sparta.

Agathias and Procopius were historians, Greek and Byzantine respectively, of the sixth century A.D.

The Archidamus referred to is Archidamus III, who was king of Sparta in the middle of the fourth century B.C.

DOCUMENT 2. Extracts from the Hague Conventions of 1907, from *The Reports to the Hague Conferences of 1899 and 1907* edited by James Brown Scott (Oxford University Press for the Carnegie Endowment for International Peace, 1917).

(a) Convention V respecting the rights and duties of neutral powers and persons in case of war on land.

With a view to laying down more clearly the rights and duties of neutral Powers in case of war on land and regulating the position of the belligerents who have taken refuge in neutral territory;

Being likewise desirous of defining the meaning of the term 'neutral', pending the possibility of settling, in its entirety, the position of neutral individuals in their relations with the belligerents;

Have resolved to conclude a Convention to this effect, and have, in consequence, appointed the following as their plenipotentiaries:

[Here follow the names of plenipotentiaries.]

Who, after having deposited their full powers, found in good and due form, have agreed upon the following provisions:

Chapter I. The Rights and Duties of Neutral Powers

Article 1. The territory of neutral Powers is inviolable.

Article 2. Belligerents are forbidden to move troops or convoys of either munitions of war or supplies across the territory of a neutral Power. . . .

Article 4. Corps of combatants cannot be formed nor recruiting agencies opened on the territory of a neutral Power to assist the belligerents. . . .

Article 6. The responsibility of a neutral Power is not engaged by the fact of persons crossing the frontier separately to offer their services to one of the belligerents.

Article 7. A neutral Power is not called upon to prevent the export or transport, on behalf of one or other of the belligerents, of arms, munitions of war, or, in general, of anything which can be of use to an army or a fleet. . . .

Article 9. Every measure of restriction or prohibition taken by a neutral Power in regard to the matters referred to in Articles 7 and 8 must be impartially applied by it to both belligerents.

A neutral Power must see to the same obligation being observed by companies or private individuals owning telegraph or telephone cables or wireless telegraphy apparatus.

Article 10. The fact of a neutral Power resisting, even by force, attempts to violate its neutrality cannot be regarded as a hostile act. . . .

Chapter III.   *Neutral Persons*

Article 16. The nationals of a State which is not taking part in the war are considered as neutrals.

Article 17. A neutral cannot avail himself of his neutrality:
  (*a*) If he commits hostile acts against a belligerent;
  (*b*) If he commits acts in favour of a belligerent, particularly if he voluntarily enlists in the ranks of the armed force of one of the parties.

In such a case, the neutral shall not be more severely treated by the belligerent as against whom he has abandoned his neutrality than a national of the other belligerent State could be for the same act.

Article 18. The following acts shall not be considered as committed in favour of one of the belligerents in the sense of Article 17, letter (*b*):
  (*a*) Supplies furnished or loans made to one of the belligerents, provided that the person who furnishes the supplies or who makes the loans lives neither in the territory of the other party nor in the territory occupied by him, and that the supplies do not come from these territories;
  (*b*) Services rendered in matters of police or civil administration. . . .

Article 20. The provisions of the present Convention do not apply except between contracting Powers, and then only if all the belligerents are parties to the Convention.

(b) Convention XIII concerning the rights and duties of neutral powers in naval war.

The High Contracting Parties ... have agreed to observe the following common rules, which cannot, however, modify provisions laid down in existing general treaties, and have appointed as their plenipotentiaries, to wit:
[Here follow the names of plenipotentiaries.]
Who, after having deposited their full powers, found in good and due form, have agreed upon the following provisions:

Article 1. Belligerents are bound to respect the sovereign rights of neutral Powers and to abstain, in neutral territory or neutral waters, from any act which would, if knowingly permitted by any Power, constitute a violation of neutrality.

Article 2. Any act of hostility, including capture and the exercise of the right of search, committed by belligerent war-ships in the territorial waters of a neutral Power, constitutes a violation of neutrality and is strictly forbidden.

Article 3. When a ship has been captured in the territorial waters of a neutral Power, this Power must employ, if the prize is still within its jurisdiction, the means at its disposal to release the prize with its officers and crew, and to intern the prize crew.
If the prize is not in the jurisdiction of the neutral Power, the captor Government, on the demand of that Power, must liberate the prize with its officers and crew. . . .

Article 6. The supply, in any manner, directly or indirectly, by a neutral Power to a belligerent Power, of war-ships, ammunition, or war material of any kind whatever, is forbidden.

Article 7. A neutral Power is not bound to prevent the export or transit, for the use of either belligerent, of arms, ammunition, or, in general, of anything which could be of use to an army or fleet.

Article 8. A neutral Government is bound to employ the means at its disposal to prevent the fitting out or arming within its jurisdiction of any vessel which it has reason to believe is intended to cruise, or engage in hostile operations, against a Power with which that Government is at peace. It is also bound to display the same vigilance to prevent the departure from its jurisdiction of any vessel intended to cruise, or engage in hostile operations, which had been adapted entirely or partly within the said jurisdiction for use in war.

Article 9. A neutral Power must apply impartially to the two belligerents the conditions, restrictions, or prohibitions made by it in regard to the admission into its ports, roadsteads, or territorial waters, of belligerent war-ships or of their prizes.

Nevertheless, a neutral Power may forbid a belligerent vessel which has failed to conform to the orders and regulations made by it, or which has violated neutrality, to enter its ports or roadsteads.

Article 10. The neutrality of a Power is not affected by the mere passage through its territorial waters of war-ships or prizes belonging to belligerents. . . .

Article 12. In the absence of special provisions to the contrary in the legislation of a neutral Power, belligerent war-ships are not permitted to remain in the ports, roadsteads or territorial waters of the said Power for more than twenty-four hours, except in the cases covered by the present Convention. . . .

Article 14. A belligerent war-ship may not prolong its stay in a neutral port beyond the permissible time except on account of damage or stress of weather. It must depart as soon as the cause of the delay is at an end.

The regulations as to the question of the length of time which these vessels may remain in neutral ports, roadsteads, or waters, do not apply to war-ships devoted exclusively to religious, scientific, or philanthropic purposes. . . .

Article 16. When war-ships belonging to both belligerents are present simultaneously in a neutral port or roadstead, a period of not less than twenty-four hours must elapse between the departure of the ship belonging to one belligerent and the departure of the ship belonging to the other.

The order of departure is determined by the order of arrival, unless the ship which arrived first is so circumstanced that an extension of its stay is permissible.

A belligerent war-ship may not leave a neutral port or road-stead until twenty-four hours after the departure of a merchant ship flying the flag of its adversary. . . .

Article 28. The provisions of the present Convention do not apply except between contracting Powers, and then only if all the belligerents are parties to the Convention.

Editor's Note to Document 2

Convention V was signed and ratified by twenty-four states including Austria-Hungary, Belgium, France, Germany, Luxembourg, Russia and the United States. Great Britain in signing the Convention made reservations to Articles 16, 17 and 18, and never ratified it.

Convention XIII was signed and ratified without reservation, by eighteen states, among them Austria-Hungary, Belgium, France, Luxembourg and Russia. Germany signed and ratified it with reservations to Articles 11, 12, 13 and 20. Great Britain signed with reservations to Articles 19 and 23, but again never ratified it. The United States did not sign, but eventually adhered, with reservations to Articles 3 and 23.

*

THE BELGIUM CASE. The next four documents focus on the case of one neutral, or more precisely neutralized, state, Belgium. The existence of Belgium as an independent state goes back only as far as the 1830s, when she broke free from Holland. After some delay, Belgian sovereignty was recognized by the Treaty of 1839, as a 'perpetually Neutral State', and guaranteed as such by the five great powers forming 'the Concert of Europe'. Document 3 shows the context in which 'the Belgian Question' arose in the 1830s and the significance of the treaty which settled it. The next extract shows how Belgian neutrality survived its first major test, the Franco-Prussian War of 1870–1. In that war, British neutrality was conditional on Belgian neutrality being maintained. The British Government had made it clear that it would intervene against whichever belligerent violated Belgian neutrality. Later, as is shown by Documents 5 and 6, the British guarantee began to be thought of as applicable only to a German violation of Belgian neutrality. Document 5 shows that by 1908 there were two somewhat conflicting views of what British policy should be if Belgian neutrality were to be threatened in any other way than by Germany, unilaterally, in a war with France. Eyre Crowe emphasizes Britain's legal and moral obligations, Hardinge the need for what today would be called 'pragmatism'; Sir Edward Grey's brief comment seems to endorse both positions. Just where the British Government stood on this question, however, is perhaps better indicated by the military conversations she had already initiated with Belgium as early as 1906. Document 6, a letter from the Belgian Chief of Staff to his own Minister of War, reports these conversations from the Belgian side. This was not, in fact, the first time that Britain's attitude towards her commitment to preserve Belgian neutrality, by force if necessary, against attack from any quarter, had shown signs of hesitation. When Lord Salisbury was Prime Minister, he had refused to reaffirm this commitment at a time when there was some talk of a threat by Germany, with whom, at that time, British relations were cordial. Indeed Britain's even-handed policy during the Franco-Prussian War was perhaps atypical; she happened not to have any strong feelings of partisanship in that war. But once Britain became aligned, in spirit if not in letter, with one of the two great military camps into which Europe was divided after 1894, the effectiveness of her guarantee to Belgium was reduced. For if a war between France and Germany were imminent, Germany, in deciding whether to attack through Belgium or respect the latter's neutrality, might regard Britain as her enemy in either case; and would certainly not feel that the British guarantee offered any security against a French violation of that neutrality.

DOCUMENT 3. (a) Extracts from *The Great European Treaties of the Nineteenth Century* by Sir Augustus Oakes and R. B. Mowat (Clarendon Press, 1918).

The union of Holland and Belgium was the result of a statesmanlike attempt on the part of the Congress of Vienna to deal with a difficult problem. The Low Countries, situated between France and the Germanic States, and possessing harbours on the Channel and North Sea, had on many occasions been the battleground of the great States of Europe. The Belgic provinces, in particular, under whatever master they happened to be, had never been able to preserve their neutrality, but had been used by one belligerent State or another in their military designs. During the War of the Austrian Succession, Belgium was for two years (1747–8) conquered and actually governed by France. The same thing had happened again between 1792 and 1814. The United Provinces had been more successful in protecting themselves, for their people were independent in spirit, and were wealthy and statesmanlike. The two groups, the United and Belgic Provinces, if joined firmly together, might have formed a very substantial State, able to defend itself, and to prevent its great neighbours from using it for their military designs. If Holland and Belgium with use and wont had gradually grown together into one State and people, the international condition of Europe in the nineteenth and early twentieth centuries would have been simplified. The Dutch and Belgians were both comfortable, peace-loving peoples, with a high standard of civilization. Being neither able nor disposed to carry on aggressive designs, all their interests were in peace, which they might have been strong enough to maintain for themselves.

But the obscure forces which produce and develop that feeling which we call national were too strong. The Dutch felt themselves to be one nation, the Belgians another. History, language, religion, and, to a certain extent, race, all accentuated the difference between them. Between 1814 and 1830 these differences grew steadily more acute, and were increased by the fact that throughout that time men of Dutch birth played a far larger part in the management of the State than did Belgians. The majority of civil servants and military officers were Dutch. When in 1830 a revolution took place in France, it acted as an inspiration to the Belgians, who forthwith proclaimed a provisional government for themselves. . . .

It was years, however, before Holland would recognize the secession and independence of Belgium. Only the entry of a French army into Belgium put a stop to the war between the two countries. At the same time the Powers, finding Holland still unwilling to agree, took the matter under their own control. The Conference at London, on October 24, drew up the well-known Protocol of 24 Articles, which was embodied on November 15 in the famous Treaty of 1831 between Great Britain, Austria, France, Prussia, Russia, and the Kingdom of Belgium. . . .

The provisions of the Treaty of 1831 were incorporated in the Treaty of 1839, which has since then regulated the position of Belgium in international law. The treaty was made between Great Britain, Austria, France, Prussia, and Russia, on the one hand, and the Netherlands on the other. By Article II the treaty and its annex were placed 'under the guarantee' of the five Powers. Holland was not one of the guarantors. By this Article, each Power undertook to guarantee the position of Belgium as defined by the whole treaty. This was not a mere *collective* undertaking, where the guaranteeing Powers bind themselves to act together as one body. It was an individual obligation imposed by each Power on itself. The guarantee with respect to Luxemburg, made in 1867, was collective. An individual guarantee is, if anything, more emphatic than a collective one, but the moral obligation imposed by one or the other is just the same. Belgium was thus put into what was considered, by the Powers, to be the very eligible position of a State, with its integrity and neutrality guaranteed. As a consequence of this, Belgium was declared 'bound to observe such neutrality towards all other States'. This obligation Belgium honourably interpreted as involving not merely a passive attitude of strict neutrality, but also as carrying with it the heavy task of actually defending herself against an aggressor by force of arms. . . .

Yet while no one has denied that under the Treaty of 1839 Belgium was a neutral and guaranteed State, doubt has been cast upon Belgium's own impartiality. It has been suggested that previously to 1914 she had formed a design to join with the Entente Powers against Germany, and that accordingly she had forfeited all right to be considered by others as a neutral State. The Treaty of 1839 contained the stipulation that Belgium should be bound to observe her own neutrality.

The ground of accusation against Belgium does not lie in the fact that she called upon England and France to assist her.

Sir,
The Belgian Government regret to have to announce to

your Excellency that this morning the armed forces of Germany entered Belgian territory in violation of treaty engagements.

The Belgian Government are firmly determined to resist by all the means in their power.

Belgium appeals to Great Britain, France, and Russia to co-operate as guaranteeing Powers in the defence of her territory.

There should be concerted and joint action, to oppose the forcible measures taken by Germany against Belgium, and at the same time, to guarantee the future maintenance of the independence and integrity of Belgium. Belgium is happy to be able to declare that she will undertake the defence of her fortified places. [Belgian Minister for Foreign Affairs to British French and Russian Ministers at Brussels 4 August 1914.]

This appeal to the other guaranteeing Powers was a natural consequence of the obligation which the Powers had put upon Belgium, that she should observe her own neutrality. The guaranteeing Powers were bound to help her, once Germany had crossed her border. It would even have been quite correct for Belgium to invite the troops of a guaranteeing Power to enter the country, as a precautionary measure, before the territory had been violated. More than this, it was suggested by the British Military Attaché at Brussels in 1906 that a guaranteeing Power could, uninvited, send a force to Belgium in order to defend her neutrality against a State which was taking steps to violate it. The Belgian Government, however, refused to entertain this view. They maintained that the troops of a guaranteeing Power could only enter the country with the explicit consent of the Belgian Government.

The charge that Belgium had as early as 1906 departed from her neutrality, and taken up an attitude hostile to Germany, is based upon certain papers found in the archives of the Foreign Office at Brussels, after the occupation of that city by the Germans on August 20, 1914. These papers contained a record of conversations between the chief of the Belgian General Staff and the British Military Attaché at Brussels. The problem discussed was the manner in which Great Britain could best co-operate with the Belgian forces in the event of an attack upon Belgium by Germany. 'Should Belgium be attacked, it was proposed to send 100,000 men.' In another interview the two officers 'examined the question of combined operations, in the event of a German attack directed against Antwerp'.

The conversations, when first published in the *Nord-deutsche Allgemeine Zeitung* on October 13, 1914, created considerable surprise, but as soon as the documents were seriously studied they were seen to constitute no departure from neutrality on the part of Belgium, and no intention to violate that neutrality on the side of England or France. The Treaty of 1839 had imposed upon Belgium the heavy burden of defending her territory against any State, however powerful, which should try to get a passage for troops, or a base of operations in her territory. Such defence, on the part of Belgium, could be of no avail without co-operation with the Powers which had guaranteed to stand by her, under the Treaty of 1839. She was therefore not merely at liberty, but morally obliged to concert a plan for such combined operations in her own defence. Therefore, with regard to the conversations between the Chief of the Belgian General Staff and the British Military Attaché, the only question which the Belgian Government can be called on to answer, is this: when they concerted a scheme for operations along with Great Britain against a possible attack by Germany, why did they not make a complementary agreement with Germany, for concerted operations against a possible attack by Great Britain or France?

Such a method would have been in line with the policy pursued by Lord Granville, the British Secretary of State in 1870, when he concluded the treaty to join France, if the Germans crossed the Belgian frontier, and to join Prussia against France, if the French invaded Belgium. That the Belgian Government did not have conversations 'all round' in 1906, was because they had reason to believe that no danger threatened them from France or England, but that serious danger threatened them from Germany. The events which took place in the summer of 1914 indicate that conversations between the Belgian and German General Staffs would only have supplied Germany with military information which the Government of that country would not have scrupled to use, for reasons of State, when the time came.

Editor's Note to Document 3 (a)

This account of the origins and meaning of Belgian neutralization contains one curious argument—that it would have been quite correct for Belgium to have invited the troops of a guaranteeing Power to enter the country before the territory had been violated. This would on the contrary have been a violation of the 1839 Treaty.

DOCUMENT 3. (b) Extracts from the Treaty signed at London, on 19 April 1939, between Great Britain, Austria, France, Prussia, and Russia, on the one part, and the Netherlands, on the other part, and from the Annex thereto.

Article VII of the Annex
Belgium, within the limits specified in Articles I, II, and IV, shall form an Independent and perpetually Neutral State. It shall be bound to observe such Neutrality towards all other States.

Article II of the Treaty Proper
Her Majesty the Queen of the United Kingdom of Great Britain and Ireland, His Majesty the Emperor of Austria, King of Hungary and Bohemia, His Majesty the King of the French, His Majesty the King of Prussia, and His Majesty the Emperor of All the Russias, declare that the Articles mentioned in the preceding Article [which include Article VII above] are considered as having the same force and validity as if they were textually inserted in the present Act, and that they are thus placed under the guarantee of their said Majesties.

DOCUMENT 4. Extract from *Albert of Belgium* by Emile Cammaerts (Ivor Nicholson and Watson, 1935).

The fact is that, owing to the growing ambitions of her powerful neighbours, Belgium was in danger of becoming once more a pawn on the European chessboard. A conflict threatened between Prussia and Austria, and it was rumoured that Bismarck was ready to allow Napoleon to annex Belgium in order to secure his alliance or his benevolent neutrality. When King Leopold I died, on December 10th, 1865, the outlook appeared so dark that *The Times* expressed a doubt as to whether the country would survive her King. The pessimists forgot that the days of a weak and ill-defined neutrality were over. Leopold had not only succeeded in strengthening the country's international position, he had created a tradition defining her duties and her rights, and these had been repeatedly recognized by the Conservative as well as by the Liberal Powers. To use the King's words in a letter to Queen Victoria, written nine years before his death: "Belgium has bound herself to remain neutral, and her existence is based upon this neutrality, which the other Powers have guaranteed and are bound to maintain if she keeps her engagements." Any breach of neutrality on her part would upset the balance of power upon which European peace depended. Her existence did not prevent all conflicts, but it prevented at least a general conflagration. As long as Belgium kept out of the struggle, England could retain her detached attitude and exert her moderating influence. It had been contended, in 1831, that neutrality was a flimsy dream; Leopold I had shown that it was a solid reality, and that it could be maintained with sincerity, loyalty and strength. All the ambitions and intrigues of the following years failed to destroy the diplomatic stronghold he had so patiently and wisely erected.

The crisis began after Sadowa. Napoleon III, who had been taken unawares by the rapid success of the Prussian arms, endeavoured to seek compensations for France in exchange for Prussian aggrandisements. A series of dilatory negotiations took place, the outcome of which was the draft of the famous secret treaty called after the French Minister, Benedetti, and only revealed to the world in July 1870. This treaty would have secured Prussian help for France when she wished to conquer Belgium.

Bismarck did not delay his consent on account of his respect for Belgian neutrality, but because he did not wish to alienate English sympathies. Writing to Count Bernsdorf, the Prussian Minister in London, in January 1867, he declared that "the importance which Belgium" had for him "derived principally and precisely from that which it had in the eyes of Great Britain. . . . He had no motive for considering the maintenance of Belgian integrity as one of the necessary factors of his own policy, or for consenting alone to any sacrifice for its safeguard, if the latter were to threaten Germany's own integrity in a struggle with the most powerful of her neighbours. . . . He was not inclined to make the existence of Belgium a primary question if, by giving way on this point, he could secure the good relations with France which were indispensable to Germany." Bismarck was of course aware of the inquiries made by Lord Stanley in Paris, during the previous year, regarding the Franco-Prussian negotiations, and of the reassuring answer he had received.

Unwilling to challenge English policy with regard to Belgium, the French Emperor hoped at least to secure the Grand Duchy of Luxemburg which the Dutch King was not unwilling to cede against financial compensations. Though Bismarck did not openly oppose the project, he declared that the matter lay with the signatories of the Treaties of 1839, which, in determining the status of Belgium, had at the same time determined that of the Grand Duchy. It was therefore found necessary to convene a Conference of the Powers in London, on May 7th 1867, and Belgium and Holland were invited to attend. Prussia agreed to the dismantling of the fortress of Luxemburg, and the Grand Duchy was declared a neutral independent State under the "collective guarantee" of the Powers.

Conversations took place at the time between the British and Belgian Governments, with regard to the nature of the guarantee given to Belgium in 1839, and of the one granted to the Grand Duchy by the recent treaty. Both Lord Stanley and Lord Derby declared that the two guarantees were entirely different; the first was binding separately upon each of the Powers, and a violation constituted a *casus belli* for each of them, while the second implied merely a collective undertaking based upon a common agreement. . . .

The Belgian Minister, Frère-Orban, went to Paris to confer with the Emperor, who broached the subject of a political union. Frère-Orban, standing on the firm ground of independent neutrality, and strongly supported by British diplomacy, succeeded in maintaining the Belgian standpoint. He finally obtained the signature of a Protocol which, while sparing Napoleon's susceptibilities, completely defeated his purpose.

(8) Such was the situation on the eve of the Franco-Prussian War. Belgian neutrality had gone from strength to strength for nearly forty years. It had been tested in fair weather and foul.

Its scope was well defined: independence at home, non-intervention abroad. There was no room for misunderstanding or misinterpretation with regard to the duties imposed by the original treaties and the binding character of the guarantee. Great Britain and Belgium were to reap the fruits of the work so patiently pursued by Palmerston and Leopold I.

After Austria's defeat in 1866, a direct conflict between France and Prussia had become unavoidable. Napoleon was driven to it by internal difficulties and his failure to restore his prestige through diplomatic success. Bismarck was well prepared for the struggle and even anxious that it should break out at the earliest opportunity. The candidature of the Prince of Hohenzollern to the throne of Spain offered a useful pretext; in July 1870, everybody realized that war was imminent.

The Emperor wrote to Leopold II assuring him of his intention to respect the Belgian status and on July 16th, de Grammont, his Foreign Minister, confirmed this declaration to Baron Beyens, Belgian Minister in Paris: "The Emperor's Government," he wrote, "is resolved to respect the neutrality of Belgian territory on condition that it shall be respected by Prussia and her Allies." Three days later the Belgian Government received the same assurances through the German Minister in Brussels. In response to a request of M. Nothomb, Belgian Minister in Berlin, Bismarck confirmed this statement in a letter dated July 22nd, repeating almost word for word the French declaration. In order to avoid any possible misunderstanding, the Belgian Government instructed their representatives in Berlin and Paris to point out that the violation of Belgian territory by one of the belligerents would not release the other from its international obligations. On both sides the answer was perfectly explicit: France and Prussia would only enter Belgium in case of violation of neutrality, in order to help the Belgian troops to repulse the invader. "Belgian neutrality," declared de Grammont, "was created not only for the security and happiness of Belgium, but for our own (France's) security; it is a rampart which you (Belgians) must defend. If you could not do so, we should be obliged to join you in defending it."

During these critical days, the Cabinets in London and Brussels remained in close touch, and English and Belgian diplomats acted in co-operation with one another, in Paris and Berlin.

The publication, on July 25th, of the famous secret treaty offered by Benedetti to Bismarck, four years before, prompted Disraeli to insist on an unequivocal declaration from the British Government concerning the Belgian guarantee, and Lord John Russell to urge that England was in duty bound to defend Belgium in case of aggression. Both Gladstone and Lord Granville were obliged to observe a certain reticence, since the negotiations between London, Paris and Berlin were not yet concluded. After the exchange of signatures, on the 9th and 11th of August, the Prime Minister was more explicit. Justifying his diplomatic intervention, he declared that "the day that witnessed Belgium's absorption would hear the death-knell of public right and public law," and that England could not be a passive witness of the worst crime "that ever stained the pages of history."

The stipulations of the new treaties, which were communicated to the Belgian Government as soon as the assent of the parties had been obtained, confirmed the assurances given by France and Prussia on July 16th and 22nd, and added that the Power defending Belgian neutrality would obtain the naval and military support of Great Britain. It was also made clear that the treaties of 1839 were not suspended by the new agreements, and would again come into force after the hostilities.

Belgium meanwhile had taken all necessary defensive measures. On July 15th, the army had been placed on a war footing, all railway lines had been guarded, and both the southern and eastern frontiers were constantly patrolled. In his speech to the Chamber on August 24th, the Prime Minister, Baron d'Anethan, said that before receiving the declarations from France and Prussia promising to respect her neutrality, Belgium had been asked whether she was able to defend it. Having answered in the affirmative, she was in duty bound to prevent any infringement of international obligations. This duty extended not only to the two belligerents, but also to all the guaranteeing Powers: "How could we ask them, in case of need, to execute their guarantee," said the Belgian Minister, "if we omitted to defend ourselves?"

The Belgian defences seemed adequate, at least on paper.

considering the size of the German and French armies engaged in the field, the addition of 100,000 men on one side or the other was of considerable importance, and both belligerents seemed convinced that the strategical advantages they might gain by the invasion of Belgian territory would not compensate for this addition to the forces of the enemy, even if the recent treaties had not removed all possible doubt concerning England's attitude.

The crisis of 1870 is a perfect example of the working of the guarantee included in the 1839 treaties. Belgium was willing and, to all appearances, able to check an aggression. The two belligerents entered into identical engagements not to violate Belgian territory and to oppose, as guarantors of its neutrality, any such invasion on the part of the other. England, as a third guarantor in Western Europe, had not only promised her help to the Belgian Government, but had bound herself to military intervention against the law-breaker. The most optimistic supporter of neutrality could scarcely have hoped to improve upon this situation. Belgian security had a threefold protection: the military defences of the country, the promise of both belligerents, and the British guarantee.

One month later, Belgium had passed unscathed through the severest conflict which had afflicted Europe since Waterloo, and her neutrality had proved a more efficient safeguard than the strongest "barrier." It was a triumph for the rule of law against the rule of force.

(9) A closer examination of the difficulties which confronted Leopold II during this period shows, however, that if circumstances had not been favourable, the result might have been very different. . . .

All through the following year, at the time of the secret negotiations conducted by the French minister Rouher with Bismarck, through Benedetti, the King urged his Government to take further military precautions. After visiting Paris and Berlin in June 1867, he addressed to Rogier, his Prime Minister, a memorandum demanding a prompt decision: "If I do not succeed, at the beginning of my reign, in instilling into the minds of my ministers my own conviction of the necessity, of the urgency of strongly reorganizing our army, I shall have to reproach myself all my life for having failed in my duty towards my country." A new military law was finally passed in 1869, but the results were disappointing since, instead of 95,000 men, the call to the colours in July 1870 only yielded 83,000. "I defy anybody," wrote the King a few months later, "to find an officer who will deny that if the army, instead of limiting itself to sentry duty, had been compelled to act, it would have been exposed to the gravest dangers and the most frightful humiliations. . . ."

To internal dissension and inadequate defence was added a third difficulty during the years which preceded the Franco-Prussian War. Great Britain, Belgium's sponsor and principal guarantor, had become unwilling to bind herself to interfere in case of aggression. Van de Weyer, the Belgian Minister in London, found Lord Stanley very sympathetic, but far less definite in his declarations than Palmerston. The latter had on several occasions assured Belgium of British support; Lord Stanley was non-committal. "We shall see," he replied to the Belgian Minister during the critical days of 1867, "and I add: put yourself promptly in a state of defence." This attitude was no doubt inspired by the desire to see the Belgians make the necessary preparations and not to rely too much on British protection, but it was also based on a new conception of the guarantee, which found expression in the course of the parliamentary debates during the crisis of 1870. While some speakers —Lord John Russell amongst them—contended that the British duty of intervention was unconditional, Gladstone considered that view to be "rigid" and impracticable. On August 10th, he explained that he could not agree with those who held "that the simple fact of the existence of a guarantee is binding on every party to it, irrespectively altogether of the particular position in which it may find itself at the time, when the occasion for acting on the guarantee arises." This contention was perfectly reasonable for circumstances might arise, such as the refusal of Belgium to defend herself, or a struggle in which all British forces would be engaged, which might render intervention inadvisable or impossible. But the fact that this interpretation of the guarantee had become the British official doctrine weakened its prestige abroad and left the door open to doubt and suspicion. . . .

DOCUMENT 5. Extract from *British Documents on the Origins of War* edited by G. P. Gooch and H. V. Temperly (Volume VIII, H.M.S.O. 1935). Document No. 311. 'Memorandum by Mr Eyre Crowe respecting Belgian Neutrality and Great Britain's Obligation to Defend it' with Minutes by Sir C. Hardinge and Sir Edward Grey.

Memorandum by Mr. Eyre Crowe.
Memorandum respecting Belgian Neutrality and Great Britain's Obligation to Defend it.[1]

... It will be convenient to consider first the 2nd alternative situation indicated in Sir E. Grey's inquiry, viz.:

"How far would England's liability under the treaty guaranteeing the neutrality of Belgium be affected, if the other Powers, or some of them, acquiesced in a violation of that neutrality?"

The case, as put, presupposes that Belgium is not a consenting party to the violation. She will, therefore, necessarily appeal to the guaranteeing Powers against the aggression of a State which is likely to be one of their number. These Powers are clearly bound in such a case to make good their guarantee, if the guarantee has any practical meaning at all. There is nothing in the words of the treaty to indicate that the guarantee is an exclusively collective one, that is to say that if one guarantor fails, none of the others are bound. Any such view would, on the contrary, make the treaty obligation of the guaranteeing Powers, in practice, nugatory. For it is obvious that the only real danger of a violation of Belgian neutrality, under the political conditions prevailing at the time of signature, and still existing practically unchanged, lies in the possible action of one of the guaranteeing Powers themselves. If it were held that the cooperation of all the guaranteeing Powers was an essential condition of the liability of any one of them to make good its guarantee, then the liability could never arise in any contingency that has any probability of presenting itself,—

---

[1] [This memorandum was written on the following questions asked by Sir Edward Grey: "How far would England's liability under the Treaty guaranteeing the neutrality of Belgium be affected, if (1) Belgium acquiesced in a violation of her neutrality; (2) if the other guaranteeing Powers or some of them acquiesced?"]

which cannot be supposed to have been the intention of the signatories.

It must therefore be concluded, and this is also the common sense view of the matter, that the acquiescence of one or more of the guaranteeing Powers in a violation of the neutrality of Belgium, protested against by Belgium herself, does not absolve the other guaranteeing Powers from the obligation to make good their guarantee. Perhaps the obligation could be most appropriately expressed in legal phraseology, by saying that the guaranteeing Powers are "jointly and severally" liable.

The conditions of the problem are materially changed in the situation which underlies the assumption made in Sir E. Grey's first question:

"How would England's liability be affected if Belgium acquiesced in a violation of her neutrality?"

The wording of article 7 of the Annex to the treaty of guarantee makes it quite clear that for Belgium to acquiesce in such violation would constitute a repudiation on her part of her engagement under that article. Technically, and on a strict construction of the treaty, there appears to me to be no doubt that even in this contingency the guaranteeing Powers remain liable for the fulfilment of the treaty stipulation that Belgium shall remain perpetually neutral.

It might, nevertheless, seem, at first sight, that, whatever the actual words of the treaty, the Powers cannot reasonably be held bound to vindicate a guaranteed right in favour of a party which freely desired to abandon such right.

A closer examination however of the political conditions in which the treaty originated will show that the question must be viewed differently. If it were the case that the neutrality of Belgium was a purely Belgian interest which the guaranteeing Powers were anxious, out of friendship for her, to uphold, then no doubt it would be absurd to expect that the Powers should go out of their way to enforce that neutrality when Belgium no longer desired it. But this is not really the situation. The neutrality of Belgium was guaranteed not merely because it was a Belgian interest, but because it was an interest of the guaranteeing Powers. Indeed it is difficult to imagine why, otherwise, so onerous an engagement should have been entered into. It follows that the obligation of the guarantee was incurred not alone, nor exclusively, as towards Belgium, but also as towards the other guaranteeing Powers. If, then, the neutrality is violated, with the connivance of Belgium, each of the guaranteeing Powers has the right to call upon its co-partners to join in enforcing the maintenance of neutrality, and such an appeal could not be refused without thereby repudiating the engagement solemnly undertaken by the fact of the guarantee.

The validity of a treaty concluded between a number of Powers does not, unless this be specifically stipulated, cease on one of the signatories violating or repudiating it. Were this otherwise, then, in the present case, the very violation of Belgian neutrality by one of the guaranteeing Powers would suffice to nullify the whole treaty. In other words, the sole contingency which the treaty was designed to meet, would, if it arose, automatically abolish or abrogate the treaty.

The case may perhaps be convincingly illustrated by a concrete example: Supposing Belgium were, with her own consent, during a Franco-German war, overrun by Germany. Would not France be entitled to call upon Great Britain to make good her guarantee that Belgium should remain perpetually neutral? Would not Holland be entitled to make the same demand?

It seems to me that only on the assumption that all the other guaranteeing Powers, and also Belgium herself, acquiesced in the violation of neutrality, would Great Britain be absolved from her liability. Even then she would of course retain her *right* to oppose the violation of neutrality, as being an infringement by the other Powers of their obligation to herself.

The above observations deal with the legal aspect of the matter.

From the point of view of policy, it is not difficult to imagine a situation in which the enforcement of Belgian guarantee by the employment of British forces would be an extraordinarily difficult and troublesome affair. If for instance both France and Germany simultaneously violated the neutrality, or, again, if France and Germany agreed, whilst remaining at peace with each other, to divide Belgium between them, how could Great Britain effectively reply to an appeal for assistance from Belgium? But difficulties of execution are no sufficient ground, legally and morally, for repudiating an obligation freely undertaken, though they may justify or excuse extreme caution in cho[o]sing the mode and time of action.

I conclude that Sir E. Grey's questions should be answered by the following proposition:

Great Britain is liable for the maintenance of Belgian neutrality whenever either Belgium or any of the guaranteeing Powers are in need of, and demand, assistance in opposing its violation.

E. A. C[ROWE].
Nov[ember] 15, 1908.

Foreign Office, November 15, 1908.
MINUTES.

The liability undoubtedly exists as stated above, but whether we could be called upon to carry out our obligation and to vindicate the neutrality of Belgium in opposing its violation must necessarily depend upon our policy at the time and the circumstances of the moment. Supposing that France violated the neutrality of Belgium in a war against Germany, it is, under present circumstances, doubtful whether England or Russia would move a finger to maintain Belgian neutrality, which [sic] if the neutrality of Belgium were violated by Germany it is probable that the converse would be the case.

C. H.

I am much obliged for this useful minute; I think it sums up the situation very well, though Sir C. Hardinge's reflection is also to the point.

E. G.

DOCUMENT 6. Extracts from letters from the Chief of the Belgian General Staff to the Belgian Minister of War, (a) 10 April 1906, (b) 24 April 1912 (from *Collected Diplomatic Documents Relating to the Outbreak of the European War* H.M.S.O. 1915).

(a) REPORT OF CONVERSATIONS BETWEEN THE BELGIAN AND
        BRITISH MILITARY AUTHORITIES, 1906
(Confidential.)

Brussels, April 10, 1906.

Sir,

I have the honour to furnish herewith a summary of the con-

versations which I have had with Lieutenant-Colonel Barnardiston, which I have already reported to you verbally.

His first visit was in the middle of January. Lieutenant-
Colonel Barnardiston told me of the preoccupation of the
British General Staff concerning the general political situation
and the existing possibilities of war. Should Belgium be attacked,
it was proposed to send about 100,000 men.

The lieutenant-colonel having asked me how we should
interpret such a step, I answered that, from the military point
of view, it could only be advantageous; but that this question
of intervention had also a political side, and that I must
accordingly consult the Minister of War.

Lieutenant-Colonel Barnardiston replied that his Minister
at Brussels would speak about it to our Minister for Foreign
Affairs.

He continued as follows: The disembarkation of the British
troops would take place on the French coast, in the neighbour-
hood of Dunkirk and Calais, in such a manner that the operation might be carried out in the quickest possible way. Landing
at Antwerp would take much longer, as larger transports would
be required, and, moreover, the risk would be greater.

This being so, several other points remained to be decided,
viz., transport by rail, the question of requisitions to which the
British Army might have recourse, the question of the chief
command of the allied forces.

He enquired whether our arrangements were adequate to
secure the defence of the country during the crossing and
transport of the British troops—a period which he estimated at
about ten days.

I answered that the fortresses of Namur and Liège were safe
against a surprise attack, and that in four days our field army
of 100,000 men would be ready to take the field. After having
expressed his entire satisfaction at what I had said, my visitor
emphasized the following points: (1) Our conversation was
absolutely confidential; (2) it was in no way binding on his
Government; (3) his Minister, the British General Staff, he, and
myself were the only persons then aware of the matter; (4) he
did not know whether his Sovereign had been consulted. . . .

At another interview Lieutenant-Colonel Barnardiston and I
examined the question of combined operations in the event of a

German attack directed against Antwerp, and on the hypothesis of our country being crossed in order to reach the French Ardennes.

Later on, the colonel signified his concurrence in the scheme I had laid before him, and assured me of the assent of General Grierson, Chief of the British General Staff.

Other questions of secondary importance were likewise disposed of, particularly those respecting intermediary officers, interpreters, gendarmes, maps, illustrations of uniforms, English translations of extracts from certain Belgian regulations, the regulation of customs dues chargeable on the British supplies, hospital accommodation for the wounded of the allied army, &c. Nothing was settled as to the possible control of the Press by the Government or the military authorities.

In the course of the last meetings which I had with the British attaché he communicated to me the daily disembarkation table of the troops to be landed at Boulogne, Calais and Cherbourg. The distance of the latter place, included owing to certain technical considerations, would cause a certain delay. The first corps would be landed on the tenth day, the second corps on the fifteenth day. Our railways would carry out the transport operations in such a way that the arrival of the first corps, either towards Brussels-Louvain or towards Namur-Dinant, would be completed on the eleventh day and that of the second corps on the sixteenth day.

I finally urged once again, as forcibly as was within my power, the necessity of accelerating the transport by sea in order that the British troops might be with us between the eleventh and the twelfth day; the very best and most favourable results would accrue from the concerted and simultaneous action by the allied forces. On the other hand, a serious check would ensue if such co-operation could not be achieved. Colonel Barnardiston assured me that everything would be done with that end in view.

In the course of our conversations I took the opportunity of convincing the military attaché of our resolve to impede the enemies' movements as far as lay within our power, and not to take refuge in Antwerp from the outset. Lieutenant-Colonel Barnardiston, on his side, informed me that he had at present little confidence in the support or intervention of Holland. He likewise confided to me that his Government intended to move the British base of supplies from the French coast to Antwerp as soon as the North Sea had been cleared of all German warships.

At all our interviews the colonel regularly communicated to me any confidential information he possessed respecting the military condition and general situation of our eastern neighbour, &c. At the same time he laid stress on the imperative need for Belgium to keep herself well informed of what was going on in the neighbouring Rhine country. I had to admit to him that in our country the intelligence service beyond the frontier was not, in times of peace, directly under our General Staff. We had no military attachés at our legations. I took care, however, not to admit to him that I was unaware whether the secret service, prescribed in our regulations, was organized or not. But it is my duty here to call attention to this state of affairs, which places us in a position of glaring inferiority to that of our neighbours, our possible enemies.

Major-General,
Chief of General Staff.

(b)　　　　　　　　　　(Translation.)
(Confidential.)

The British military attaché asked to see General Jungbluth. These gentlemen met on the 23rd April.

Lieutenant-Colonel Bridges told the general that Great Britain had, available for dispatch to the Continent, an army composed of six divisions of infantry and eight brigades of cavalry, in all 160,000 men. She had also all that she needed for home defence. Everything was ready.

The British Government, at the time of the recent events, would have immediately landed troops on our territory, even if we had not asked for help.

The general protested that our consent would be necessary for this.

The military attaché answered that he knew that, but that as we were not in a position to prevent the Germans passing through our territory, Great Britain would have landed her troops in any event.

As to the place of landing, the military attaché was not explicit. He said the coast was rather long; but the general knows that Mr. Bridges made daily visits to Zeebrugge from Ostend during the Easter holidays.

The general added that, after all, we were, besides, perfectly able to prevent the Germans from going through.

April 24, 1912.

PART II

The First World War

The First World War was precipitated by the assassination of the Austrian Crown Prince, Archduke Franz Ferdinand, on 28 June 1914 in the Serbian town of Sarajevo. Serbia was a protégé of Russia, and because of its appeal to Slavs within the Austro-Hungarian Empire, a thorn in the latter's flesh. After some delay, the Austrian government, supported and even egged on by Germany, presented to Serbia an ultimatum which would have made that small country an Austrian satellite, if it had been accepted. It was not accepted in full, but the Serbian reply was conciliatory, agreeing to investigate all alleged participants in the crime, to punish those found guilty, and to submit to arbitration any further questions of difference between Serbia and Austria. Even the German Kaiser conceded that there was now no valid cause for war. Nevertheless, as soon as the Austrians received the Serbian reply, they declared war. First Russian, and then German, mobilization followed; and Germany went on to demand of France that her government abandon its alliance with Russia and pledge its neutrality. When that was refused, she attacked France through Belgium. At this point, the British Empire came into the war on the side of France and Russia; and eventually the remaining powers of any political consequence—Italy, Japan, Turkey and the United States—all came in on one side or other. 'If war breaks out', Sir Edward Grey prophesied, 'it will be the greatest catastrophe that the world has ever seen.' The prophecy was apt.

It was in such circumstances that the law of neutrality, as set forth in the Hague Conventions and elsewhere, was put to the test from 1914 to 1918. It was a severe one, for many if not all of them. The stakes were so high for the belligerents that they were tempted to gain whatever advantage could be seized by violating the rights of neutrals. The latter's fate depended on two considerations: firstly, on how close their geographical position and their activities brought them to the main battle-fields of the war, on land and on sea; and secondly on their capacity to defend themselves when their neutral rights were infringed, and, in the last resort, on whether they were sufficiently strong to make the infringing state think twice about bringing them into the war on the opposing side.

In this chapter we shall look at what happened to four countries whose governments were determined to remain neutral when war broke out: Belgium, China, the United States and Norway. The first documents take up the story of Belgium. As we saw in the last chapter, the 'perpetual' neutralization provided by the Belgian Treaty of 1839 did not by itself assure Belgium of security in the event of a war in Western Europe; and the conditions in which Belgium survived intact the Franco-Prussian War of 1870–71 no longer held. Nevertheless the German ultimatum, and the entry of German troops into Belgium that followed immediately on it, came as a great shock to the Belgian people, though not as so great a shock to their government. It was obviously a breach of the 1839 Treaty, and thus of international law; and, in the remarkable speech of the German Imperial Chancellor Bethmann Hollweg to the Reichstag (the German Parliament), it was admitted to be such. This speech is one of the few occasions in twentieth-century history in which a statesman has publicly and expressly at the time admitted that his own policy is a breach of international law. The excuse he gave, both to the Belgians and to his own legislators, was that it was, for Germany, a matter of life and death. This excuse was to be used again and again to cover breaches of neutral rights by one or other side in the four years of war that followed.

It is doubtful whether *anything* could have saved Belgian neutrality in a war between France and Germany in 1914. The Schlieffen Plan, on which German strategy for a war against France and Russia was based, provided that Germany would first attack in the West, and, since 1904, it had been accepted by the German generals preparing for the possibility of such an attack, that it would be routed through Belgium. One thing only might have made the German government insist on modifying these plans: that is, if it had known that by violating Belgian neutrality, Germany would have brought Britain into a war in which she would otherwise have remained neutral. In fact, in a conversation with the German Ambassador on 29 July, the British Foreign Minister, Sir Edward Grey, indicated in politely diplomatic language that if war broke out between Germany and France, Britain would support France in any case (see Document 7); and a few days later Grey refused to commit himself when the German Ambassador asked whether Britain would remain neutral in such a conflict if Germany respected Belgium's neutrality. Thus, the British guarantee to Belgium had now disappeared; or rather it was extended in effect to guarantee France as well. It is possible that, had Germany known earlier of Grey's determination to bring Britain on France's side in any war with Germany, the German leaders might have shrunk from the war, and might not have encouraged Austria-Hungary to be so severe on Serbia; but once such a war occurred, Grey's policy meant that there was no incentive for Germany to forgo the strategic advantages of attacking through Belgium. It would perhaps be truer to say, no apparent incentive; for without the widespread indignation aroused in Britain by the violation of Belgian neutrality, the British government might not in the event have supported Grey in entering a war between France and Germany on the former's side. But the German government assumed, rightly or not, that Grey spoke for Britain.

A. THE END OF BELGIAN NEUTRALITY

DOCUMENT 7. Extract from telegram sent by the German Ambassador to Britain (Prince Lichnowsky) to the German Foreign Secretary (von Jagow) 29 July 1914, from *Outbreak of the World War: German Documents collected by Karl Kautsky* (Carnegie Endowment for International Peace, 1924).

The worst and most scandalous piece of English	Sir E. Grey just sent for me again. The Minister was entirely calm, but very grave, and received me with the words that the situation was continuing to

grow more acute. Sazonov had stated that after the declaration of war he will no longer be in a position to negotiate with Austria direct, and *had requested them here to take up the mediation efforts again.* The Russian Government regards the cessation of hostilities for the present as a necessary preliminary to mediation.

Sir E. Grey repeated his suggestion already reported, that we take part in a mediation *à quatre*, such as we had already accepted in principle. It would seem to him to be a suitable basis for mediation, if Austria, after occupying Belgrade, for example, or other places, should announce her conditions. Should Your Excellency, however, undertake mediation, a prospect I was able early this morning to put before him, this would of course suit him equally well. But *mediation* seemed now to him to be urgently necessary, if *a European catastrophe were not to result.*

Sir E. Grey then said to me that he had a friendly and private communication to make to me, namely, that he did not want our warm personal relations and the intimacy of our talks on all political matters to lead me astray, and he would like to *spare himself later the reproach (of) bad faith.* The British Government desired now as before to cultivate our previous friendship, and it could *stand aside as long as the conflict remained confined to Austria and Russia. But if we and France should be involved,* then the situation would immediately be altered, and the British Government would, *under the circumstances, find itself forced to make up its mind quickly.* In that event it

Marginal notes (left):

pharisaism that I ever saw! I will never enter into a naval convention with such scoundrels.

That sets me out of the running.

Good.

We have been trying to accomplish this for days, in vain!

Instead of mediation, a serious word to St Petersburg and Paris, to the effect that England would not help them would quiet the situation at once.

Aha! The common cheat!

This means, we are to leave Austria in the lurch. Mean and Mephistophelian! Thoroughly English, however.

Marginal notes (right):

In spite of the Czar's appeal to me!

It remains.

64

Already made up.	*would not be practicable to stand aside and*
This means they will attack us.	*wait for any length of time.* 'If war breaks out, it will be *the greatest catastrophe* that the *world has ever seen.*' It was far from his desire to express any kind of a threat;
He has shown bad faith all these years just the same, down to his latest speech.	he only wanted to protect me from disappointments and *himself* from the *reproach of bad faith*, and had therefore chosen the form of a private explanation. . . .

An absolute failure.

England reveals herself in her true colours at a moment when she thinks that we are caught in the toils and, so to speak, disposed of! That mean crew of shopkeepers has tried to trick us with dinners and speeches. The boldest deception, the words of the King to Henry for me: 'We shall remain neutral and try to keep out of this as long as possible.' Grey proves the King a liar, and his words to Lichnowsky are the outcome of a guilty conscience, because he feels that he has deceived us. At that, it is as a matter of fact a threat combined with a bluff, in order to separate us from Austria and to prevent us from mobilising, and to shift the responsibility for the war. He knows perfectly well that, if he were to say one single, serious, sharp and warning word at Paris and St Petersburg, and were to warn them to remain neutral, that both would become quiet at once. But he takes care not to speak the word, and threatens us instead! Common cur! England *alone* bears the responsibility for peace and war, not we any longer! That must also be made clear to the world.

Editor's Note to Document 7

The comments in small type, above and in the margins are by the German Emperor, Kaiser Wilhelm II Words italicized in the text are those underlined by him in the original

DOCUMENT 8. The German Ultimatum to Belgium, 2 August 1914. From *Collected Diplomatic Documents Relating to the Outbreak of the European War* (H.M.S.O. 1915).

Note presented by Herr von Below Saleske, German Minister at Brussels, to M. Davignon, Belgian Minister for Foreign Affairs.

Imperial German Legation in Belgium. Brussels, August 2, 1914. (Translation.) (Very Confidential.)
Reliable information has been received by the German Government to the effect that French forces intend to march on the line of the Meuse by Givet and Namur. This information leaves

no doubt as to the intention of France to march through Belgian territory against Germany.

The German Government cannot but fear that Belgium, in spite of the utmost goodwill, will be unable, without assistance, to repel so considerable a French invasion with sufficient prospect of success to afford an adequate guarantee against danger to Germany. It is essential for the self-defence of Germany that she should anticipate any such hostile attack. The German Government would, however, feel the deepest regret if Belgium regarded as an act of hostility against herself the fact that the measures of Germany's opponents force Germany, for her own protection, to enter Belgian territory.

In order to exclude any possibility of misunderstanding, the German Government make the following declaration:—

1. Germany has in view no act of hostility against Belgium. In the event of Belgium being prepared in the coming war to maintain an attitude of friendly neutrality towards Germany, the German Government bind themselves, at the conclusion of peace, to guarantee the possessions and independence of the Belgian Kingdom in full.

2. Germany undertakes, under the above-mentioned condition, to evacuate Belgian territory on the conclusion of peace.

3. If Belgium adopts a friendly attitude, Germany is prepared, in co-operation with the Belgian authorities, to purchase all necessaries for her troops against a cash payment, and to pay an indemnity for any damage that may have been caused by German troops.

4. Should Belgium oppose the German troops, and in particular should she throw difficulties in the way of their march by a resistance of the fortresses on the Meuse, or by destroying railways, roads, tunnels, or other similar works, Germany will, to her regret, be compelled to consider Belgium as an enemy.

In this event, Germany can undertake no obligations towards Belgium, but the eventual adjustment of the relations between the two States must be left to the decision of arms.

The German Government, however, entertain the distinct hope that this eventuality will not occur, and that the Belgian Government will know how to take the necessary measures to prevent the occurrence of incidents such as those mentioned. In this case the friendly ties which bind the two neighbouring States will grow stronger and more enduring.

DOCUMENT 9. 'The Night of August 2 1914'. Further extracts from *Albert of Belgium* by Emile Cammaerts.

(1) Brussels, that summer Sunday, looked particularly happy. The fine weather had caused the usual flow of trippers to the neighbouring countryside. Trains and trams—motors were still scarce in those days—leading to the Forêt de Soignes towards Tervueren and Waterloo were crowded to overflowing. The town itself was not deserted, for crowds of peasants and provincials had taken this opportunity of paying a visit to the Capital, strolling through the Grand' Place or hailing each other across the boulevards. The cafés were busy quenching the thirst of the people, and the children lately released from school took a lively share in the general merriment.

Prospects were good. Tradespeople congratulated themselves on their profits, and even the farmers, gratified by a record crop, refrained from uttering their usual complaints. The political struggle between Socialists and Conservatives pursued its normal course, but the agitation for universal suffrage, which had culminated in the general strike of 1913, had lost a great deal of its bitterness. It was generally felt that the worst was over and that a satisfactory solution of social and linguistic difficulties was within sight.

Those who troubled their heads about international affairs —a small minority in those days of complacent neutrality— were vaguely aware of a crisis. The ultimatum sent by Austria to Serbia on July the 23rd, followed five days later by the declaration of war, had caused a certain stir, and the military preparation going on in Germany and France were somewhat disturbing, but these were considered as mere precautions. There had been other crises in recent years, Tangiers, Algeciras, Agadir, which had been successfully overcome, in spite of the forebodings of the pessimists. Neither did the mobilization of the Belgian Army, started two days previously, trouble the equanimity of the ordinary citizen. On the contrary, the movement of troops added new interest to the holiday mood of the crowd. Supposing the conflict were to spread to Western

Europe, Belgium would at worst be obliged to guard her fron-tiers—as in 1870. England would once more keep a stern watch over her neutrality. Those who had glanced through their news-papers in the morning, had learnt with some indignation that the Germans had seized the railways of the neutralized Grand Duchy of Luxemburg, and occupied the Capital; but even this news did not seriously shake their confidence. The measure might be merely defensive and its scope was no doubt limited. Luxemburg was on the direct road to France, and its neutrality was not built on such solid foundations as that of Belgium. . . .

(2) The placid mood of the Belgian people had not been shared by the officials of the Foreign Office, who realized from the first that the Austrian ultimatum to Serbia might jeopardize the country's security.

From July the 23rd, foreseeing the danger to which Belgium was exposed, they had eagerly considered the various circum-stances under which a violation of the treaties of 1839 might occur. A number of notes on the subject had been prepared some years before. To the Belgian diplomats of pre-war days, a cynical violation of the treaties devoid of all legal excuse seemed indeed unlikely. They discussed the attitude to be taken in case of unwarranted invasion by Germany, France or England (and no distinction was made between the three Powers), and they also dealt with more complex problems. What would happen, for instance, in case of simultaneous invasions from two or more sides, each invader accusing the other of having ignored his obligations and justifying his own attitude by the necessity of parrying the blow? Such academic discussions, however, were soon to be swept away by a succession of alarming events.

On July 28th, a telegram from Comte Dudzeele, the Belgian Minister in Vienna, announced the declaration of war by Austria-Hungary to Serbia. The same evening, the ministerial Council, over which King Albert presided, resolved to place the army on a "strengthened peace footing," that is to say, to provide it with effectives similar to the forces maintained nor-mally, in time of peace, by other nations in frontier areas.

On July 31st, the Government was informed that a state of "Danger of War" (*Kriegsgefahr*) had been proclaimed in Ger-many and that Holland was arming. The Council ordered general mobilization to start on August 1st at midnight. The same evening, Sir Francis Villiers, the British Minister in Brussels, explained to the Foreign Minister, M. Davignon, the steps taken by Sir Edward Grey to ascertain the intentions of France and Germany with regard to Belgian neutrality. Meanwhile, Baron van der Elst [Secretary-General at the Ministry of Foreign Affairs] had called on the German Minister in Brussels in order to obtain further information. He reminded Herr von Below of the declaration made in 1911 by the German Chancellor through his Minister in Brussels: Germany had no intention of violating Belgian neutrality, but a public declaration to that effect would weaken her military situation. Baron van der Elst also alluded to the statement made in 1913 by Herr von Jagow before the Budget Commission of the Reichstag, recognizing the treaties of 1839. The German Minister answered that personally he was convinced that the feelings of his country towards Belgium remained unaltered.

On August 1st, in the morning, M. Klobukowski, the French Minister in Brussels, declared to M. Davignon that the Government of the Republic would respect Belgian neutrality, thus confirming the French answer to Sir Edward Grey's Note of the previous day. Reassured on this side, the Belgian Foreign Minister sent once more to the German Legation in order to inform Herr von Below of the French answer and give him an opportunity of making the intentions of his Government better known. The German Minister remained non-committal, but reiterated his opinion that Belgium had nothing to fear from Germany.

. On August 2nd, the very day on which the ultimatum was delivered, Herr von Below repeated this statement to M. Davignon himself and, questioned by a representative of the *Soir*, indulged in a picturesque metaphor: "Your neighbour's roof will perhaps burn, but your house will be saved." Was it an allusion to the future fate of France, or perhaps to that of Luxemburg which had already been occupied by German troops early that morning? It must be stated, in all fairness, that Herr von Below might have been sincere. The ultimatum had been sent to him, it is true, on July 29th, but he had been ordered not to break the seal of the envelope before being instructed to communicate its contents to the Belgian Government. It is more difficult to explain the reason which prompted the German Military Attaché in Brussels to answer the inquiries of the editor of the *Vingtième Siècle*, made on the same day, by denying that Germany had declared war on Russia, and that German troops had entered the Grand Duchy.

The Belgian authorities were in no doubt, by that time, as to the failure of the efforts made to prevent or limit the conflagration. Germany was already at war with Russia, and the occupation of Luxemburg made it plain that a conflict with France was imminent. But there was still a chance that, owing to British pressure upon the belligerents, Belgian neutrality would be respected as it had been in 1870. Germany had given, as a pretext for her invasion of Luxemburg, the necessity of securing the railways which she exploited in that country, against a possible attack by the French. Would she provoke British hostility, add to the number of her enemies, and challenge world opinion by violating Belgian territory?

The answer was soon to come. At about 7.20 p.m. Herr von Below called on M. Davignon at the Ministry of Foreign Affairs. After handing him the German ultimatum, he briefly outlined its proposals and retired, after ten minutes, without further comment. Baron de Gaiffier, *Directeur de la Politique*, and his collaborators, had been warned of the visit, and rushed to M. Davignon's study. They found him holding a paper in his hand:

"It is bad, very bad," said the Minister, who was extremely pale, "here is the German Note . . . they demand that we give free passage to the Army.

—And what did you say?

—I took the paper and said that I would examine it, with the King and my colleagues. We have twelve hours in which to answer. But I was unable to refrain from expressing my indignation. I told Herr von Below that we could have expected anything but this: Germany, who pretended to be our devoted friend, urging dishonour upon us! Let us translate quickly and call M. de Broqueville. . . ."

A long silence followed. The meaning of the document was only too plain. According to Belgian information, and to the definite declaration of the French Government, the suspicions expressed in the first paragraph served merely as a pretext for the German demand. The allusion to the line of the Meuse left no doubt as to the extent of the projected military movements.

Germany intended to use the road from Liège to Namur under the silenced guns of the very forts which she had urged Belgium to build in 1887. As to the promises made in paragraphs 1, 2 and 3, they were nullified by the blatant threat contained in paragraph 4. Besides, what value could be attached to such engagements made by a Power who entirely ignored the formal and solemn treaties concluded in 1839, confirmed in 1870, and strengthened by a score of public declarations made recently by the Emperor himself and his ministers?

It has since been disclosed that the text of the ultimatum had been prepared as early as July 26th—on the morrow of the Serbian reply to Austria-Hungary—by General von Moltke, the German Chief of Staff. In this first draft, Belgium was promised territorial compensation at the expense of France, and an allusion was made to an impending Franco-British invasion of Belgian territory. Herr von Below, in his last instructions, had been ordered to shorten the duration of the ultimatum from twenty-four to twelve hours, and to add a suggestion which appeared particularly ominous: the Belgian Government was advised to retire to Antwerp and to allow the German authorities to deal with any trouble which might arise in the Capital.

The sense of relief felt in Belgian diplomatic circles after the first shock brought by the ultimatum was over, strange as it may appear, was not without some foundation. "The situation was clear," writes M. de Bassompierre. "It lent itself neither to hesitation nor to interpretation." Under certain circumstances, Belgium might have been obliged to appreciate the motives which prompted her guarantor's actions and to choose between two belligerents who had penetrated her territory, or she might have been driven into a futile struggle against two or three Powers through strict adherence to the letter of the law. Now, the case was plain. On one side, the French Ministers' declaration of July 31st, officially confirmed the next day, stating that in case of international conflict the Government of the Republic would respect Belgian neutrality; on the other, an unequivocal demand, accompanied by threats, to allow German troops to enter Belgian territory, a demand based not even on a supposed breach by France of her obligations, but on her presumed intention of breaking them.

The silence was at last broken by Baron van der Elst who

asked the question which was in every mind—"Are we ready?" M. de Broqueville who had remained throughout quite calm, answered slowly: "Yes, we are ready. Mobilization, started yesterday morning, is almost completed. To-morrow the army will be able to move, but we have not yet received our heavy guns."

The time was then ten minutes past eight. It was decided that the King must be warned without delay, and asked to summon a Ministerial Council at nine o'clock. The Prime Minister left at once for the Royal Palace.

DOCUMENT 10. Extracts from a speech by the German Imperial Chancellor (von Bethmann Hollweg) to the German Reichstag, 4 August 1914. From *Collected Diplomatic Documents Relating to the Outbreak of the European War* (H.M.S.O. 1915).

A stupendous fate is breaking over Europe. For forty-four years, since the time we fought for and won the German Empire and our position in the world, we have lived in peace and have protected the peace of Europe. In the works of peace we have become strong and powerful, and have thus aroused the envy of others. With patience we have faced the fact that, under the pretence that Germany was desirous of war, enmity has been awakened against us in the East and the West, and chains have been fashioned for us. The wind then sown has brought forth the whirlwind which has now broken loose. We wished to continue our work of peace, and, like a silent vow, the feeling that animated everyone from the Emperor down to the youngest soldier was this: Only in defence of a just cause shall our sword fly from its scabbard.

The day has now come when we must draw it, against our wish, and in spite of our sincere endeavours. Russia has set fire to the building. We are at war with Russia and France—a war that has been forced upon us. . . .

From the first moment of the Austro-Servian conflict we declared that this question must be limited to Austria-Hungary and Servia, and we worked with this end in view. All Governments, especially that of Great Britain, took the same attitude. Russia alone asserted that she had to be heard in the settlement of this matter. . . .

The Emperor drew the Czar's attention to the solidarity of the interests of all monarchs in face of the murder of Serajevo. He asked for the latter's personal assistance in smoothing over the difficulties existing between Vienna and St. Petersburgh. About the same time, and before receipt of this telegram, the Czar asked the Emperor to come to his aid and to induce Vienna to moderate her demands. The Emperor accepted the role of mediator.

But scarcely had active steps on these lines begun, when Russia mobilized all her forces directed against Austria, while Austria-Hungary had mobilized only those of her corps which were directed against Servia. To the north she had mobilized only two of her corps, far from the Russian frontier. The Emperor immediately informed the Czar that this mobilization of Russian forces against Austria rendered the role of mediator, which he had accepted at the Czar's request, difficult, if not impossible.

In spite of this we continued our task of mediation at Vienna and carried it to the utmost point which was compatible with our position as an ally.

Meanwhile Russia of her own accord renewed her assurances that she was making no military preparations against us.

We come now to July 31st. The decision was to be taken at Vienna. Through our representations we had already obtained the resumption of direct conversations between Vienna and St. Petersburg, after they had been for some time interrupted. But before the final decision was taken at Vienna, the news arrived that Russia had mobilized her entire forces and that her mobilization was therefore directed against us also. The Russian Government, who knew from our repeated statements what mobilization on our frontiers meant, did not notify us of this mobilization, nor did they even offer any explanation. It was not until the afternoon of July 31st that the Emperor received a telegram from the Czar in which he guaranteed that his army would not assume a provocative attitude towards us. But mobilization on our frontiers had been in full swing since the night of July 30th–31st.

While we were mediating at Vienna in compliance with Russia's request, Russian forces were appearing all along our extended and almost entirely open frontier, and France, though indeed not actually mobilizing, was admittedly making military preparations. . . .

Therefore, on July 31st we called upon Russia to demobilize as the only measure which could still preserve the peace of Europe. . . .

Therefore, the time limit having long since expired, the Emperor was obliged to mobilize our forces on the 1st August at 5 p.m.

At the same time we had to make certain what attitude France would assume. To our direct question, whether she would remain neutral in the event of a Russo-German War, France replied that she would do what her interests demanded. That was an evasion, if not a refusal.

In spite of this, the Emperor ordered that the French frontier was to be unconditionally respected. This order, with one single exception, was strictly obeyed. France, who mobilized at the same time as we did, assured us that she would respect a zone of 10 kilometres on the frontier. What really happened? Aviators dropped bombs, and cavalry patrols and French infantry detachments appeared on the territory of the Empire! Though war had not been declared, France thus broke the peace and actually attacked us. . . .

Gentlemen, we are now in a state of necessity (*Notwehr*), and necessity (*Not*) knows no law. Our troops have occupied Luxemburg and perhaps have already entered Belgian territory.

Gentlemen, that is a breach of international law. It is true that the French Government declared at Brussels that France would respect Belgian neutrality as long as her adversary respected it. We knew, however, that France stood ready for an invasion. France could wait, we could not. A French attack on our flank on the lower Rhine might have been disastrous. Thus we were forced to ignore the rightful protests of the Governments of Luxemburg and Belgium. The wrong—I speak openly—the wrong we thereby commit we will try to make good as soon as our military aims have been attained.

He who is menaced as we are and is fighting for his highest possession can only consider how he is to hack his way through (*durchhauen*).

Gentlemen, we stand shoulder to shoulder with Austria-Hungary.

As for Great Britain's attitude, the statements made by Sir Edward Grey in the House of Commons yesterday show the standpoint assumed by the British Government. We have informed the British Government that, as long as Great Britain remains neutral, our fleet will not attack the northern coast of France, and that we will not violate the territorial integrity and independence of Belgium. These assurances I now repeat before the world, and I may add that, as long as Great Britain remains neutral, we would also be willing, upon reciprocity being assured, to take no warlike measures against French commercial shipping.

Gentlemen, so much for the facts. I repeat the words of the Emperor: "With a clear conscience we enter the lists." . . .

*

B. CHINA

Belgium's neutral status, despite the wide international recognition it had enjoyed from 1839 onwards, and despite the international guarantees that were supposed to uphold it, disappeared in the first week of the war; but other neutral states were more fortunate. Latin America, for instance, largely escaped the pressures of the belligerents. For them, the maintenance of neutrality offered few problems, at least until the U.S.A. entered the war. The three other states we shall examine in this chapter were less fortunate. They all suffered some considerable infringements of their neutral rights. Yet two of them, China and Norway, endured these injuries without entering the war; and the third neutral, the U.S.A. itself, which did in the end enter the war, ostensibly in defence of its rights as a neutral, had in fact been less affected than either.

The case of China shows that violation of neutral rights in this war was not confined to the German side. China was only peripherally affected by the war; such involvement as there was arose out of the fact that Germany was among the European powers that had secured 'concessions' and 'leases' of territory, from China, and thus the expulsion of Germany from these outposts by the other beneficiaries of such concessions, and particularly by Japan, was a part, though a very subsidiary part, of the war. The Chinese could do nothing to protect their territory; internal conditions were still chaotic after the collapse of the Manchu Dynasty in 1911. Document 11 describes the action taken by Britain's ally Japan, and assesses the extent to which it violated China's neutrality.

DOCUMENT 11. Extract from 'Japanese violation of Chinese Territory' from *International Law and the World War* by J. W. Garner (Longmans, 1920).

Another example of the violation of neutral territory by a belligerent, and one which has been regarded by some as analogous to the German invasion of Belgium, was the marching of Japanese troops in September 1915, across a portion of the territory of China in order to facilitate the military operations of Japan against the German leased territory of Kiau-Chau. Upon the outbreak of the war in 1914 the Chinese government issued a neutrality proclamation announcing its intention of treating all belligerents impartially. The German government is said to have indicated its willingness to keep its naval squadron away from Tsing-tau and to place Tsing-tau with the Shantung railway under the jurisdiction of the Chinese government or to allow it to be neutralized. The Chinese government, however, agreed not to oppose belligerent action within the territory leased to Germany and to consider hostilities carried on therein as not taking place within Chinese territory.

Tsing-tau, embracing the larger part of the leased territory of Kiau-Chau, lies on the south side of the Shantung promontory, the German sphere of influence running westward. On the north side of the promontory, about seventy miles from Tsing-tau, is Lung-Kau, a Chinese harbor, in which Japanese troops were landed against the protest of Chinese officials, and from which place they later marched across Chinese territory to the rear of Tsing-tau. They also seized the custom-house and post-office and stretched a railway and telegraph line across the country in disregard of the rights of China and despite the protests of Chinese authorities.

§ 461. Chinese Concession of a "War Zone." It being apparent that the Japanese forces were indisposed to respect the neutrality of China in the region of Tsing-tau and being unable to compel respect for its sovereignty, the Chinese government thereupon, following the advice of its Japanese legal adviser,

Professor Ariga, consented to recognize the existence of a "war zone" embracing an area of Chinese territory with a radius extending thirty miles from Tsing-tau. Within this region hostilities would be permitted, the concession being made with a view to limiting the sphere of Japanese activities in northern Shantung. The proposal recited that the allied forces of Great Britain and Japan had, to the regret of China, begun operations at Lung-Kau and other places outside the German leased territory, although both powers were in friendly relations with the Chinese government. Therefore China, following the precedent of the Russo-Japanese war of 1904 when the area of operations in the Liao-Tung peninsula was limited, proposed a similar restriction on the area of operations of the Japanese forces. The Chinese government would accordingly "not accept responsibility" for the passing of troops through or the conduct of operations at Lung-Kau, Kiau-Chau, and the adjacent districts, but in other portions of China strict neutrality would be enforced. It was charged that Japan showed no respect for the zone thus defined by the Chinese government.*

The German minister at Peking protested against the Chinese concession thus granted to Japan as a violation of neutrality and informed the Chinese government that it would be held responsible for all injuries sustained by Germany in consequence of the Japanese invasion of Chinese territory. The Chinese government in its reply pleaded its inability to oppose an effective resistance to the action of the Japanese forces and charged Germany with having first violated the neutrality of China by fortifying Tsing-tau. Finally the Chinese government called the attention of the German government to the fact that Tsing-tau had never been ceded to Germany, but only leased to her, in consequence of which the territory was still under the legal sovereignty of China. . . .

* "They landed their troops at Lung-Kau, marched into the hinterland, and instead of working toward Tsing-tau, the Japanese army turned its back on the German garrison and marched westward, thus violating the neutrality of China. Though the latter protested vehemently, Japan went ahead and marched her troops still farther westward, out of the war zone, to Tsinanfu, the capital of Shantung. . . . China in

deadly fear of a revolutionary uprising against the invader and with the one object of saving, if possible, her people of Shantung from the horrors of war, declared a war zone. To this zone Japan paid not the least attention, but marched her troops about as if Shantung was in reality Japanese territory. She seized the Shantung railway, a Chino-German enterprise, the valuable coal mines belonging to the company and committed many acts of violence and force upon the once peaceful Shantung communities." Jones, *The Fall of Tsing-tau*, pp. 173–174.

C. AMERICA

The position of the United States as a neutral was at the very opposite pole to that of China. She had no fear of invasion in the course of the war, being situated so far from the main theatres of operations. Also, she was strong enough to impose terms on the belligerents about the treatment of her shipping and even about their policy towards ships of other nations on which her citizens sailed. The two speeches of President Wilson reproduced here, one soon after the war had broken out in Europe, and the other in recommending to Congress the Declaration of War which, when passed, finally brought America officially into the war in April 1917, illustrate the transformation in Wilson's policy over the intervening two and a half years. The reasons for this change from neutrality to belligerence were not necessarily those proclaimed by Wilson. A Norwegian scholar, Nils Ørvik, suggests that a more careful examination of the actions and reactions of America in these years of neutrality shows that Wilson's policy was not so much the preservation of America's neutral rights, as the preparation of American public opinion for a situation in which America might have to enter the war in order, as he saw it, to save Britain and France from defeat by Germany. In other words, for Wilson, the saving of Britain and France was a vital American interest, just as it has been since the Second World War; but by laying claim to the widest conceivable interpretations of her rights as a neutral, Wilson was providing himself with a more popularly acceptable excuse for entering the war when Germany violated these rights. Certainly, up to February 1917, Germany took some care to meet American demands. In that month, Germany announced a policy of unrestricted submarine warfare, and the U.S.A. broke off diplomatic relations.

DOCUMENT 12. Extracts from two speeches by President Woodrow Wilson, (a) 18 August 1914 (b) 2 April 1917.

(a) MY FELLOW COUNTRYMEN:

I suppose that every thoughtful man in America has asked himself, during these last troubled weeks, what influence the European war may exert upon the United States, and I take the liberty of addressing a few words to you in order to point out that it is entirely within our own choice what its effects upon us will be and to urge very earnestly upon you the sort of speech and conduct which will best safeguard the Nation against distress and disaster.

The effect of the war upon the United States will depend upon what American citizens say and do. Every man who really loves America will act and speak in the true spirit of neutrality, which is the spirit of impartiality and fairness and friendliness to all concerned. The spirit of the Nation in this critical matter will be determined largely by what individuals and society and those gathered in public meetings do and say, upon what newspapers and magazines contain, upon what ministers utter in their pulpits, and men proclaim as their opinions on the street.

The people of the United States are drawn from many nations, and chiefly from the nations now at war. It is natural and inevitable that there should be the utmost variety of sympathy and desire among them with regard to the issues and circumstances of the conflict. Some will wish one nation, others another, to succeed in the momentous struggle. It will be easy to excite passion and difficult to allay it. Those responsible for exciting it will assume a heavy responsibility, responsibility for no less a thing than that the people of the United States, whose love of their country and whose loyalty to its Government should unite them as Americans all, bound in honor and affection to think first of her and her interests, may be divided in camps of hostile opinion, hot against each other, involved in the war itself in impulse and opinion if not in action.

Such divisions among us would be fatal to our peace of mind and might seriously stand in the way of the proper performance of our duty as the one great nation at peace, the one people holding itself ready to play a part of impartial mediation and speak the counsels of peace and accommodation, not as a partisan, but as a friend.

I venture, therefore, my fellow countrymen, to speak a solemn word of warning to you against that deepest, most subtle, most essential breach of neutrality which may spring out of partisanship, out of passionately taking sides. The United States must be neutral in fact as well as in name during these days that are to try men's souls. We must be impartial in thought as well as in action, must put a curb upon our sentiments as well as upon every transaction that might be construed as a preference of one party to the struggle before another.

My thought is of America. I am speaking, I feel sure, the earnest wish and purpose of every thoughtful American that this great country of ours, which is, of course, the first in our thoughts and in our hearts, should show herself in this time of peculiar trial a Nation fit beyond others to exhibit the fine poise of undisturbed judgment, the dignity of self-control, the efficiency of dispassionate action; a Nation that neither sits in judgment upon others nor is disturbed in her own counsels and which keeps herself fit and free to do what is honest and disinterested and truly serviceable for the peace of the world.

Shall we not resolve to put upon ourselves the restraints which will bring to our people the happiness and the great and lasting influence for peace we covet for them?

(b) GENTLEMEN OF THE CONGRESS:

I have called the Congress into extraordinary session because there are serious, very serious, choices of policy to be made, and made immediately, which it was neither right nor constitutionally permissible that I should assume the responsibility of making.

On the third of February last I officially laid before you the extraordinary announcement of the Imperial German Government that on and after the first day of February it was its purpose to put aside all restraints of law or of humanity and use its submarines to sink every vessel that sought to approach either the ports of Great Britain and Ireland or the western coasts of Europe or any of the ports controlled by the enemies of Germany within the Mediterranean. That had seemed to be the object of the German submarine warfare earlier in the war, but since April of last year the Imperial Government had somewhat restrained the commanders of its undersea craft in conformity with its promise then given to us that passenger boats should not be sunk and that due warning would be given to all other vessels which its submarines might seek to destroy, when no resistance was offered or escape attempted, and care taken that their crews were given at least a fair chance to save their lives in their open boats. The precautions taken were meager and haphazard enough, as was proved in distressing instance after instance in the progress of the cruel and unmanly business, but a certain degree of restraint was observed. The new policy has swept every restriction aside. Vessels of every kind, whatever their flag, their character, their cargo, their destination, their errand, have been ruthlessly sent to the bottom without warning and without thought of help or mercy for those on board, the vessels of friendly neutrals along with those of belligerents. Even hospital ships and ships carrying relief to the sorely bereaved and stricken people of Belgium, though the latter were provided with safe conduct through the proscribed areas by the German Government itself and were distinguished by unmistakable marks of identity, have been sunk with the same reckless lack of compassion or of principle.

I was for a little while unable to believe that such things would in fact be done by any government that had hitherto subscribed to the humane practices of civilized nations. International law had its origin in the attempt to set up some law which would be respected and observed upon the seas, where no nation had right of dominion and where lay the free highways of the world. By painful stage after stage has that law been built up, with meager enough results, indeed, after all was accomplished that could be accomplished, but always with a clear view, at least, of what the heart and conscience of mankind demanded. This minimum of right the German Government has swept aside under the plea of retaliation and necessity and because it had no weapons which it could use at sea except these which it is impossible to employ as it is employing them without throwing to the winds all scruples of humanity or of respect for the understandings that were supposed to underlie the intercourse of the world. I am not now thinking of the loss of property involved, immense and serious as that is, but only of the wanton and wholesale destruction of the lives of non-combatants, men, women, and children, engaged in pursuits which have always, even in the darkest periods of modern history, been deemed innocent and legitimate. Property can be paid for; the lives of peaceful and innocent people cannot be. The present German submarine warfare against commerce is a warfare against mankind.

It is a war against all nations. American ships have been sunk, American lives taken, in ways which it has stirred us very deeply to learn of, but the ships and people of other neutral and friendly nations have been sunk and overwhelmed in the waters in the same way. There has been no discrimination. The challenge is to all mankind. Each nation must decide for itself how it will meet it. The choice we make for ourselves must be made with a moderation of counsel and a temperateness of judgment befitting our character and our motives as a nation. We must put excited feeling away. Our motive will not be revenge or the victorious assertion of the physical might of the nation, but only the vindication of right, of human right, of which we are only a single champion.

When I addressed the Congress on the twenty-sixth of February last I thought that it would suffice to assert our neutral rights with arms, our right to use the seas against unlawful interference, our right to keep our people safe against unlawful violence. But armed neutrality, it now appears, is impracticable. Because submarines are in effect outlaws when used as the German submarines have been used against merchant shipping, it is impossible to defend ships against their attacks as the law of nations has assumed that merchantmen would defend themselves against privateers or cruisers, visible craft giving chase upon the open sea. It is common prudence in such circumstances, grim necessity indeed, to endeavor to destroy them before they have shown their own intention. They must be dealt with upon sight, if dealt with at all. The German Government denies the right of neutrals to use arms at all within the areas of the sea which it has proscribed, even in the defense of rights which no modern publicist has ever before questioned their right to defend. The intimation is conveyed that the armed guards which we have placed on our merchant ships will be treated as beyond the pale of law and subject to be dealt with as pirates would be. Armed neutrality is ineffectual enough at best; in such circumstances and in the face of such pretensions it is worse than ineffectual: it is likely only to produce what it was meant to prevent; it is practically certain to draw us into the war without either the rights or the effectiveness of belligerents. There is one choice we cannot make, we are incapable of making: we will not choose the path of submission and suffer the most sacred rights of our nation and our people to be ignored or violated. The wrongs against which we now array ourselves are no common wrongs; they cut to the very roots of human life.

With a profound sense of the solemn and even tragical character of the step I am taking and of the grave responsibilities which it involves, but in unhesitating obedience to what I deem my constitutional duty, I advise that the Congress declare the recent course of the Imperial German Government to be in fact nothing less than war against the government and people of the United States; that it formally accept the status of belligerent which has thus been thrust upon it; and that it take immediate steps not only to put the country in a more thorough state of defense but also to exert all its power and employ all its resources to bring the Government of the German Empire to terms and end the war. . . .

Our object now, as then, is to vindicate the principles of peace and justice in the life of the world as against selfish and autocratic power and to set up amongst the really free and self-governed peoples of the world such a concert of purpose and of action as will henceforth insure the observance of those principles. Neutrality is no longer feasible or desirable where the peace of the world is involved and the freedom of its peoples, and the menace to that peace and freedom lies in the existence of autocratic governments backed by organized force which is controlled wholly by their will, not by the will of their people. We have seen the last of neutrality in such circumstances. We are at the beginning of an age in which it will be insisted that the same standards of conduct and of responsibility for wrong

done shall be observed among nations and their governments
that are observed among the individual citizens of civilized states.

DOCUMENT 13. Extracts from 'The Position of America as the
Greatest Neutral' from *The Decline of Neutrality 1914–41* by Nils
Ørvik (Grundt Tanum, 1953, and Cass).

The Germans started using submarines against neutral vessels
February 19, 1915. But they had too few submarines then to
effectively terrorize the seas, and most Americans took little
interest in this campaign before the sinking of the British liner,
Lusitania, in May, 1915. This event stirred up America, particularly, since more than a hundred United States citizens went
down with the ship. The State Department sent a strong protest
to Germany and the Germans actually changed the manner in
which they conducted their submarine warfare. They continued
to be very cautious up to 1916, when conditions were changed
because of the new use of the armed merchant men. Count
Bernstorff, the German ambassador to the United States, wrote
to Lansing on March 8, 1916, that England had made it
impossible for submarines to act in accordance with the old
rules of visit and search 'by arming nearly all merchantmen and
by ordering the use of guns in merchant vessels for attack'. . . .
    The arming of merchantmen was no new measure in 1915.
What was new was the use of these ships. Up to that time, the
armament had been considered to be exclusively for defensive
purposes. However, on February 10 and 15, 1915, the British
Admiralty issued orders to their merchantmen to try to ram
submarines if escape seemed impossible and to fire at them on
sight. These instructions reached the State Department via the
American Embassy in Berlin. This made the offensive character
of the armed merchantmen rather obvious. There was a special
provision in the instructions stating that 'the ship pursued
should open fire in self-defense, notwithstanding the submarine
may not have committed a definite hostile act'. . . .
    Those who saw the gun-crews of the British merchant marine
in action have since testified that they were extremely efficient.
'They handled their guns so skillfully that it was almost certain
destruction for the submarine to emerge above the sea level in
sight of the merchant ships.' Naturally it was unreasonable to

expect the submarines to conform to the old rules of visit and search under such circumstances; it would be suicide to give warning as the heavily armed cruisers could afford to do. It was, therefore, possible to find some logic in the German complaints. In October, 1915, Lansing took the view that if the United States insisted that submarines must give warning 'we should also insist that merchantmen be not armed.' If not, the advantage was all with the merchantmen and against the submarines. . . .

Millis says the proposal had not the slightest chance of success. From what Lansing says in his *War Memoirs*, there is reason to believe that even he did not take it seriously. Wilson let it be known that Lansing's proposal was purely tentative, and that according to custom, merchant vessels had the right to arm themselves defensively. Thus, if a submarine attacked an unresisting merchantman, with loss of American lives, it would be considered a breach of the formal assurances given by the German Government.

This statement that merchantmen had a right to arm for defensive purposes was sent by Lansing to the diplomatic officers in European countries on February 16, 1916. A week before, February 8, 1916, the German Government had announced that very soon it would regard armed merchant vessels as ships of war and treat them accordingly. On this issue Morrissey says that 'the United States asserted rights which never before had been claimed by a neutral government,' because it was impossible for a neutral to discriminate between defensive and offensive armaments. In her opinion the United States followed a policy of avowed discrimination between the belligerents.

Therefore, the submarine question cannot be dealt with separately, but must be seen in relation to the stand which the United States took on the issue of the armed merchantmen. In the period following the sinking of the *Lusitania*, where a great many American lives were lost, two more Americans were killed when the British liner *Arabic* was sunk. There were also other minor incidents, but sentiments were not brought to a high pitch until the attack on the unarmed French channel steamer, *Sussex*. This ship was torpedoed (not sunk) on March 24, 1916, by a German submarine which did not give warning. A great number of the passengers were killed or injured, but considering the events that followed, it is worth noting that *no* American lives were lost by the explosions on the *Sussex*, although quite a few were injured.

Nevertheless, in spite of the fact that no American had lost his life on this occasion, in America the torpedoing of this steamer marked the decisive turn of the development towards war. Shortly afterwards Lansing sent a sharp note to Gerard for the communication to the German Minister for Foreign Affairs. He claimed that unless the Imperial Government would abandon its present methods of submarine warfare 'the Government of the United States can have no choice but to sever diplomatic relations with the German Empire altogether.' Mr. Gerard was instructed to say that it had become painfully evident to the Government of the United States that this German practice was utterly 'incompatible with the principles of humanity, the long established and incontrovertible rights of neutrals and the sacred immunities of non-combatants'.

These lofty statements were answered by Germany on May 4, 1916. The Germans said that the submarine question should not be allowed to interfere with the maintenance of peace between the two countries. They took the opportunity, however, of pointing to the inhumanity of the Allied starvation blockade of Germany.

Thus, in order to keep the United States out of war, Germany yielded to the American claims. Consequently, no American ships were sunk without warning until the Germans reintroduced unrestricted warfare in 1917. This gave the United States an acceptable casus belli and she entered the war on the side of the Allies. In this connection Lansing says in *War Memoirs*, that the 'submarine warfare may have been a blessing in disguise'. . . .

From then on the United States turned against the neutrals with no less severity than the other belligerents. Before America declared war, the neutrals had been able to get along by obtaining from the United States what was refused them by the Allies. After April 6, 1917, they were completely at the mercy of the belligerents and had to accept unconditionally the terms offered. The American pressure in order to stop all exports to Germany actually brought the Scandinavian countries on the verge of starvation.

D. NORWAY

The final document in this chapter concerns Norway. It is an account by Professor Ørvik of how his own country managed to survive the war. Norway was heavily dependent on trade, and vulnerable both to the British Navy and to the German submarine fleet. Forty-nine per cent of her merchant tonnage, a greater proportion than that of any belligerent, was sunk by German submarines. More than two thousand Norwegian sailors died in this process. Yet Norway maintained throughout the war this passive and agonized neutrality.

DOCUMENT 14. Chapter II 2 'Weak Power Neutrality' from *The Decline of Neutrality* by Nils Ørvik (Grundt Tanum, 1953 and Cass).

The small neutral countries were not given much of a choice as to the maintenance of their neutrality. Squeezed, battered, and beaten from both sides, they were compelled to do what was expedient, rather than what was desirable from their own point of view. But all neutrals did not submit to the same extent. Their actual bargaining power became the decisive factor in their gradual submission to belligerent pressure. The weaker they were, the greater were their humiliations.

To illustrate this fact it will be necessary to elaborate in some detail on what happened to the northern neutrals during this period. The Scandinavian countries were almost completely at the mercy of the Allies as far as trade was concerned. Previous reference has been made to the restriction on their import, but they were not much better off when it came to export. Before long the British had established control organizations in all these northern countries. By means of these half-camouflaged institutions they were able to control all neutral export and import, particularly observing that nothing was re-exported to places where it could reach the enemy.

Sweden, was better off than the rest, and, in fact, came very near to being economically self-sufficient. Even so, she had to submit to measures that greatly reduced her sovereignty and her right of self-determination. An organization called Transito had been established in October of 1915 to control and regulate the transit over Swedish territory of goods to and from Russia. This institution was camouflaged as a joint stock company, but was actually controlled by the British Government and operated under orders from the British Legation at Stockholm. It did not limit its activities to the transit only, but had decisive influence on nearly all matters of import and export. The activities of this organization caused the Swedish Prime Minister, in December, 1915, to issue a declaration that the government would not permit the establishment, under foreign leadership, of a state within the state. The King made an announcement to the same effect in January, 1916, and in April a bill was passed that provided penalty for those who tried to place the economic life of Sweden under foreign supervision. Nevertheless, Transito continued to operate effectively until the end of the war.

This indeed serves to illustrate the weakness of the neutral position. When such encroachments on an independent state's right to selfdetermination could go on in a relatively strong and well-to-do state such as Sweden, how then should the other northern neutrals be able to run their own affairs?

As long as the transit to Russia continued, Sweden had considerable bargaining power, of which she made efficient use. On one occasion she let the Allies inside her territorial waters and used the sheltered waterway, Kogrundsrennan in return for a certain amount of grain. The Schwartz-Lindemann and the Eden-Hellner governments, which followed the fall of Hammarskjöld, were in a less favorable bargaining position when they took over in 1917. By that time, the Bolshevik revolution had greatly reduced the importance of the transit to Russia.

Sweden and to some extent also Denmark, due to their strategic positions and domestic production, were thus able to gain something from both belligerents by bargaining. Norway, however, was greatly dependent upon the import of all sorts of foodstuffs as well as raw materials for industrial production. As shipping was her main source of income, she was from the very beginning in a difficult position, especially because her trade and commerce had for centuries been primarily tied up with Great Britain and the Western world. The situation did not appear serious at the beginning, since England stuck fairly close to the Declaration of London. But in October 1914, it became evident that this would not be the case in the future, and with the closing of the North Sea, November 5, 1914, Norway's foreign trade came to a great extent under British control.

The German submarine declaration of February 4, 1915, also caused great losses to the Norwegian Merchant Marine. In 1915, more than fifty Norwegian ships were sunk by German torpedoes, with heavy losses in lives, but this did not decrease the activity of Norwegian shipping. During 1915, Allied control became effective even within the country itself, and by 1916, the businessmen in Norway were forced to take a stand for or against Germany so far as trade was concerned. By an indiscriminate use of blacklists, the merchants were pressed into the British-controlled system, and all sales to them were made on very strict conditions. In order to buy British goods, neutral merchants had to guarantee that the goods would only be used for specified purposes. A strict neutral position was, therefore, unattainable for the Norwegian businessmen, even if they had wanted to preserve it. The Germans used the same methods, but could not enforce it to the same extent.

While Denmark effected a general trade agreement with Great Britain, Norway obtained only branch agreements which were much less favorable. Trade relations became more complicated and unstable, as each group of importers separately had to come to terms with the British government. According to the provisions of the branch agreements, the British gained the privilege of inspecting the closest secrets and most confidential figures of the concerned industries. The first agreement of this kind was reached between Great Britain and the Norwegian cotton goods manufacturing union. It made the union responsible for the conduct of its members; whose behaviour would consequently determine future trade. The conditions were made increasingly harder as time went on, and in some of the agreements made in 1916, British authorities actually got complete administrative domination even over Norwegian owned firms. In spite of the extremely humiliating provisions which the importers had to accept, the British made matters worse by claiming that the Norwegian Government should give its 'unofficial approval' to the agreements.

The Fish Agreement and the Submarine Warfare in the Arctic.

The most important of all these was the famous Fish Agreement of 1916. Fish is known to be Norway's most important export commodity, and before the war it was sent all over the world, particularly to South-European countries. Due to war costs and risks, the fish rose so high in price that those countries could no longer afford to buy it; but as the effect of the British blockade became felt in Germany in 1915, that country before long conquered the whole Norwegian fish market.

This could not escape the attention of the British, and since they furnished Norway with 85% of the means necessary for sustaining the fisheries, Great Britain had the power to stop the Norwegian fisheries completely if she should choose to apply full pressure.

For different reasons she did not do so. Instead, ten million pounds were appropriated to buy the Germans out of the Norwegian market. This was done by making a Norwegian fish merchant an agent of the British Government. At first the Germans did not know who was behind the merchant, but as prices rose and the Norwegian refused to sell to them, they would soon find out.

Later Great Britain questioned whether the same effect could be obtained in a cheaper way. As a result of this consideration, an agreement was made with the Norwegian Government on August 5, 1915, according to which the Norwegians were totally prohibited from exporting any kind of fish except canned goods. As a special grace, however, fifteen percent of the total catch might be exported to 'any other country'. The remaining eighty-five percent the British would still buy, but at their own prices, and they might end their purchasing obligations after four weeks' warning.

The Fish Agreement was definitely a violation of the principles of economic neutrality and as such inconsistent with Norway's duties as a neutral. This was an obvious fact to the Norwegian Government as well as to the British; and as a consequence, German reprisals had to be expected. It meant the risk of getting into the war, a risk Norway would never have taken if she had had a free choice. Additionally, the agreement also meant a financial loss to the national economy. The government, therefore, did not dare to announce the agreement publicly, but tried for a while to keep it secret. This was, of course, not possible because no plausible explanations could be given the Germans when they were denied further purchases of fish.

The Germans then on the twenty-first of September, 1916, told the Norwegian minister in Berlin, Thor von Ditten, that they did not consider these explanations satisfactory and that reprisals might be expected at any time. A few days later a submarine campaign was started against Norwegian shipping in the Arctic waters off the coast of Northern Norway. By this campaign, the Germans wanted to strike a blow at Norwegian shipping and stop the traffic between Great Britain and Archangelsk. From September 26 to October 4, they sank eleven Norwegian ships in this area. Due to the cold, many of the sailors froze to death and the rest suffered greatly before they were rescued.

These sinkings caused great indignation in Norway, and public opinion demanded that the government should do something to stop them. Since the submarines were likely to get up to the northern area through Norwegian territorial waters, the government issued a proclamation providing that war submarines were prohibited access to Norwegian territorial waters, except when it was necessary in order 'to save human lives'.

This measure was more an expression of the indignation which was felt all over Norway than a move of wise diplomacy. The other neutral countries had prohibited submarines within their territorial waters except in the case of bad weather or shipwreck. The Norwegian proclamation thus went much further, and the German Government sent an indignant answer and intensified their submarine warfare in the North. From the twentieth to the thirty-first of October, the Germans sank a total of thirty-three Norwegian ships at a value of twenty-five million crowns. What they wanted was a revision of the Fish Agreement and by the submarine activity force Norway to continue the fish export to Germany; but if Norway were to do so, the Allies would stop her imports and destroy her fisheries and industry.

The Allies also felt that the situation was critical. On the twenty-ninth of October, the French Prime Minister offered the Norwegian fleet ten submarines, and in November, the British put twelve airplanes at the disposal of the Norwegians. Fortunately, these offers were declined by the Norwegian Minister of Defense.

More important was the support given by the Swedish and Danish Governments. The strong position which particularly Sweden took in this question may have had some weight with the Germans. They may have understood that the Norwegians were pressed to a point where they in desperation might enter the war on the other side, and as the Swedes and Danes had taken a unified attitude, these powers, might also be drawn in.

What motives the Imperial Government may have had, it altered its position by the end of November, 1916. The German Assistant Secretary of State told von Ditten that if the Norwegians would base the fifteen percent fish export to Germany on the average export for the last five years, maybe an agreement could be reached. This hint was enthusiastically grasped by Norway. Simultaneously, the Norwegians changed their stand on the submarine issue. The proclamation was not officially revoked, but it was put out of force by a secret instruction to the Norwegian Navy. On these conditions, an agreement could be reached, and on the ninth of February, the German Minister to Norway, Michahelles, communicated that the Imperial Government '*betrachtet den Zwischenfall als erledigt*'.

Copper and Coal.

About the same time, Norway had perhaps her most serious controversy with Great Britain; this time the issue was copper. Norway exported copper ore and imported electrolytic copper, primarily from the United States. Great quantities of the copper ore had for years been exported to Germany, but in the spring of 1916, the British Government informed the Norwegians that it disapproved of this traffic. As a consequence an agreement was made, whereby the Allies permitted eight thousand tons of copper to reach Norway. In return they were to get the copper ore. The British understood this to include all kinds of copper ore, while the Norwegian Foreign Minister held that ore with less than one-half percent copper might be exported elsewhere.

He, therefore, permitted great quantities of this to be exported to Germany.

In the agreement of August 30, the British also had provided for a first claim to all supplies and production of copper in Norway until a certain amount was covered. To be sure of getting it all, they gave the Spanish-English company, Rio Tinto, the right of buying the rest. The provisions were not quite clear, and Ihlen, the Norwegian Foreign Minister, construed this to mean that the British had renounced their right to a first call for the contract with Rio Tinto. Thus he permitted increased sales of copper ore to Germany, with compensation in metallic copper, but on a much smaller scale. This had been made to bring about an understanding with Germany on the submarine issue, and was probably an absolutely necessary concession to make the Germans negotiate at all. Nevertheless, on the twenty-fourth of November, the British claimed that the export of copper to Germany should be stopped immediately. Yet, this Ihlen could not do, because it would undoubtedly have broken the negotiations with the Germans, which were evidently progressing satisfactorily. The export of copper ore to Germany was therefore continued.

On December 1, 1916, Lloyd George took over the government in England, and shortly afterwards the Norwegian Government was warned that if the export of copper ore to Germany was allowed to continue, the coal export to Norway would be stopped. Ihlen tried to delay this prohibition from taking effect, but immediately before Christmas the British allowed no more coal to reach Norway.

The agreement with Germany was, however, not yet concluded and Norway could, therefore, not yield to the Allied demand, but had to go on without coal. It had a very serious effect on the country's economic life and was painfully felt all over the country. Schools, churches, and theaters had to close. The gas was on only certain hours a day. The ships could not get into the ports, because the ice-breakers lacked coal to keep the passage open.

By the beginning of January, 1917, the agreement with Germany was reached, and on January 24, Ihlen let the British know that he was willing to stop the export of copper ore to Germany if they would recall the ban on exports of coal to

Norway. This was done on the seventeenth of February. These episodes illustrate the dilemma that a small country had to face during the Great War. . . .

Norway's greatest asset was her merchant marine, but it could not always be used effectively for bargaining purposes because its services were imperative for paying for the export. In fact, Norway had to sail in order to live. The Allies got an effective control over her shipping through 1915 and 1916, and there was not much Norway could do about it. However, the Germans thought they could do something, and one of the aims of the unrestricted submarine warfare of January 31, 1917, was to scare the neutrals away from trade with Great Britain.

In the beginning it looked as if they should be successful. The Swedes and the Danes held back their ships, and during the first nineteen days of February, only five American ships set out for ports within the danger zone. The Norwegian passenger liners suspended their sailings for a while, but the tramp steamer lines decided to go on regardless of the markedly increased risks. The British were, however, still fearful that if the losses were too great Norway might withdraw her merchant marine, and on February 3, 1917, the British Minister of Blockade, Lord Robert Cecil, suggested to the Norwegian Government that the British should buy a greater part of the Norwegian tonnage.

This was rejected by the Norwegian Government on February 9, 1917. The official reason was that such a sale would be considered an unneutral act by Germany. The fact was that if Norway should sell her merchant fleet, she would lose what little bargaining power she had; and finally, the Norwegian shipping interests would be set aside with no chances for making large profits. These were actually the major considerations.

The fact that Norway continued to sail when the others did not, made the British grant special privileges to Norwegian ships in regard to control and custom duties. But the losses were heavy; of the 590,545 tons which were the total world war losses in March, 1917, Norway alone lost 106,111 tons. There was a popular demand that the Norwegian ships should be armed, but the government refused to give its permission. Instead, British armed ships took over the most dangerous routes across the North Sea.

While the Danish and Dutch ships were requisitioned, the

Norwegians got a so-called tonnage agreement. This was made by the Norwegian Shipowners Association and a British shipping company which acted as an agent for the British Government. It provided for an exchange of tonnage and the lease of some Norwegian ships for the duration of the war. From April, 1917, all ships to or from Norway were protected by British convoys. This greatly reduced sinkings.

All in all Norway lost 49·3 per cent of her merchant marine. No other merchant marine in the world lost that much, including the belligerents. Italy lost 46·9%; France, 39·2%, and Great Britain, 37·6%. Due to the sinkings, more than two thousand Norwegian sailors lost their lives.

It is obvious that the neutrality Norway claimed to maintain was not a real one. Although Norway must be recognized as a nonbelligerent, since no battles were fought within her territory and she did not participate in any acts of war, yet how much was left of her declared status? How many of those rules were enforced and respected? She was not impartial, nor was she passive; thus, what remained of her neutrality?

A few studies have been made of the attitude of the men that led the government in those days; but nothing has been brought forth so far to indicate that the administration tried to influence the Storting and the public opinion to favor one side in particular. In the case of Ihlen, the Foreign Minister, it is even today hard to determine where his own private sympathies lay.

It must be admitted that the Norwegian people were pro-British, as decidedly as the greater part of the Swedish people were pro-German. Both had been so for centuries, and this could not be changed by the war. Yet, even if they had their sympathies, there is every reason to believe that they did not want them to interfere with the policy of the country. They were not carried away by their sentiments to join any of the sides of the war. Common sense would forbid such actions by a small country. By getting in, she might lose all her independence, sovereignty, and domestic prosperity; by staying out and dealing impartially with both antagonists, she could press prices high and prosper—as Norway did when the British and the Germans competed for her fish market. There can be little doubt that the small countries which had the choice, preferred to stay neutral, because small and weak as they were, neutrality in its classic definition seemed to guarantee them just what they were afraid to lose: prosperity, sovereignty, political and economic independence. In spite of this, they were un-neutral, because they were too weak to resist the force of the belligerents, and consequently had to yield. What they lacked was not the will, but the force.

Great Britain could probably have destroyed the Norwegian fisheries completely any time she wanted to, but 'as it would have aroused severe criticism in the other neutral countries, and the reaction of Norway could not be predicted, England first found it wiser to buy the fish in the open market.' Vigness says, 'Great Britain, as every Norwegian knew, possessed the power to bring about economic destruction of Norway any time she so willed.' Dr. O. Thommesen, famous editor and columnist, said that 'a war with Germany would bring fearful misfortune upon us, but a war with England would be suicide.'

Dr. Paul Vigness, who has made a special study of the Norwegian neutrality during the First World War states that Norway, even 'if she was exposed to the worst provocations, never was carried away from her the determined will to keep the peace.' That may be all right so far as will is concerned, but he also thinks that Norway had demonstrated to the world that it is possible even under such circumstances 'to keep peace with honor'. To this statement there can be raised some doubt. Of course Norway desired to preserve the peace, but she also wanted to carry on her economic life as an independent sovereign nation and make decisions for herself. This she could not do. She was forced to accept such terms as she could get.

Because war as an instrument of practical politics was out of the question, Norway was left with one alternative: to keep peace at the sacrifice of her full sovereign status. She had to take what she was given, and what little bargaining power she had did not prove sufficient to preserve her the right of self-determination in her economic life.

PART III

The Inter-war years

The First World War began as a war of statesmen, and ended as a war of peoples, even of ideologies. The enormous loss of life made it necessary for the governments of Britain and France to claim that they were fighting 'to make the world safe for democracy'; the collapse of Russia, their autocratic ally, and the entry of two further democracies, Italy and the United States of America, made this claim plausible. This slogan implied that this would be 'a war to end war'; once victory had been won, the world would be so organized that it could never happen again.

How was this to be done? The currently popular remedy for war was 'collective security'; all states would simultaneously commit themselves to resist an aggressor, whether he should be one of themselves or an outsider. This simple principle was embodied in the Covenant of the League of Nations (see Document 15). The crucial articles are 10 and 16. In Article 10, the commitment lies in the word 'preserve'. The detailed sanctions which members obliged themselves to take against a covenant-breaker in Article 16 came into effect only if the state going to war had either ignored or flouted the elaborate machinery for peaceful settlement provided by Articles 12, 13, and 15 (not quoted here). The machinery did not, however, provide a binding solution in all cases. It could still happen, though it never did, that two states which had followed the procedures laid down in these articles and observed the prescribed delays, went to war without either having broken the Covenant. (These were the 'gaps' in the Covenant.) In such a case, other members of the League could be neutral, provided neither state threatened the 'territorial integrity' or 'existing political independence' of the other. But by and large the Covenant abolished neutrality.

Article 17 even extended the sanctions obligations of the preceding article to conflicts between non-members. And Article 11, though it provided a more flexible basis for the League to handle any 'war or threat of war', seemed to envisage a collective rather than an individual response from member states. The plain meaning of the Covenant was that in most cases, when a war occurred, League members had a duty not to stay on the sidelines, but to join in upholding whoever was in the right—an almost complete reversal of the position under the Hague Conventions.

On paper, these were incredibly far-reaching obligations. For instance, as a member of the League, Luxembourg undertook (regardless of what the others did) to 'preserve . . . the territorial integrity and existing political independence' of say, Haiti against the United States, Esthonia against Soviet Russia, or Egypt against Britain, if any such attack should occur—obviously impossible obligations. In practice, it was fairly clear that each member would fight only if there was general agreement to do so among states other than the aggressors, and that there was not going to be general agreement to fight Britain, France or America. The theory of 'collective security' is supposed to operate against 'the unknown enemy'—the 'aggressor' who is deemed innocent and therefore anonymous until he commits his crime. But the states that devised the Covenant were the victors in a war for which they blamed the other side; and it was Germany, and to a lesser extent Austria and Hungary, whose aggression they chiefly feared; and also that of Russia under its new and communist régime.

Thus in specific rather than general terms the Covenant was a device to ensure that suspect states like Germany could be treated as friends so long as they behaved themselves, but as enemies of the whole international community if they did not. And since Germany's rights and duties, which determined what constituted 'behaving herself', were defined by the Treaty of Versailles, which many outside Germany regarded as unjust, there were some qualms even among those who saw these obligations in realistic rather than literal terms.

DOCUMENT 15. Articles 10, 11, 16 and 17 of the Covenant of the League of Nations.

Article 10

The Members of the League undertake to respect and pre-serve as against external aggression the territorial integrity and existing political independence of all Members of the League. In case of any such aggression or in case of any threat or danger of such aggression, the Council shall advise upon the means by which this obligation shall be fulfilled.

Article 11

1. Any war or threat of war, whether immediately affecting any of the Members of the League or not, is hereby declared a matter of concern to the whole League, and the League shall take any action that may be deemed wise and effectual to safe-guard the peace of nations. In case any such emergency should arise, the Secretary-General shall, on the request of any Member of the League, forthwith summon a meeting of the Council.

2. It is also declared to be the friendly right of each Member of the League to bring to the attention of the Assembly or of the Council any circumstance whatever affecting international rela-tions which threatens to disturb international peace or the good understanding between nations upon which peace depends.

Article 16

1. Should any Member of the League resort to war in dis-regard of its covenants under Articles 12, 13 or 15, it shall, *ipso facto*, be deemed to have committed an act of war against all other Members of the League, which hereby undertake im-mediately to subject it to the severance of all trade or financial relations, the prohibition of all intercourse between their nationals and the nationals of the Covenant-breaking State, and the prevention of all financial, commercial or personal inter-course between the nationals of the Covenant-breaking State and the nationals of any other State, whether a Member of the League or not.

2. It shall be the duty of the Council in such case to recom-mend to the several Governments concerned what effective military, naval or air force the Members of the League shall severally contribute to the armed forces to be used to protect the covenants of the League.

3. The Members of the League agree, further, that they will mutually support one another in the financial and economic measures which are taken under this article, in order to minimise the loss and inconvenience resulting from the above measures, and that they will mutually support one another in resisting any special measures aimed at one of their number by the Covenant-breaking State, and that they will take the necessary steps to afford passage through their territory to the forces of any of the Members of the League which are co-operating to protect the covenants of the League.

4. Any member of the League which has violated any covenant of the League may be declared to be no longer a Member of the League by a vote of the Council concurred in by the Representatives of all the other Members of the League represented thereon.

Article 17

1. In the event of a dispute between a Member of the League and a State which is not a member of the League or between States not members of the League, the State or States not members of the League shall be invited to accept the obligations of membership in the League for the purposes of such dispute, upon such conditions as the Council may deem just. If such invitation is accepted, the provisions of Articles 12 to 16 inclusive shall be applied with such modifications as may be deemed necessary by the Council.

2. Upon such invitation being given, the Council shall immediately institute an enquiry into the circumstances of the dispute and recommend such action as may seem best and most effectual in the circumstances.

3. If a State so invited shall refuse to accept the obligations of membership in the League for the purposes of such dispute, and shall resort to war against a Member of the League, the provisions of Article 16 shall be applicable as against the State taking such action.

4. If both parties to the dispute when so invited refuse to accept the obligations of membership in the League for the purposes of such dispute, the Council may take such measures and make such recommendations as will prevent hostilities and will result in the settlement of the dispute.

*

Even in specific terms, these obligations looked onerous to many of the League's members or prospective members. The next four documents show how four states, separately and at different times, refused to abandon their neutrality altogether, as the price of League membership. Of the four, America alone never joined. This was largely for internal reasons. President Woodrow Wilson had been, probably more than any other statesman, the architect of the League; but by the United States Constitution, all Treaties have to be ratified by the Senate, by a two-thirds majority, before they can be strictly binding on the U.S.A.; and there were many senators opposed to the obligations themselves, or to the very idea of a League, or simply to President Wilson's visionary leadership. The result was that when the final vote was taken, such drastic reservations and conditions had been attached to the Treaty that twenty-three of Wilson's supporters voted against it. They believed that the United States could not ask the other members to amend the Covenant in the way the resolution was demanding, and that it was better to wait until a different constituted Senate, in different circumstances, voted to accept the Covenant as it stood. That day never came. America remained outside the League throughout its history: the chair reserved for her stayed empty. And so long as America remained outside the League, neutrality could not be obsolete.

Document 16 shows some of the reservations to the Covenant made in the final proposal on which the Senate voted on 19 March 1920. If two-thirds of the Senators had supported that proposal, and its reservations had been accepted by other members of the League, the United States would have been entitled, as a League member, to remain neutral when the Covenant was broken. But would the other League members have agreed to American membership on such conditions? and if they had, would the history of the League, and of the world as a whole, have been very much different? Documents 17 and 19 give us some clue to the answer to the first question. Switzerland and Germany both asked to be treated as special cases when they applied for League membership. In the first extract, F. P. Walters, the League's historian, describes the compromise proposed by Switzerland and accepted by the League Council. This was a straightforward case.

Germany, however, disarmed at the end of the war like the

other defeated states, asked for a wider dispensation than Switzerland. At this moment of history, in ironic contrast to the situation in 1914 or 1939, she could plausibly claim to find herself 'in complete military impotence in the centre of a heavily-armed Europe'.

What chiefly worried her leaders, particularly her foreign secretary and former chancellor, Gustav Stresemann, was the prospect of being called on by the League to take sanctions against Russia. In these days Russia was perhaps the League's likeliest collective enemy. Many League members, from Finland to Romania, ruled over land formerly Russian. The Western powers did not trust Soviet Russia; they were prepared, and even eager, to defend these states against a Russian attack. Germany however had found an ally in Russia, her fellow outcast from the League. Stresemann therefore wanted to insist that by joining the League Germany was not renouncing neutrality in any war between the League and Russia.

In a letter to Sir Eric Drummond, Secretary-General of the League (see Document 19), Gustav Stresemann eloquently pleaded that Germany, because of her special position, should retain the option of full neutrality. Note his argument that neutrality offered 'protection' for a neutral state.

The League Council replied on 14 March 1925. It refused to concede this option to Germany, but welcomed the prospect of German membership and assured her that no excessive demands would be made of her. Stresemann appeared satisfied with this reply although, for other reasons, Germany did not apply for membership until nearly a year later (8 February 1926), and was not admitted until the following September.

The three cases mentioned so far were all of states who expressed their reservations about collective security before entering the League. The last example, however, shows a state already a member of the League, Canada, having second thoughts about collective security. The occasion of this speech was the vote of the League Assembly recommending the Geneva Protocol, which would have plugged some of the gaps in the Covenant, and thus have reduced still further the scope for neutrality. The Geneva Protocol never came into effect for several reasons, of which the attitude of Canada and the other Dominions was one, but the tone of this speech indicates that

Canada's hesitations extended to the Covenant itself. Now that America was outside the League, Canada did not want to be involved automatically in the quarrels of others, to forswear, that is, her neutrality in advance.

DOCUMENT 16. Extracts from the Resolution of Ratification of the Treaty of Versailles, as amended by, and put to, the United States Senate, 19 March 1920.

Resolution of ratification.

Resolved (two-thirds of the Senators present concurring therein), That the Senate advise and consent to the ratification of the treaty of peace with Germany concluded at Versailles on the 28th day of June, 1919, subject to the following reservations and understandings, which are hereby made a part and condition of this resolution of ratification, which ratification is not to take effect or bind the United States until the said reservations and understandings adopted by the Senate have been accepted as a part and a condition of this resolution of ratification by the allied and associated powers and a failure on the part of the allied and associated powers to make objection to said reservations and understandings prior to the deposit of ratification by the United States shall be taken as a full and final acceptance of such reservations and understandings by said powers. . . .

2. The United States assumes no obligation to preserve the territorial integrity or political independence of any other country by the employment of its military or naval forces, its resources, or any form of economic discrimination or to interfere in any way in controversies between nations, including all controversies relating to territorial integrity or political independence, whether members of the league or not, under the provisions of article 10, or to employ the military or naval forces of the United States, under any article of the treaty for any purpose, unless in any particular case the Congress, which, under the Constitution, has the sole power to declare war or authorize the employment of the military or naval forces of the United States, shall, in the exercise of full liberty of action, by act or joint resolution so provide. . . .

11. The United States reserves the right to permit, in its discretion, the nationals of a covenant-breaking State, as defined

in article 16 of the covenant of the League of Nations, residing within the United States or in countries other than such covenant-breaking State, to continue their commercial, financial, and personal relations with the nationals of the United States.

Editor's Note to Document 16

Forty-nine Senators voted for this resolution, and thirty-five against. The resolution was not adopted, having failed to secure a two-thirds majority.

DOCUMENT 17. Extract from *A History of the League of Nations* by F. P. Walters (Oxford University Press for the Royal Institute of International Affairs, 1952).

The Council then considered a request from Switzerland to be permitted to maintain neutrality in regard to any military action by the League, and nevertheless to be accepted as a Member. Like other neutrals, Switzerland was called upon to declare within two months of the coming into force of the Covenant whether she chose to be an original Member of the League or not. Under the Swiss Constitution, a question of such importance could only be settled after holding a national referendum. The government was solidly for joining: there was a large majority on the same side in the Federal Parliament, but in the country itself there was strong opposition. If entry into the League meant the total abandonment of the neutrality which had for centuries been the established tradition of Switzerland, the government itself would be against it, and, in any case, the popular vote would register an overwhelming negative. In these circumstances Switzerland proposed, first to the Allied Council in Paris, and then to the Council of the League, that she should join on the express understanding that if ever the League were compelled to use coercion against a State guilty of aggression, she should not be expected either to participate in any military action, or to allow the passage of troops across her territory; but that she would take her full part in the economic and financial sanctions which the Covenant in such a case made obligatory for all Members. The Swiss proposal was accepted by the Council; three months later, on May 16th, 1920, the referendum was duly held, and the Swiss people decided by a narrow majority to join the League. This result was achieved only after a hard-fought political campaign, in which several cantons were induced by their pro-German sentiment to vote against joining, while both the extreme left and the extreme right put up a bitter opposition to the policy of the Federal Government.

No other country ever gave such thorough consideration to the question of entering the League; nor has any people or government a higher standard of integrity than those of Switzerland. Yet when the test came some fifteen years later, the Swiss government repudiated the promise they had given in London; and Switzerland, almost alone among League Members, declined to share in the economic sanctions which aimed at preventing Mussolini's conquest of Ethiopia.

DOCUMENT 18. Extract from the speech of Senator Dandurand (Canada), to the League Assembly, on the resolution approving the Geneva Protocol, 2 October 1924.

It is my firm conviction that Canada, faithful to her past, will be prepared to accept compulsory arbitration and the compulsory jurisdiction of the Permanent Court of International Justice. Further, I believe she would be prepared to accept all the sanctions that might be imposed in case she refused to accept the decisions of the court of the arbitrators.

As to disarmament, we have already attained the ideal toward which you are striving.

There remains the question of sanctions. Prepared to accept sanctions against herself, in what measure can Canada pledge herself to impose them upon others?

We have already demonstrated that in times of serious crisis we have a full appreciation of our international responsibilities. Canada, in complete independence, entered the great war, out of sentiment, not out of interest or necessity, and to-day she is raising in taxes for the payment of interest on her war debt and war pensions a sum exceeding her whole annual revenues before the war. Nearly five hundred thousand men, out of a population of eight millions, crossed the Atlantic and sixty thousand of them did not return.

When the war was over, we signed at Versailles the Covenant

of the League of Nations. We will be loyal to that Covenant. We are not forgetful, however, of the conditions under which we signed it. Canada was then far from thinking that she would have the whole burden of representing North America when appeals would come to our continent for assistance in maintaining peace in Europe.

The falling away of the United States has increased, in our eyes, the risks assumed, and the history of Europe in the past five years has not been such as to lessen that apprehension.

The heavy sacrifices to which we agreed for the re-establishment of peace in Europe led us to reflect on what the future might hold in store.

May I be permitted to add that in this Association of Mutual Insurance against fire, the risks assumed by the different States are not equal? We live in a fire-proof house, far from inflammable materials. A vast ocean separates us from Europe. Canada therefore believed it to be her duty to seek a precise interpretation of what appeared to her to be the indefinite obligations included in Article 10 of the Covenant.

We besought you to make more precise the scope of the obligations flowing from this clause, in order that the geographical situation and special conditions of each State might be taken into account, and that it would appear quite clearly that our own Parliament retained the decision as to the measure of its participation in the conflict. That interpretation secured the support of the fourth Assembly, with a single dissenting vote.

We hope that it will be possible to find, in the Protocol which is presented to us, the policy expressed in last year's resolution interpreting Article 10.

I recognise that the closely elaborated plan before us forms a logical and harmonious whole, corresponding to the needs of Europe and designed mainly for application to that continent.

Our Government and our Parliament will have to consider in what measure this Protocol will meet the conditions of our country, and decide whether it can undertake to subscribe to its obligations.

We can assure our colleagues that this study will be made with the fullest sympathy and in the same spirit that has animated the members of this Assembly, who have conscientiously striven to find the most certain method of ensuring the peace to the world.

The Canadian delegation, animated by the same sentiments, will vote for the resolutions before it. (*Applause.*)

DOCUMENT 19. Extract from a Letter of Gustav Stresemann (Foreign Minister of Germany), to Sir Eric Drummond (Secretary-General of the League), 12 December 1924, from *Gustav Stresemann: His Diaries, Letters and Papers* edited by Eric Sutton (Macmillan, 1935).

Article 16 regulates the procedure to be adopted in the case of a violation of peace, against the guilty State. It obliges the members of the League to take measures of an economic and military character, such as hitherto were in general only possible as the result of a declaration of a state of war. In any event, the States taking part in such measures must be continually prepared to be treated by the State in question as though they were Powers carrying on a war. It is at once obvious that the principle that lies at the basis of these coercive proceedings can only be practically realized if it is accompanied by arrangements and Treaty agreements calculated to provide the members of the League involved with the greatest possible measure of security against the warlike proceedings of the disturber of the peace. This is not the case under the terms of the Covenant of the League. The conduct of military operations against the disturber of the peace is indeed contemplated in principle, but has hitherto not been more exactly regulated. It is not subjected to the central authority of the League, but left to the free disposition of the individual members. Moreover, the success of these measures becomes in certain circumstances doubtful when they are applied to States which, as is still the case to-day, have at their disposal unlimited and powerful armaments of war.

That this offers the possibility of certain dangers for nearly all the States that are members of the League is obvious. But these dangers will be intensified beyond endurance for a country that, like Germany, lies in a central position and is entirely disarmed. In order to make clear the condition of affairs that has been called into being by the one-sided disarmament of Germany, it is merely necessary to call the following facts to mind: Germany, a country with more than sixty million inhabitants, with a land frontier of 5000 kilometres, and a coastline of more than 2000 kilometres in extent, disposes of an army of 100,000 men in all. Universal military service is abolished, and the formation of reserves is not permitted. This force, quite apart from its numerical strength, cannot in any way be compared with the armies of other countries. It is lacking in all the equipment necessary for modern warfare. It possesses neither heavy artillery nor aeroplanes nor tanks. The fortresses on the western frontier are dismantled, and the few fortresses still remaining to Germany are completely out of date. In the west, 55,000 square kilometres of German soil is demilitarized, not, however, in Germany's favour but one-sidedly in favour of her neighbours. State armament factories do not exist in Germany. The productive capacity of the existing arms and munition factories, the number and character of which is exactly laid down, only suffices to deal with the current needs of peace-time. Any rapid adaptation of other factories for military purposes, in the case of war, has been made impossible by the demolitions effected under the provisions of the Treaty of Versailles. All mobilization measures are forbidden. The strength of the fleet is far below the disarmament limit of the Washington Agreement of February 6th, 1922. On the other hand, apart from their fleets, the other European States may equip themselves for war to a degree that is completely unlimited. Their production of up-to-date war material is subject to no restriction whatever. There are States adjoining Germany which even in peace-time possess more than 5000 tanks, 1500 military aeroplanes, and 350 batteries of heavy artillery. All of them dispose of large reserves of material against the event of war. A neighbouring State with less than eight million inhabitants has a standing army of 80,000 men; another with less than fourteen million inhabitants has a standing army of over 150,000 men; a third neighbouring State with less than thirty million inhabitants has a standing army of 275,000 men; and a fourth, with less than forty million inhabitants, has a standing army of more than 700,000 men. All these armies are based on the system of universal military service, which ensures the application of the whole power of a nation in the event of war.

Thus Germany finds herself in complete military impotence

in the centre of a heavily armed Europe. If the measures contemplated under Article 16 lead to acts of war, Germany is not
in a position to make any real resistance to a military invasion
of her territory. Germany would be completely dependent on
the military protection of her fellow members of the League,
though these would not be under any obligation to provide
such protection. The country would, in most cases that could
be imagined, become the scene of European wars conducted
under the auspices of the League. Even when the disturber of
the peace was not an immediate neighbour, there is good reason
to fear that, if the course of the military operations turned out
unfavourably, the war would be carried on to the defenceless
territory of Germany. And even presupposing the loyal fulfilment of League obligations, it must not be forgotten that the
foreign League forces would not defend German soil with the
same self-sacrifice with which they would defend their own land.
That German troops could play no appreciable part in such
conflicts needs no further emphasis in view of their small numbers and their lack of all the modern means of warfare.

All this is a necessary consequence of the fact that the whole
organization of the League is scarcely compatible with the
military preponderance of individual States, whether they are
members of the League or not. It presupposes as a basis an
armed equipment of all States, in the assessment of which the
geographical position and the size of the States is taken into
more or less equal consideration. This presupposition will not
even be fulfilled, so far as concerns Germany, if the disarmament
of the other States were carried out within the terms of the
League programme, since this programme defines a limit for the
reduction of military resources that does not prejudice the
requirements of national security nor the possibility of participation in the coercive measures. The level of general armaments
will still even then be far above the level of the state of German
armaments.

In the view of the German Government there is only one way
out of the difficulties in which Germany is involved by this dis-
parity in regard to her participation in any coercive measures.
In the event of international conflicts the German Reich must
be allowed to determine for herself the extent of her active
participation. In this, Germany is asking for no favour. What

she asks for is the consideration of her special position in the assessment of her duties as a member of the League. Otherwise, by her entry into the League, she would be forced to surrender the ultimate means of protection for a defenceless people, neutrality.

In what form this request on Germany's part could be met, the German Government cannot foresee. We are not authentically informed as to how the application of coercive measures will be arranged or planned in an individual case. However, the German Government assumes from your courteous communication of October 27th of this year, entitled "Protocol for the Peaceful Settlement of International Disputes", that the League has already been engaged in deliberations tending in the same direction. By the terms of Section 2 of Article 11 of this protocol, in the share assigned to individual States in the application of coercive measures, account is to be taken of their geographical and military position. But, apart from the fact that the protocol has not come into force, the above reservation is clearly not to affect the obligation of all members of the League to take part in measures of blockade, to afford active economic support to the campaign, and to permit the troops taking part to march through their territory. In this way all members of the League will be deprived of the possibility of neutrality. Thus, even when the protocol comes into force, Germany will still be exposed to all the dangers that have been briefly enumerated above.

The German Government confidently anticipate that the League of Nations will recognize the justice of these apprehensions and find a way to remove them. It is felt that it is possible to consider German interests without in any way imperilling the organization of the League or the fulfilment of its tasks. May I ask you, Sir, to lay the matter before the competent committees of the League as soon as may be practicable?

*

So far, we have looked at only the *theory* of neutrality in the inter-war years—how various states insisted on retaining their option of neutrality in *future* conflicts, either by keeping out of the League, in the case of the U.S.A., or by somehow reconciling this policy with League membership. What this meant in practice—how far members of the League would actually go in involving themselves in any war arising out of a breach of the

Covenant, and how far non-members like America would succeed in keeping out of it—was not apparent in the relatively peaceful 1920s, but had to wait for the turbulent events of the 'thirties. When Japan annexed Manchuria in 1931–2, the only action taken by the League was the dispatching of the Lytton Commission, which eventually produced a report critical of Japan, and whose adoption by the Assembly provoked Japan's withdrawal from the League. There was thus nothing for would-be neutrals to be dragged into. The Italian invasion of Ethiopia in 1935 raised more serious problems for them, for the vast majority of League members agreed to impose economic sanctions—substantial though by no means total—on Italy. These sanctions did not include oil; military action, and even the closing of the Suez Canal to Italy, were ruled out; and as a result they were quite ineffective in stopping her. Still, each state, particularly those concerned to preserve their neutrality, had to decide whether to go along with the others and impose sanctions, or to break sanctions by trading with Italy. Of the four states whose policies we have already examined, Switzerland, despite its promise, failed to impose sanctions on Italy (see Document 17); Canada fully supported Britain, and at one time even proposed to extend the sanctions to cover oil; Germany, now under Nazi rule, rearming, and outside the League, had her own quarrel with Italy and prevented her from buying extra supplies of the materials that the sanctions denied her. More important than these where economic pressures were concerned was the attitude of the U.S.A. The sanctioning states were not imposing a blockade—they did not try to stop Italy's trade with other countries by force—and if Italy could buy what she needed in the American market much of the effect of sanctions would be lost. (Not all, though. At Suez, in 1956, Britain could still buy oil from the western hemisphere when her Middle East supplies were interrupted, but at a price which, in the absence of special arrangements by the U.S. Government, she found crippling.) Once again there was a difference of view between President (now Franklin D. Roosevelt) and Congress. The next two documents show one of a succession of Neutrality Acts by which Congress sought to tie the President's hands (see Document 20), and the way in which Roosevelt and his Secretary of State, Cordell Hull, interpreted

it (see Document 21). This last extract is taken from a book by
two whole-hearted advocates of 'Neutrality for the United
States'; a further extract from this book appears in the next
chapter (see Document 24). These two extracts, as well as
showing how Roosevelt deviated from a policy of strict neutrality, and perhaps from his constitutional duty to carry out the
Congressional Resolution unamended, make out a vigorous case
against that policy; but there were many in America who
welcomed any steps Roosevelt took to align their country
closely with the League, and later with Britain and France
against Hitler. In reading documents 20 and 21, it is important
to distinguish between trade in 'arms, ammunition, or implements of war' whose export in time of war is prohibited by the
Neutrality Act, and trade generally, which is not affected.
Borchard and Lage accuse Roosevelt of confusing the two. A
general trade embargo, even if applied to both sides, would
have hit Italy more than Ethiopia; an arms embargo, the
reverse, since Italy could make her own arms if she had the
necessary raw materials, while Ethiopia could not. Moreover,
Italy's trade with the U.S.A., which was much greater than that
of Ethiopia anyway, was enhanced in importance while the
sanctioning countries were limiting their trade with her. It is
also important to distinguish between a neutral United States
permitting both sides to buy arms from private firms operating
within its territory, which but for the Neutrality Act would have
been legitimate, and the government itself supplying arms to one
side, which by international law is not.

In spite of Roosevelt's alleged distortion of the Neutrality Act,
Italy, according to Walters, 'found no difficulty in securing
(from the American market) whatever additional supplies she
could pay for'. America's neutrality, which followed logically
from her refusal to join the League, helped to permit Italy to
annex Ethiopia. But the halfheartedness of Britain and France
probably helped more. But for the obligations of the League
Covenant, they too, no doubt, would have remained neutral.
They wanted Italian support against Germany, rather than the
other way round, and France in particular had a demilitarized
frontier with Italy that she was very anxious to keep demilitarized. This was a traditional balance-of-power policy of
coalescing with not particularly congenial states against any

one power that threatened to dominate the system; and in 1935 the major threat obviously came from Germany. Such neutrality would have been tactical, however. It differed from that of traditional neutrals such as Switzerland, even from the doctrinaire neutrality of the U.S.A.

DOCUMENT 20. Joint Resolution of the United States Congress, 31 August 1935 (The Neutrality Act).

Providing for the prohibition of the export of arms, ammunition, and implements of war to belligerent countries; the prohibition of the transportation of arms, ammunition, and implements of war by vessels of the United States for the use of belligerent states; for the registration and licensing of persons engaged in the business of manufacturing, exporting, or importing arms, ammunition, or implements of war; and restricting travel by American citizens on belligerent ships during war.

Resolved by the Senate and House of Representatives of the United States of America in Congress assembled, That upon the outbreak or during the progress of war between, or among, two or more foreign states, the President shall proclaim such fact, and it shall thereafter be unlawful to export arms, ammunition, or implements of war from any place in the United States, or possessions of the United States, to any port of such belligerent states, or to any neutral port for transshipment to, or for the use of, a belligerent country.

The President, by proclamation, shall definitely enumerate the arms, ammunition, or implements of war, the export of which is prohibited by this Act.

The President may, from time to time, by proclamation, extend such embargo upon the export of arms, ammunition, or implements of war to other states as and when they may become involved in such war. . . .

SEC. 3. Whenever the President shall issue the proclamation provided for in section 1 of this Act, thereafter it shall be unlawful for any American vessel to carry any arms, ammunition, or implements of war to any port of the belligerent countries named in such proclamation as being at war, or to any neutral port for transshipment to, or for the use of, a belligerent country.

Whoever, in violation of the provisions of this section, shall take, attempt to take, or shall authorize, hire, or solicit another to take any such vessel carrying such cargo out of port or from the jurisdiction of the United States shall be fined not more than $10,000 or imprisoned not more than five years, or both; and, in addition, such vessel, her tackle, apparel, furniture, equipment, and the arms, ammunition, and implements of war on board shall be forfeited to the United States.

When the President finds the conditions which have caused him to issue his proclamation have ceased to exist, he shall revoke his proclamation, and the provisions of this section shall thereupon cease to apply.

SEC. 4. Whenever, during any war in which the United States is neutral, the President, or any person thereunto authorized by him, shall have cause to believe that any vessel, domestic or foreign, whether requiring clearance or not, is about to carry out of a port of the United States, or its possession, men or fuel, arms, ammunition, implements of war, or other supplies to any warship, tender, or supply ship of a foreign belligerent nation, but the evidence is not deemed sufficient to justify forbidding the departure of the vessel as provided for by section 1, title V, chapter 30, of the Act approved June 15, 1917 (40 Stat. . . . U. S. C., title 18, sec. 31), and if, in the President's judgment, such action will serve to maintain peace between the United States and foreign nations, or to protect the commercial interests of the United States and its citizens, or to promote the security of the United States, he shall have the power and it shall be his duty to require the owner, master, or person in command thereof, before departing from a port of the United States, or any of its possessions, for a foreign port, to give a bond to the United States, with sufficient sureties, in such amount as he shall deem proper, conditioned that the vessel will not deliver the men, or the cargo, or any part thereof, to any warship, tender, or supply ship of a belligerent nation; and, if the President, or any person thereunto authorized by him, shall find that a vessel, domestic or foreign, in a port of the United States, or one of its possessions, has previously cleared from such port during such war and delivered its cargo or any part thereof to a warship, tender, or supply ship of a belligerent nation, he may prohibit the departure of such vessel during the duration of the war.

SEC. 5. Whenever, during any war in which the United States is neutral, the President shall find that special restrictions placed on the use of the ports and territorial waters of the United States, or of its possessions, by the submarines of a foreign nation will serve to maintain peace between the United States and foreign nations, or to protect the commercial interests of the United States and its citizens, or to promote the security of the United States, and shall make proclamation thereof, it shall thereafter be unlawful for any such submarine to enter a port or the territorial waters of the United States or any of its possessions, or to depart therefrom, except under such conditions and subject to such limitations as the President may prescribe. When, in his judgment, the conditions which have caused him to issue his proclamation have ceased to exist, he shall revoke his proclamation and the provisions of this section shall thereupon cease to apply.

SEC. 6. Whenever, during any war in which the United States is neutral, the President shall find that the maintenance of peace between the United States and foreign nations, or the protection of the lives of citizens of the United States, or the protection of the commercial interests of the United States and its citizens, or the security of the United States requires that the American citizens should refrain from traveling as passengers on the vessels of any belligerent nation, he shall so proclaim, and thereafter no citizen of the United States shall travel on any vessel of any belligerent nation except at his own risk, unless in accordance with such rules and regulations as the President shall prescribe: *Provided, however*, That the provisions of this section shall not apply to a citizen traveling on the vessel of a belligerent whose voyage was begun in advance of the date of the President's proclamation, and who had no opportunity to discontinue his voyage after that date: *And provided further*, That they shall not apply under ninety days after the date of the President's proclamation to a citizen returning from a foreign country to the United States or to any of its possessions. When, in the President's judgment, the conditions which have caused him to issue his proclamation have ceased to exist, he shall revoke his proclamation and the provisions of this section shall thereupon cease to apply.

DOCUMENT 21. Extract from *Neutrality for the United States* by E. Borchard and W. P. Lage (Yale University Press, 1940).

. . . The main feature of the Neutrality Act of August 31, 1935, was a mandatory embargo on "arms, ammunition and implements of war," strictly defined by the Arms Traffic Convention of 1925 to include little else besides lethal weapons. It also provided for setting up a national munitions control board which would regulate and supervise the export of munitions and implements of war from the United States by a registration and license system. The resolution further provided—and Secretary Bryan must have nudged President Wilson as they watched the proceedings from the Elysian fields—that American citizens take passage on belligerent vessels at their own risk. Submarines of a foreign nation might not enter American ports or territorial waters, if the President so proclaimed, and American ports could not be used as a base for supplying men or cargo to any belligerent warship at sea. This resolution, passed in the closing days of the 73rd Congress, was to remain in force until February 29, 1936, before which date new legislation was contemplated.

There is evidence that although the August, 1935, Resolution was signed by the President, it did not fully meet his approval. He criticized the inflexible provisions of the embargo and urged that in the light of unforeseeable situations he should have discretion in coöperating with peacefully minded governments in order to promote peace. In signing the resolution the President stated:

The latter section [arms embargo] terminates at the end of February, 1936. This Section requires further and more complete consideration between now and that date. Here again the objective is wholly good. It is the policy of this government to avoid being drawn into wars between other nations, but it is a fact that no Congress and no executive can foresee all possible future situations. History is filled with unforeseeable situations that call for some flexibility of action. It is conceivable that situations may arise in which the wholly inflexible provisions might drag us into war instead of keeping us out. The policy of the Government is definitely committed to the maintenance of peace and the avoidance of any entanglements which would lead us into conflict. At the same time it is the policy of the Government by every peaceful means and without entanglement to cooperate with other similarly minded governments to promote peace.[1]

While it is undoubtedly true that history is filled with unforeseeable situations, it is not possible to apply arms embargoes discriminatorily or flexibly without inviting all the risks of actual unneutrality. And it was unneutrality that the resolution was designed to avoid and prevent. In the light of the consistent demand for a policy enabling the United States to coöperate with other nations in punishing aggressors, a demand which the committee had considered, the whole purpose of the resolution was to make certain that the embargo would be applied against both belligerents without discrimination. If, on the other hand, the President had in mind the possibility that it would be undesirable to apply the embargo against all the belligerents in any particular war, he would also be departing from the express intention of the resolution, which was to make the arms embargo mandatory in the event of any foreign war. It is not possible to tell which aspect of the embargo the President was objecting to—its applicability to all belligerents or its mandatory imposition in every war. And just how the inflexible provisions could drag us into war he did not explain.

Perhaps the President did not realize that a discretionary arms embargo would expose him to the importunities of those who believe that it is a practical peace policy to help a favored nation and hurt the disfavored. If the arms embargo injured the favored nation they would urge the President not to proclaim it; if it helped, they would be silent. And it is far easier to exert influence on the Executive than on Congress. Less propaganda is required.

Inasmuch as embargoes are usually hostile acts, the grant of discretion to the President and the opportunity for unneutrality involved would transfer to the President the power actually to make war. Wars rarely break out without prior unfriendly acts;

[1] Press Releases XIII (31 August 1935), 162-3.

a discriminatory arms embargo could readily provoke open hostilities. Just as dangerous, as we shall see, was the demand made on Congress in 1936 to give the President discretionary power to impose commodity embargoes. Even the power to apply arms and commodity embargoes to both belligerents would not preclude unneutrality if the President has the power to choose the commodities to go on the embargo list, for commodities can be selected whose lack would hurt one belligerent more than the other. And if that happened, the handicapped belligerent would be certain to regard the discrimination as intentional.

Italian-Ethiopian Embargo

IN October, 1935, the Italians entered upon the war that had for a year been threatened against Ethiopia. The League declared Italy to be the aggressor (October 9, 1935) and appointed a Committee to bring about coördination in the application of sanctions, which were to become effective November 18, 1935. Difficulties at once arose, notably between Great Britain and France. The common phenomenon of Great Powers proving unable to agree on any major policy became at once apparent. The difference served at least to limit the scope of the sanctions. Each day a Geneva dispatch to the *New York Times* informed the American public of the changing list of commodities which it was proposed to embargo against Italy. Imports from Italy were in the main banned. Loans and credits to Italy were prohibited. Besides armaments, transport animals, rubber, bauxite, aluminum, iron ore and scrap iron, nickel and various ores used for steel-making, tin and tin ores were embargoed.

On October 5 the President ruled that Americans traded with, and traveled on the ships of, belligerents at their own risk.[1] The injunction against general trade was unauthorized, but was hailed by advocates of the League of Nations as an abandonment of the freedom of the seas, a doctrine which unfortunately they seem to believe is a detriment to peace. It became apparent, too, that inasmuch as practically the only trade between the United States and the belligerents was with Italy and the only

[1] *Press Releases*, XIII (5 October 1935), 251, 256.

belligerent ships on which Americans could take passage were Italian, the administration's request operated to handicap Italy alone. And it was made very clear that it was the sanctionists' desire to discourage trade with Italy. On October 10 the Secretary of State reinforced the President's proclamation by supporting embargoes as well as by further discountenancing American trade with the belligerents.[1]

On October 26 Secretary Hull addressed the President of the Committee of Coördination of the League of Nations, expressing "sympathetic interest" with "the individual or concerted efforts of other nations to preserve peace or to localize or shorten the duration of war." This was generally, and probably correctly, interpreted to express sympathy with the policy of suppressing Italy.[2] On October 30 the President issued a further warning against "transactions of any character with either of the belligerent nations" except at the trader's risk. The statement was made that this restriction of trade was designed to shorten the war.[3] The Secretary of State on the same day reiterated his purpose "to discourage dealings with the two belligerent nations."[4] It was conceded that this restriction of ordinary trade was not authorized by the Neutrality Act of August 31, 1935, but it was argued that it was within the "spirit" of that act and was justified "upon the further purpose not to aid in protracting the war." It was urged that trade and the profits accruing from it would be obtained "at the expense of human lives and human misery." But misery is promoted not by supplying but by withholding commodities that countries at war most urgently need.

In executing its policy, the government cautioned our citizens not to trade in any commodities with either of the belligerents, although at that time even League of Nations' sanctions had not come into force and it was not then known to what materials such sanctions would apply. The injunction was accompanied by pressure on the shippers of commodities, such as oil, which eventually the League decided not to embargo at all. In his address of November 6 Secretary Hull indicated his desire for

[1] *Press Release*, XIII (10 October 1935), p. 303–4.
[2] *New York Times*, 27 October 1935.
[3] *Press Releases*, XIII (2 November 1935), p. 338.
[4] *Ibid.*, p. 339.

an embargo extending beyond "arms, ammunition and imple-ments of war" as a part of our general neutrality legislation. He added that:

Our foreign policy would indeed be a weak one if it began or ended with the announcement of a neutral position on the outbreak of a foreign war. I conceive it to be our duty and in the interest of our country and of humanity, not only to remain aloof from disputes and conflicts with which we have no direct concern, but also to use our influence in any appropriate way to bring about the peaceful settlement of international differences.

He desired "a virile policy tempered with prudent caution . . . for after all if peace obtains, problems regarding neutrality will not arise."[1]

On November 15, 1935, shortly before the League sanctions were to come officially into effect, it was announced in Washing-ton that the shipment to the belligerents of oil, copper, trucks, tractors, scrap iron and scrap steel—in some respects going beyond, in others short of, the lists suggested from Geneva—would be disapproved. Traders with Italy were warned that they were violating American policy. American ships under mortgage to the United States Shipping Board were required to desist from trade with the belligerents, which in effect always meant Italy alone. On November 27 the administration limited itself to requesting shippers to desist from trade in "abnormal" quantities beyond pre-war levels, but no administrative machinery was supplied for determining what that level was or for enforcing the limitation.

On November 30, the *New York Times'* correspondent reported from Geneva that the League was encouraged by the activities of the United States in enjoining American trade in "copper, trucks and tractors," because Secretary Hull had classed them as "essential war materials" on November 15. But the suggestion that "oil, copper, trucks, tractors, scrap iron and scrap steel" constitute "essential war materials" is legally unsustainable. All these commodities are used for civilian pur-poses. At most, they might be goods conditionally contraband only. Heretofore belligerents have issued contraband lists;

[1] *Press Releases*, XIII (9 November 1935), pp. 367, 369.

neutrals have not been keen to cut off their own trade. In all these warnings against American trade with Italy, the United States was in advance of the League of Nations, enjoining trade in commodities which the League ultimately declined to control.

Possibly this government pressure on American traders would have gone on but for the fact that the news from Geneva was not encouraging. There was some dissent among League members to the Geneva policy. Sanctions were limited to a few commodities, and were administered in such a way that they could have a crippling effect on Italy only after a considerable time. Irate, Great Britain took drastic measures by enlarging its Mediterranean fleet, and the threat of a conflict between Italy and Great Britain almost overshadowed in importance the Ethiopian War then in progress. Thus, the anti-Italian policy of Washington involved the danger of this country's becoming embroiled on Great Britain's side if British-Italian hostilities developed—a serious possibility at the time.

Finally on December 12 the celebrated Hoare-Laval Agreement was concluded, which would have saved everyone's face; but the "peace" advocates of England would not accept so sensible a solution. Like other moralists, they demanded righteousness in all its perfection. But the announcement of the Hoare-Laval Agreement and the manifest difficulties of the sanctions policy caused Washington to withdraw its demands on American traders, and the possible threat of a foreign war extending to America was diminished.

*

After Ethiopia, the U.S.A. moved, gradually but perceptibly, towards involvement, even military involvement, in the world outside the western hemisphere. A landmark in this journey was Roosevelt's 'quarantine' speech of October 1937 (see Document 22). The speech contained no specific change in policy—America had already followed a 'non-recognition' policy towards annexations achieved by force, such as that of Manchuria. But its tone was significant. Roosevelt's Secretary of State, Cordell Hull, thought that the hint of collective action contained in the 'quarantine' analogy aroused such alarm among the 'isolationists' that it set back the 'internationalist' campaign for six months. This is doubtful. Roosevelt went on to win two more Presidential elections, making four in all; he can hardly have been so out of touch with public opinion as Hull suggests. In any case, even if it was a false move domestically, Roosevelt's speech showed the way American policy was moving.

In Europe, in contrast, the Ethiopian fiasco made neutrality seem more popular. The alternative of collective security no longer seemed to exist. The Spanish Civil War; the Anschluss by which Austria was incorporated into Germany; above all Munich—these events were not even brought before the League, and no effort was made by countries not concerned to protect the victims of pressure, intervention, or attack. Only in the case of the Russian attack on Finland in 1939, after the war with Germany had started, was there any attempt at collective action by the League. Russia was expelled—the one member so treated in the League's history; and only Sweden's resolute neutrality prevented Britain and France from sending military help to the Finns. But this was part of Sweden's neutrality in the Second World War, and belongs to the next chapter.

DOCUMENT 22. Speech of Franklin D. Roosevelt, at Chicago, 5 October 1937 (The Quarantine Speech) from *The Public Papers and Addresses of Franklin D. Roosevelt*, vol. 6 (1937), edited by S. I. Rosenman (Macmillan, New York, 1941).

. . .

The political situation in the world, which of late has been growing progressively worse, is such as to cause grave concern and anxiety to all the peoples and nations who wish to live in peace and amity with their neighbors.

Some fifteen years ago the hopes of mankind for a continuing era of international peace were raised to great heights when more than sixty nations solemnly pledged themselves not to resort to arms in furtherance of their national aims and policies. The high aspirations expressed in the Briand-Kellogg Peace Pact and the hopes for peace thus raised have of late given way to a haunting fear of calamity. The present reign of terror and international lawlessness began a few years ago.

It began through unjustified interference in the internal affairs of other nations or the invasion of alien territory in violation of treaties; and has now reached a stage where the very foundations of civilization are seriously threatened. The land-marks and traditions which have marked the progress of civilization toward a condition of law, order and justice are being wiped away.

Without a declaration of war and without warning or justification of any kind, civilians, including vast numbers of women and children are being ruthlessly murdered with bombs from the air. In times of so-called peace, ships are being attacked and sunk by submarines without cause or notice. Nations are fomenting and taking sides in civil warfare in nations that have never done them any harm. Nations claiming freedom for themselves deny it to others.

Innocent peoples, innocent nations, are being cruelly sacrificed to a greed for power and supremacy which is devoid of all sense of justice and humane considerations.

To paraphrase a recent author "perhaps we foresee a time when men, exultant in the technique of homicide, will rage so hotly over the world that every precious thing will be in danger, every book and picture and harmony, every treasure garnered through two millenniums, the small, the delicate, the defenseless —all will be lost or wrecked or utterly destroyed."

If those things come to pass in other parts of the world, let no one imagine that America will escape, that America may expect mercy, that this Western Hemisphere will not be attacked and that it will continue tranquilly and peacefully to carry on the ethics and the arts of civilization.

If those days come "there will be no safety by arms, no help from authority, no answer in science. The storm will rage till every flower of culture is trampled and all human beings are leveled in a vast chaos."

If those days are not to come to pass—if we are to have a world in which we can breathe freely and live in amity without fear— the peace-loving nations must make a concerted effort to uphold laws and principles on which alone peace can rest secure.

The peace-loving nations must make a concerted effort in opposition to those violations of treaties and those ignorings of humane instincts which today are creating a state of international anarchy and instability from which there is no escape through mere isolation or neutrality. . . .

There is a solidarity and interdependence about the modern world, both technically and morally, which makes it impossible for any nation completely to isolate itself from economic and political upheavals in the rest of the world, especially when such upheavals appear to be spreading and not declining. There can be no stability or peace either within nations or between nations except under laws and moral standards adhered to by all. International anarchy destroys every foundation for peace. It jeopardizes either the immediate or the future security of every nation, large or small. It is, therefore, a matter of vital interest and concern to the people of the United States that the sanctity of international treaties and the maintenance of international morality be restored.

The overwhelming majority of the peoples and nations of the world today want to live in peace. They seek the removal of barriers against trade. They want to exert themselves in industry, in agriculture and in business, that they may increase their wealth through the production of wealth-producing goods rather than striving to produce military planes and bombs and machine guns and cannon for the destruction of human lives and useful property.

In those nations of the world which seem to be piling armament on armament for purposes of aggression, and those other nations which fear acts of aggression against them and their security, a very high proportion of their national income is being spent directly for armaments. It runs from thirty to as high as fifty percent. We are fortunate. The proportion that we in the United States spend is far less—eleven or twelve percent. . . .

I am compelled and you are compelled, nevertheless, to look ahead. The peace, the freedom and the security of ninety percent of the population of the world is being jeopardized by the remaining ten percent who are threatening a breakdown of all international order and law. Surely the ninety percent who want to live in peace under law and in accordance with moral standards that have received almost universal acceptance through the centuries, can and must find some way to make their will prevail.

The situation is definitely of universal concern. The questions involved relate not merely to violations of specific provisions of particular treaties; they are questions of war and of peace, of international law and especially of principles of humanity. It is true that they involve definite violations of agreements, and especially of the Covenant of the League of Nations, the Briand-

Kellogg Pact and the Nine Power Treaty. But they also involve problems of world economy, world security and world humanity.

It is true that the moral consciousness of the world must recognize the importance of removing injustices and well-founded grievances; but at the same time it must be aroused to the cardinal necessity of honoring sanctity of treaties, of respecting the rights and liberties of others and of putting an end to acts of international aggression.

It seems to be unfortunately true that the epidemic of world lawlessness is spreading.

When an epidemic of physical disease starts to spread, the community approves and joins in a quarantine of the patients in order to protect the health of the community against the spread of the disease.

It is my determination to pursue a policy of peace. It is my determination to adopt every practicable measure to avoid involvement in war. It ought to be inconceivable that in this modern era, and in the face of experience, any nation could be so foolish and ruthless as to run the risk of plunging the whole world into war by invading and violating, in contravention of solemn treaties, the territory of other nations that have done them no real harm and are too weak to protect themselves adequately. Yet the peace of the world and the welfare and security of every nation, including our own, is today being threatened by that very thing.

No nation which refuses to exercise forbearance and to respect the freedom and rights of others can long remain strong and retain the confidence and respect of other nations. No nation ever loses its dignity or its good standing by conciliating its differences, and by exercising great patience with, and consideration for, the rights of other nations.

War is a contagion, whether it be declared or undeclared. It can engulf states and peoples remote from the original scene of hostilities. We are determined to keep out of war, yet we cannot insure ourselves against the disastrous effects of war and the dangers of involvement. We are adopting such measures as will minimize our risk of involvement, but we cannot have complete protection in a world of disorder in which confidence and security have broken down.

If civilization is to survive the principles of the Prince of

Peace must be restored. Trust between nations must be revived.

Most important of all, the will for peace on the part of peace-loving nations must express itself to the end that nations that may be tempted to violate their agreements and the rights of others will desist from such a course. There must be positive endeavors to preserve peace.

America hates war. America hopes for peace. Therefore, America actively engages in the search for peace.

DOCUMENT 23. Extract from *Undeclared War* by Elizabeth Wiskemann (Macmillan, 1939).

Love of peace and horror of destruction have combined with the failure of the League of Nations to undermine the meagre beginnings of international co-operation, political or economic; the Swiss have returned to greater insistence upon their neutrality, and other small nations, the Low Countries, the Scandinavians and the Balts, increasingly aware of the fact that the Nazi criterion of force by definition destroys the independence of the weak, have hastened to take refuge behind the same principle, while the Balkan countries try to poise themselves between the Axis Powers and the West. In the East of Europe this policy is easily understood in view of an inherited dislike for Russia and the fears induced by her social system, but it is seldom realized to how great an extent the pursuit of neutrality suits Germany's plan. All genuine ideas of international co-operation are condemned by Hitler's doctrine; in *Mein Kampf* and elsewhere it is made plain that Nazi Germany must first become dominant—then he will see.... Neutrality tends towards acceptance of Germany's condemnation of international action, towards acceptance of Germany's encirclement cries which mean nothing but dislike of the tardy appreciation of her aggressive designs. During 1938 Germany's encirclement of Czechoslovakia was skilful and complete (the Ruthenian-Roumanian frontier excepted), yet even the Germans scarcely believed that Prague cherished aggressive intentions. The Czechs, nevertheless, were required to drop their alliances and become "neutral," or, in other words, helpless. National Socialist Germany knows very well that one cannot be neutral towards totalitarianism—it is something which, by definition, one must accept or reject. In the name of "moral" neutrality Germany claims the submission of all the small States, for any sign of resistance to her doctrines on their part she condemns as unwarrantably "provocative" action; the power she has gained by her influence on the press in the Scandinavian, Baltic and Balkan countries has been seen. Another Nazi method in the undeclared war has been to exploit Europe's thirst for peace by denouncing all ideas of international co-operation as chestnut tactics on the part of Great Britain and France. Divide to destroy. If each small country waits till its own territory is openly attacked or a prey to "spontaneous revolt" from within, each separately is helpless before Germany, and every vow to defend that territory to the "last drop of blood" is as aimless as suicidal mania.

PART IV

The Second World War

The neutral island facing the Atlantic
The neutral island in the heart of man
Are bitterly soft reminders of the beginnings
That ended before the end began.

So wrote Louis MacNeice sadly of his own Ireland, in the middle of the Second World War, reproaching it finally with the thought that:

to the west off your own shores the mackerel
Are fat—on the flesh of your kin.[1]

The British, too, felt betrayed by Ireland's policy of neutrality. Indeed, the Allies generally regarded the neutrals with contempt. Sometimes, perhaps, their neutrality was useful to the Allied cause. This was true, certainly, of Sweden after the Nazi occupation of Norway and of Switzerland after the fall of France. But where it was not, they were prepared to disregard it. Churchill was about to land British troops in Norway when the Nazis forestalled him; Britain and Russia jointly invaded Iran, to end German influence there and provide a safe channel for Allied help to Russia.

But the Allies' treatment of neutrals was restrained indeed compared with that of the Axis powers. After occupying Norway and Denmark in April 1940, Germany again violated the neutrality of Belgium and Luxembourg, and this time added the Netherlands to her victims, in her *Blitzkrieg* against France. The whole of the Balkans, except for some isolated strongholds of resistance, came under direct or indirect Axis control. Only

[1] "Neutrality", from *The Collected Poems of Louis MacNeice*, edited by E. R. Dodds, Faber, 1949.

Ireland, Portugal, Spain, Sweden, and Switzerland of the European states, preserved their neutrality throughout the war.

Taken together the four cases studied in this chapter give a rather flattering picture of the chances of neutrality in the Second World War. They include two of the five successful European neutrals—Sweden and Switzerland: and only one failure—Norway. This imbalance is natural; the longer a neutral stays neutral the more chance it has to demonstrate both the problems, and the art, of being neutral under pressure. But anyone who reads these three accounts should not forget that there were, among the would-be neutrals, more Norways than Switzerlands.

The remaining example takes up again the rather different story of the United States, a country whose military and economic strength and geographical position, made it singularly immune from direct attack. The problem for the Roosevelt Administration in the months after the British and French declaration of war on Germany was not how to maintain its neutrality in a world war, but how far it could aid the Allied cause without provoking retaliation by the Axis, or disaffection among the isolationists at home. This further extract from Borchard and Lage, which goes only up to April 1940, shows how unneutral America was able to be (see Document 24).

The pressures felt by Norway, Sweden and Switzerland in this war have many points of similarity. In each case, the belligerents' demands on them fell into three categories: demands for trade agreements, demands for transit of forces or supplies, or other military use of their territory; and demands for the suppression of critical comment in the press and radio.

The chief differences lay in the resources with which the neutrals could oppose these demands. Sweden and Switzerland had two assets which Norway did not; substantial armies, and resources valuable to a belligerent which could be destroyed or seriously damaged at a moment's notice if war came. But if there is anything in the 'balance of power' theory, Norway was in a better position than either Sweden or Switzerland to play off the Allies against the Axis. For, after the occupation of Norway, Sweden was virtually surrounded by Axis powers, as was Switzerland after the fall of France. Ireland, similarly, was a neutral enclave behind Allied lines. Yet although neither

Germany nor Britain wanted Norway to go over to the others, each was prepared to invade her; and because Norway could offer only negligible resistance, the balance was unstable: whichever side struck first gained whatever was to be gained from occupation.

Sweden and Switzerland, like other successful neutrals, had to make concessions, in their case largely to the Axis powers. This was more difficult for them because public opinion in both countries was overwhelmingly in favour of the allies (though this was not true of all neutrals—in Spain's case, for instance, the régime at least was strongly sympathetic to the Axis powers, with whose help it had won power in the Spanish Civil War). Both certainly breathed more easily when they saw the Axis powers defeated, although by being neutral they had contributed little if anything to this outcome. Yet it is worth considering the arguments of both Ambassador Hägglöf, on behalf of Sweden (see Document 27), and of Max Petitpierre of Switzerland, in the next chapter (see Document 28) that their countries' neutrality was of benefit to their occupied neighbours and to the world as a whole.

DOCUMENT 24. Extract from *Neutrality for the United States*, by E. Borchard and W. P. Lage (Yale University Press, 1940).

Poland. Meanwhile, events in Europe were going from bad to worse. Germany's demands for the return of Danzig were becoming sharper. When Poland viewed this as a threat to her independence, she received a guaranty of protection from Britain and France. Germany's plan embraced, first, a road across the Corridor, and finally, as Poland refused, annexation of the whole Polish Corridor. While Britain and France were seeking to enlist Soviet Russia in guaranties of military coöperation, on August 20 the Germans concluded a trade agreement and, a few days later, a nonaggression pact with Russia. On September 1 Germany marched into Poland and, after two days' delay, Great Britain and France declared war on Germany.

On September 5 the President proclaimed the Neutrality Act of 1937 in force and outlined certain duties imposed on American citizens under international law. On October 18 he issued a proclamation barring belligerent submarines, military and commercial, from American ports. He was silent, however, as to the Allied merchantmen which were then entering American ports heavily armed.[1] That the President was not unaware of the implications of such armament is indicated by his detention in New York harbor of the German liner *Bremen* for two days in late August on the ground that if she left with arms the United States might be held responsible under the *Alabama* rule for any depredations she might commit. In admitting Allied armed merchantmen, however, the President revived the distinction between offensive and defensive armament, discredited even by Secretary Lansing on January 18, 1916, by announcing that "purely defensive armament against warships and submarines" was unobjectionable.[2]

It was known that large orders for airplanes had been placed here by Great Britain and France early in 1939. Unless the Neutrality Act were changed, these could not be delivered after the outbreak of war. For this and other reasons, the President was determined to have the act amended to accord with his wishes. He succeeded.

On the opening day of an extraordinary session of Congress called for the purpose, the President delivered a stirring address again manifesting his dislike for the "aggressor"—clearly indicated, but not named—and for the arms embargo; what he sought was "greater consistency through the repeal of the embargo provisions and a return to international law." To bolster his argument he derided the "artificial legal distinction" between munitions and other articles, although this distinction was made not merely by the Act of 1935, which he now deprecated, but by the international law he purported to extol. He pointed out the "material . . . advantage" of giving employment here rather than sending raw materials abroad for processing; he intimated that legislative restrictions would impair his exercise of discretion under "international law." Contrary to his former devotion to the "Peace Act" of 1937, he now pictured that legislation as impairing "the peaceful relations of the United States with foreign nations."[3] He repeated his

---

[1] Although the power to bar both submarines and armed merchantmen is included in the same clause of the act.

[2] *New York Times*, 30 August 1939, p. 4.

[3] Address, 21 September 1939, *Cong. Rec.* (daily), LXXXV, pp. 8–10.

statement of the previous January that the attempt to "legislate neutrality . . . may operate unevenly and unfairly—may actually give aid to an aggressor and deny it to the victim"—a Geneva misconception of the function of neutrality, and indeed an implicit attack upon the whole philosophy of neutrality. . . .

With minor modifications, the bill forthwith introduced by Senator Pittman followed closely his bill of the previous spring. Again, the only serious debate turned on the lifting of the arms embargo. It was hard to conceal the fact, though a valiant effort was made, that the motive for the change was a desire to help Great Britain and France. This accorded with the emotional views of most American citizens, but little mention was made of the fact that such a change for such a motive would violate international law and cause America to incur grave risks of involvement. The law does not deny a neutral the privilege of changing his law in time of war, but it may not be changed with the motive of helping one belligerent at the expense of the other; nor may the neutral *weaken* his neutrality, without exposing himself to charges of unneutrality from the handicapped belligerent. . . .

The peculiar defect in the proposed change was that it undertook to lift the embargo during a foreign war with the knowledge, if not, indeed, the intention that it would help one set of belligerents only. This seems a clear violation of international law. Just as the United States Government as a neutral government may not legally furnish arms to either belligerent, so it may not by deliberate change in its law help its citizens to furnish such arms, particularly when the effect is discriminatory.

Arguments were advanced, however, to show that the proposed change was purely a matter of American policy which no one could question and that the cash-and-carry provisions as to all commodities afforded a compensating restriction upon the existing law. But the tightening of certain provisions in order to promote abstention does not justify a loosening of other provisions calculated to assist one side only. We can only hope that the handicapped belligerents will not be in a position to exert reprisals. At the moment, the greater danger arises from the United States itself, for if the aid given Great Britain and France does not prove sufficient, the urge to increase it may become irresistible and active intervention may well result. On January 4, 1940, presumably the best the President could say for non-intervention was that "the overwhelming majority of our fellow citizens do not abandon in the slightest their hope and their expectation that the United States will not become involved in military participation in these wars." Perhaps this was an admission that the United States is already being involved in economic and other participation "short of war."

Special exemptions in the new act, passed on November 4, permit trade in American vessels, without prior transfer of title except for munitions, with belligerent states outside Europe. Most trade to Canada is unrestricted, except that title to munitions must be transferred and American vessels are forbidden to enter ports eastward of the Bay of Fundy. Bonds of belligerent governments may not be sold in the American market, as the 1937 act had already provided, and credit may not be extended to belligerent governments or their agents; but credit may be freely extended to private purchasers (except for buying arms and munitions). . . .

Unneutral Acts. The United States is permitting finished bombing planes to be supplied to Great Britain and France. To avoid conflict with American statutes, they are being flown from California to the Canadian border by American pilots, title is solemnly transferred, they are pushed or pulled across the border on wheels, and then the flight continues across Canada to the East coast. Just as no warship may be supplied by a neutral to a belligerent, so no finished bombing plane may be supplied. Article 46 of the Draft Convention adopted at The Hague, 1923, though unratified, prohibits such supply and merely codifies, it is believed, pre-existing law. It is now reported that the British Government is supplying funds for the enlargement of American powder and aircraft plants under contract to supply Britain and France with their entire output. This, too, is believed to be a violation of American neutrality, in that the funds of a belligerent are used to make the United States a base of military supplies.

On June 23, 1939, Ambassador Kennedy in London signed an agreement with the British Government providing for exchange of British rubber for American cotton, the declared purpose being "to acquire reserves of cotton and rubber, respectively, against the contingency of a major war emergency."[1] Neither the cotton nor the rubber was to be disposed of or released by the receiving government on the general market "except in the event of such an emergency." The agreement was ratified by the President on July 17, 1939, and was to come into force on August 25; it was proclaimed on September 6, 1939.

Meanwhile, however, Britain had declared war on Germany on September 3, and on the fifth this country had proclaimed its neutrality. As a result, it became legally impossible for this country to fulfill its obligations under the agreement without violating its neutrality, for a neutral government, as such, cannot supply either belligerent nation with any commodities, certainly not contraband, without committing an unneutral act. Nevertheless, the cotton has been shipped.

The United States has protested to Great Britain against diversion of American ships from the high seas to the dangerous "combat areas," against the prohibition of the export of goods from Germany, and against the search of American mails.[2] Great Britain, not unnaturally, is using an unwise admission of Secretary Lansing in May, 1916, to the effect that money orders, checks, and negotiable instruments may be considered merchandise, as a reason for rejecting the American protest on the mails. Thus, American surrenders of the period 1914–17 are coming home to roost, and to impair further the rights of neutrals. As Secretary Hull soundly remarked, but in another connection:

To waive rights and to permit interests to lapse in the face of their actual or threatened violation—and thereby to abandon obligations—in any important area of the world, can serve only to encourage disregard of law and of the basic principles of international order, and thus contribute to the inevitable spread of international anarchy throughout the world. For

---

[1] Press Releases, XX, pp. 547–9.

[2] There is no justification for the apparent concession by the Department of State (Bulletin II [Jan. 6, 1940] 3; British answer Jan. 20, 1940, *New York Times*, Jan. 21, 1940; cf. *idem*, March 29, 1940) that letter mail on an American vessel or plane voluntarily entering a belligerent port or letter mail in ordinary transit through belligerent territory may be examined or censored. Cf. *Reports to the Hague Conferences* (Oxford University Press, 1917), pp. 741, 733, 735, 221; Scott, *Hague Peace Conferences* (Baltimore, 1909), p. 616.

this country, as for any country, to act in such manner *anywhere* would be to invite disregard and violation of its rights and interests *everywhere*, by every nation so inclined, large or small.[1]

DOCUMENT 25. Extract from 'Norway: Political Antecedents to the German Invasion' by Agnes H. Hicks, from *Survey of International Affairs 1939–46: The Initial Triumph of the Axis* edited by Arnold Toynbee and Veronica M. Toynbee (Oxford University Press for the Royal Institute of International Affairs, 1958).

Down to the summer of 1939, the Norwegian Government, supported by the majority of the people, had been observing a correct attitude towards all foreign Powers. Norway had extricated herself from the commitment, under the Covenant of the League of Nations, to take part in imposing sanctions, and she stood outside all European power combinations; but she had arrangements for collaborating with her Scandinavian neighbours in fields other than the military one. Her Labour Government was mainly pacifist, but there were signs that the party was becoming divided against itself, as some members realized that developments in Germany might threaten Norway's democratic institutions. Unfortunately the war overtook Norway before this feeling could crystallize into effective action. The Norwegians had pursued an anti-defence policy too long to be able to change their attitude quickly. Moreover, there was still some sympathy for Germany among the bourgeois parties and some appreciation of German ideas, and these views were being expressed in a few Right-wing newspapers. Nor could the neglect of years be made good quickly. Defence was totally inadequate; there was not even any unity of direction. Defence arrangements were under the command of the Defence Department with a non-military chief. It is true that a Defence Council had been set up in 1934, but it had not met since 1937 and did not meet again until 1 September 1939. The state of civil defence was deplorable. Measures had been limited to passive anti-aircraft defence, such as bomb shelters. With the exception of Oslo, Bergen, and four or five of the larger towns, no town had active anti-aircraft defences. The Committee set up by the

[1] Department of State, Publication No. 1146.

Storting after the war to investigate the responsibility of the Government of the day for the inadequacy of Norway's state of defence reported that Koht, Nygaardsvold, and the Minister of Defence were all equally to blame. Nor could the whole Government be acquitted on the ground that they had the majority of the Storting behind them. A large number of members supported them, not because, but in spite, of the weakness of their defence policy.

As far as the supply situation was concerned, the measures taken were more effective. A Crisis Committee (*Kriseutvalg*) had been appointed by Royal decree in March 1938 to safeguard civil supplies, and a sum of Kr. 15 million had been voted by the Storting for the purpose. This Committee remained in being until the autumn of 1939, when it was replaced by a newly formed Supply Department. On 30 June 1939 goods to the value of Kr. 10 million had been bought, and purchases continued, thanks to the liberal interpretation given to the original grant by the Storting. Existing food supplies were calculated to be sufficient for from three to nine months, and artificial manure supplies for from one to two and a half years. Petrol supplies were estimated to be sufficient for two months' consumption, but they were requisitioned for defence in September 1939, and rationing was introduced at once.

King Haakon formally proclaimed Norway's neutrality on 1 September 1939 and Norway was a party to the declarations of Scandinavian neutrality on 1 and 3 September. Consultations between the Scandinavian states on questions arising out of their neutrality continued to be held from time to time. Germany assured Norway immediately that her neutrality would be respected, provided that she maintained a strictly neutral policy, and Great Britain gave a similar promise on 22 September, 'so long as Germany respects Norway's neutrality'. The Norwegian 'neutrality watch' was called up on 1 September. It was strengthened in Northern Norway on 19 October, largely on account of the Russo-Finnish war.

Certain changes were made in the Cabinet immediately. The two main changes were that the Prime Minister was relieved of departmental duties and that a Supply Department under Trygve Lie was set up. In December the Defence Minister, Monsen, retired owing to ill health and was succeeded by

Colonel Birger Ljungberg. The appointment of a soldier to this post was due to a desire to remove questions of defence from the arena of party politics in view of the gravity of the international situation. Ljungberg's appointment proved a mistake, however, as he was unequal to his task, while his appointment lulled the Government into an unjustified sense of security. Early in January 1940 a suggestion to form a Coalition Government was mooted, but it was rejected because the Prime Minister was strongly opposed to it. Thus the Labour Government remained in office until the invasion.

Norway's geographical position caused her soon to begin to experience the effects of the war at sea, in spite of the promises of the belligerents. The Germans sank Norwegian ships, while the British restricted Norway's foreign trade. Nevertheless, Norway continued to maintain commercial relations with both belligerents—though this to a decreasing extent, and at the price of incurring both German and Franco-British displeasure. Germany warned Norway and other neutrals against complying with British demands for facilitating the British blockade of Germany, and she protested against the agreement concluded with Great Britain by the Norwegian National Association of Shipowners, under which half the Norwegian merchant fleet was chartered to the Allies. The Allies showed increasing irritation at the shipments of North Swedish iron ore to Germany through Norwegian territorial waters.

On 19 September 1939 Churchill made his first attempt to deprive Germany of Swedish ore supplies by submitting to his colleagues in Whitehall a proposal to mine the Norwegian Leads and thus force the ore ships into non-territorial waters. He was well aware of the objections to this course and of the possibility of German retaliation against Norway, but he felt that the needs of war made such action necessary for Great Britain. On this occasion his proposal was not adopted; but he renewed it on 27 November, and on 16 December circulated a memorandum on the subject, which the Cabinet considered on the 22nd. During the same period the Allied press published reports of German sinkings of certain Allied ships off the Norwegian coast; but it transpired later on that there had been only one case in which the sinking had actually been the work of a German U-boat operating inside Norwegian territorial waters. On 6 January 1940 the Norwegian Government were officially advised that 'the British Government were taking appropriate measures to prevent the use of Norwegian territorial waters by German ships and trade', and that, for this purpose, it would be necessary for British naval forces at times 'to enter and operate in Norwegian waters'. At Koht's request King Haakon interceded with King George about this, and the resolution was cancelled. The British Government, however, did not cease to feel concern over German shipments of ore from Sweden through Norwegian territorial waters, and an attempt, on Koht's part, to persuade Sweden to divert some of them from the Norwegian port of Narvik, on the North Sea, to the Swedish port of Luleå, on the Baltic, was unsuccessful, largely, it may be assumed, because this diversion might have had an adverse effect on Sweden's relations with the Allies. At the end of January 1940 Great Britain suggested that Norway herself might mine her territorial waters, and the Norwegian Government promised to consider the proposal. But it was not submitted to the Defence Department until 20 March, and, in the latter half of March, Koht suggested to the British Government and also to the Allied press that it was in the Allies' interest to let the matter rest, since shipments of ore to Great Britain had increased, while shipments to Germany had decreased. Meanwhile, the Russo-Finnish War (30 November 1939–12 March 1940) had exposed Norway, and also Sweden, to the risk of partial occupation by Allied forces who, on their way to bringing help to Finland, were incidentally to secure control of Narvik and of the Swedish iron ore mines.

There were also minor violations of Norwegian neutrality during this period, in the shape of flights by belligerent aircraft over Norwegian territory. Such incidents were always followed by prompt Norwegian protests to the offending Power when it was possible to identify the trespassing aircraft. The German Government usually denied the facts, while the British (and, during the Finnish war, the Russians) usually admitted the trespass and expressed regret. More serious consequences might have followed from the entry of belligerent warships into Norwegian waters; but, at this stage, this rarely occurred. One of the more spectacular cases was that of the *City of Flint*, an American merchantman captured by the German navy. In the absence of any provision under international law directing the release of a neutral ship captured by a belligerent Power when such a vessel entered neutral waters, the Norwegians allowed the ship to proceed along the Norwegian coast. When, however, her German captain anchored at Haugesund, the legal position changed, and the Norwegian authorities promptly released the ship and interned her German officers and prize crew. Violent German protests, accompanied by threats, gradually subsided when it was realized in Berlin that the Norwegians intended to stand by their rights under international law. Norwegian action in this case was creditable to the Norwegian Government; but in other cases, notably that of the German auxiliary naval vessel *Westerwald*, Norway showed unnecessary subservience to Germany. The most important naval action affecting Norwegian neutrality in this phase of the war was carried out by the British navy on 16 February 1940 when the destroyer *Cossack* entered Jøssingfjord and forced her way alongside the German naval vessel *Altmark* (which had acted as an auxiliary to the *Graf Spee*). A boarding party led by Captain (later Admiral of the Fleet Sir) Philip Vian overpowered the German crew and liberated 299 British prisoners of war, captured by the *Graf Spee*, who had been concealed on board the *Altmark*. During the action some shots were fired and four Germans were killed. On the merits of the case the British action undoubtedly deserved sympathy, and the British Government had an arguable legal case. The Norwegian White Book claims that the Norwegians were justified in permitting the *Altmark* to enter the 'outer' territorial waters of Norway, but criticizes the Commanding Admiral—who was supported by the Foreign Affairs Committee—for allowing her to pass the naval port of Bergen. His decision not to resist 'the British breach of neutrality' is, on the other hand, approved, in the same Norwegian White Book, on the grounds that 'a neutral state is not obliged under international law to use force against obviously superior forces if its neutrality is infringed', and that, moreover, 'we were anxious to avoid Norway's being drawn into the war on Germany's side as a direct consequence of a fight in the Jøssingfjord'. In a statement in the Storting, Koht declared that resistance would have been senseless. This pronouncement was contradicted by Koht's notifications to British and German diplomats that, 'whatever happened', Norway would 'shoot' from now onwards. But both the British and the German Government had come to feel, by now, that Norway was unable—and perhaps even unwilling—to defend her neutrality, and German threats to Norway became ominous. Hitler now definitely decided to invade Norway, while the British decided to mine the Norwegian Leads, with the hope of provoking a German attack on Norway that would open the way for Allied troops to land in Norway, not as invaders, but as a rescue party. Koht now urged the Allies, through Washington, to show greater understanding for the dangers of Norway's position; but the Allies' tone towards Norway also changed, and British statesmen now repeatedly declared that the Scandinavian states ought not to remain neutral but ought, for their own sake, to join the West European Powers.

While Norway was implicated in the war at sea from the very outbreak of hostilities, her policy of neutrality underwent its first serious trial on the military-political side when Russia attacked Finland. Popular feeling in Norway was all on Finland's side, but nobody in a responsible political position was prepared to act on this feeling. The Prime Minister, in particular, threw the whole weight of his authority on the side of remaining neutral in the strictest sense of the word and Koht carried out this policy willingly. Moreover, Bräuer, the German Minister in Oslo, repeatedly warned the Norwegian Government that any official move to render military assistance to Finland would lead to German reprisals. Consequently the Government disregarded the wishes of a minority in the Storting, headed by J. L. Mowinckel and Hambro and enjoying widespread support among the people, that a policy more in line with popular sentiment should be pursued. In spite of this cautious attitude the Soviet Government protested on 6 January against the anti-Russian press campaign in Norway. The Norwegian Government's reply was firm and dignified. The accusations were rejected as incorrect and the firmness of Norway's resolve to maintain her neutrality was emphasized. Officially the Russian Government found the reply satisfactory, but unofficially Moscow Radio, on 15 January, described it as unsatisfactory. Thus Norway was never allowed to forget that her ship of state was navigating dangerous waters; but this did not prevent the Norwegians from giving Finland all the help in their power within the rules of neutrality. Koht stated at Geneva on 14 December that although compared with Swedish help to Finland Norway's help looked little, 'nevertheless it is true that never in Norway have we had collections which brought in such great value both in monies and goods as those to help Finland'. Moreover, when at the end of December 1939 the Allies asked, in a note to Norway (and Sweden), for facilities to send war materials to Finland across Scandinavian territory, these facilities were conceded by both countries as not constituting a breach of neutrality. On the other hand an Allied request on 2 March, that, in the event of a Finnish appeal for Allied military aid, Allied troops should be granted passage through the Scandinavian countries, was refused—by Sweden on 2 March and by Norway on 4 March. The only occasion on which a slight relaxation of Koht's strict conception of neutrality was noticeable was when he took part in deliberations on the possibility of a defensive alliance between the Scandinavian states and Finland after the conclusion of the Russo-Finnish Peace Treaty of 12 March 1940, but, when the Soviet Government made it clear that such a pact would be regarded as a breach of the treaty on Finland's part, the suggestion was dropped.

Norwegian trade negotiations with the belligerents came to a head in Oslo a week after the *Altmark* affair. The German-Norwegian agreement—which was approved by the British delegates—was signed on 23 February, while the Anglo-Norwegian agreement was not completed until 11 March, as it required the consent of the British Dominions. On 2 April 1940, in the House of Commons, Chamberlain alluded to the trade position, stressing that 'all the war trade agreements into which we have entered contain stipulations regulating the exports of neutral countries' own domestic produce to Germany'. It will be seen that he did not expressly mention ore shipments, because these were, in fact, Swedish exports, but Koht took the view that, under the rules of neutrality and in view of assurances given by Norway to Germany on 1 September 1939, Norway was bound to permit and protect 'peaceable transport' inside her waters. British control over this traffic was tightened up, however, and occasionally British warships penetrated into Norwegian waters.

Meanwhile, Germany and the Allies had been working out

simultaneous and parallel military designs upon Norway, after the Allies' previous designs (in connexion with their dream of bringing aid to Finland against the Soviet Union) had been overtaken and put out of court by Finland's capitulation.

On 21 March Reynaud became President of the French Council of Ministers and at once began to press the British Government again to adopt an aggressive policy in Scandinavia.

It was now decided to start by solving the original problem of the passage of the iron ore south from Narvik by the original method, namely, the mining of the Leads so as to drive enemy shipping out of Norwegian territorial waters. . . . This was to be followed by the laying of minefields in Norwegian waters, of which no previous warning would be given to the Norwegian Government. This in turn, it was supposed, might be followed by German counter-action against Norwegian territory; and this, by the acceptance by Norway of an Allied occupation of Narvik and the three southern ports. . . . Expectations about Sweden were less clear, but it was hoped that circumstances would enable the force landed at Narvik to reach the orefields as the champions of Sweden against aggression, actual or hypothetical. [From the official (British) History of the Second World War.]

On the other side the Germans had been pushing ahead with their plans for the occupation of Norway. Their operations were originally intended to begin on 20 March; the British plan, which was accepted by the Supreme War Council on 28 March, called for the dispatch of 'justificatory' notes to Norway and Sweden on 1 or 2 April, to be followed by mine-laying on 5 April. The persistence of ice in the Baltic caused the Germans to postpone their date until 9 April; and the British date was also postponed for a few days in consequence of French objections to an associated British plan for sowing mines in the Rhine. British notes to the Norwegian and Swedish Governments were delivered on 5 April, and by that time the press in the two Scandinavian capitals was already commenting adversely on the supposed Allied intentions. The mine-laying was due to follow on 8 April. It thus came about that German and Anglo-French naval forces were converging simultaneously on Norway for the execution of their respective plans. The German plan was, however, for a series of decisive blows delivered at a number of different points simultaneously before dawn on 9 April, while the British plan was 'for a succession of conditional landings, which would only take place if evidence of a suitably hostile German reaction to the minelaying were available immediately, and in that event would follow it an an interval ranging from one to four and a half days'.

When Norway entered the crisis of April 1940 only a small part of her defensive power was mobilized. No mines had been laid, coastal fortresses were only partially manned, and no more than a small proportion of the army was under arms. In spite of the disquieting developments before April, Norway's measures for defence retained the character of a 'neutrality watch' to the end. Koht—and his opinion was shared by Mowinckel and Hambro—considered the position to be less dangerous than it had been in 1914–18, and Hambro believed that the Allies' superiority in the air and Germany's lack of petrol would make any effective action on Germany's part impossible. In consequence the Government was not disposed to yield to its military advisers' pressure to increase Norwegian preparedness, particularly as, according to the Norwegian White Book, some pressure was exercised at the time by Hambro, Mowinckel, and Jens Hundseid to *limit* military dispositions. This allegation has, however, been contradicted by Hambro. The Defence Minister —according to a statement by General Laake, the General in Command—usually left decisions in such matters to the other members of the Cabinet or to the Foreign Political Department, while military circles were insufficiently informed on the political and military-political situation. The Admiral in Command, Admiral Diesen, stated after the war that he had thought the landing of enemy troops in Norway highly unlikely and had therefore not proposed full mobilization of coastal fortifications, and had even arranged to send home the majority of the troops attached to them. . . .

DOCUMENT 26. Extract from 'Switzerland' by Constance Howard, from *Survey of International Affairs 1939–46: The War and the Neutrals* edited by Arnold Toynbee and Veronica M. Toynbee (Oxford University Press for the Royal Institute of International Affairs, 1956).

(c) Switzerland in Hitler's Europe, 1940–4

(1) *Swiss Reactions to German Victories*

The entry of Italy into the war and the surrender of France completely changed Switzerland's position. Except for a narrow corridor leading from Geneva into unoccupied France she was entirely surrounded by the Axis homelands and Axis-occupied territory. Her chances of being able to pursue an independent economic and political foreign policy were clearly limited. Great Britain, too, might soon be defeated or forced to surrender, leaving a triumphant and victorious Germany free to consolidate her dominion over Europe.

In these circumstances it is, perhaps, not surprising that a number of people felt that Switzerland should qualify herself for a favourable position in Hitler's New Europe by political and economic adaptation. During the summer months of 1940 there was much public and press discussion of *Erneuerung* (renewal) and *Anpassung* (adaptation) of Swiss institutions and policies. In a broadcast to the people on 25 June Pilet-Golaz spoke of the need for economic adaptation. He warned his countrymen that they would have to accept changes in their way of life. They must give up ease and accept a greater solidarity. Moreover, the Government would no longer be able to explain and justify their decisions to the public. Pilet-Golaz's somewhat equivocal speech was later the subject of much hostile criticism. It is difficult to determine exactly what he had in mind, but it is certain that his words were not the rallying call which the occasion demanded.

The historic role of the old Swiss patriots who had called on their countrymen to defend their independence with their lives was reserved for General Guisan. Guisan was immensely popular with both the army and the public. On 25 July he summoned all the senior army officers to a meeting on the Rütli Meadow. In a stirring address the General told them to ignore the defeatists and to remain steadfast in resistance. Guisan believed that Switzerland could and would refuse to surrender, even if it meant withdrawal of the army into the mountain strongholds, and the abandonment of her towns and villages to the enemy. A 'national redoubt' had been created for this purpose, based on the natural fortresses of the Gotthard, Sargans, and Saint Maurice. Information on the High Command's plans for resistance was in turn passed on to the soldiers by their officers, and to civilian elements by the 'Armée et Foyer' section of the Staff. This section had been originally designed to strengthen the morale of the army, but its work had been widened to include education of civilians through the organization of lectures and information courses. Although, in the event, the Swiss were not called on to make the hard choice between surrender and continued resistance with the sacrifice of most of their country, morale throughout the country was enormously improved by the decision to resist at all costs. . . .

While the Swiss were determined to maintain their political independence and to defend their neutrality, the Government were obliged to make a number of concessions to Germany and Italy. Thus they accepted the German demand to hand over war material belonging to interned Polish and French soldiers after the defeat of France. In the spring of 1941 representations were made to the British Government by the Swiss Federal Council asking for the discontinuance of news bulletins broadcast to Switzerland.

Another concession to the Axis Powers was the imposition of the blackout in Switzerland on 9 November 1940. Hitherto Switzerland had been fully lighted. Not only was she entitled to lights as a neutral country; the illumination of her towns and villages would enable belligerent airmen to recognize a neutral territory and would protect her from being bombed by mistake. Since the summer of 1940, however, British bombers had repeatedly crossed Swiss territory on their way to attack north Italian towns and, in spite of repeated protests from the Swiss Government, this violation of Swiss air by British aviators continued. The Italians complained that Swiss illumination gave an unfair advantage to British bomber crews as it helped them to find their targets in northern Italy.

In July 1941 the Federal Government found it necessary to issue an order putting into effect laws to prevent insults to foreign diplomats or heads of state, national flags and emblems, and even foreign individuals on account of their nationality. Infringement of the law was punishable by imprisonment or fines. During the same month a Swiss delegate attended a meeting of the Axis-controlled International Cinema Chamber which was designed to prevent the exhibition of films displeasing to other members of the Chamber. An announcement that the Swiss delegate had signed the Chamber's statute met with much public criticism and was subsequently denied by the Government.

A much more formidable problem which confronted the Swiss Government during the war years was control of the highly organized fifth column consisting of Germans resident in Switzerland. After the outbreak of war the Germans worked hard to increase the size and efficiency of their organizations in Switzerland. Before the war, in spite of pressure from the Fatherland, only a minority of the Germans in Switzerland had belonged to one of the Nazi organizations. After the German victories in 1939 and 1940 the numbers enrolled increased rapidly and continued to grow, although at a diminishing pace, until the end of 1942. Many were inspired to enrol themselves under the Nazi banner through motives of patriotism and pride of race, while others did so in order to safeguard their future by showing themselves loyal supporters of the Führer. It was significant of the value placed on this fifth column that after the outbreak of war only a relatively small number of the Germans living in Switzerland were called up for service with the German armed forces, and among these only a few were known workers for National Socialism. It was even more significant that ardent Nazis were later withdrawn from the front and given important work in the Party groups in Switzerland.

An endless procession of spokesmen from Germany arrived in Switzerland to instruct and exhort their countrymen at the numerous rallies and meetings, which increased in frequency and size with the growth of membership in the German National Socialist groups. The Swiss Government, unable to ban the assemblies, did their best to regulate them. A decree was passed in July 1940 under which a permit had to be obtained from the Swiss authorities by organizers of political meetings. The Germans, however, were not prepared to accept these restrictions on their activities and speech. Unauthorized assemblies were held and speakers did not confine their speeches within the prescribed limitations. In these circumstances permission to address meetings was withdrawn from a number of the most outspoken propagandists. A particularly large and aggressive assembly presided over by Gauleiter

Bohle on 4 October 1942 aroused much public indignation in Switzerland, and led the Federal Council to prohibit in future large gatherings arranged by foreign organizations. By this date, however, Germany was moving over to the defensive: although the Germans were still masters of the Continent there was an increasing probability that this mastery would not permanently endure.

Throughout the war the Swiss had also to contend with the activities of spies, saboteurs, and informers. German espionage services had been elaborately organized to form a network covering the whole of Switzerland, with its key points resting on the German Legation and Consulates where the Foreign Intelligence Service of the OKW (*Abwehr*) and the SS Security Service (*Sicherheitsdienst*) had introduced special agents for this work. While the Germans made use of German nationals resident in Switzerland as well as of disloyal Swiss, the principal agents were in general sent from Germany. Agents were introduced into Switzerland, by illegal as well as by legal means, in order to obtain detailed military, political, and economic information. Information collected was frequently relayed home by means of the diplomatic courier, but clandestine wireless sets were also made use of and various different methods were employed for smuggling papers, plans, and photographs across the frontier. The Swiss authorities were unable to take firm action against the instigators of these activities in the Legation and Consulates owing to diplomatic immunity and fear of antagonizing Germany.[1]

(3) *Economic Adaptation*

Although the Swiss, with the exception of a minority of fanatics and defeatists, were resolved to maintain their political independence, economically they were obliged to align themselves much more closely with Hitler's Europe. After the fall of France Switzerland was economically at the mercy of the Axis,

---

[1] [Original note.] Germany was not, of course, the only country to conduct espionage and propaganda activities on Swiss soil, but the scale of her activities as well as the intentions underlying them placed her in a different category from the other states. Germany was, in fact, the only country presenting a direct threat to Swiss independence.

which controlled practically all the ways in and out of Switzerland. In a trade agreement reached on 9 August 1940 Germany undertook to supply her with certain quantities of raw materials, of which the most vital were coal and iron. In return Swiss industry was to supply Germany with goods required for her war effort, and transport facilities were to be afforded her for the exchange of goods with Italy. In addition the Swiss Government were obliged to enter into a clearing agreement allowing Germany a credit of 150 million Swiss francs, and to submit the goods that she exported to German control. Only an extremely restricted list of goods could be exported without the German *Geleitschein* or transit permit.

During the ensuing months renewed pressure was brought to bear on the Swiss in order to force them into closer economic relations with Germany. When they showed reluctance the Germans threatened to withhold supplies of coal and iron and to withdraw the permits which allowed the Swiss a limited export trade, a threat which was temporarily put into effect in the spring of 1941 when certain export permits were withdrawn. In face of this pressure the Swiss Government agreed to increase the clearing credit to 317 million Swiss francs in February 1941 and to 350 million in July, when a new trade agreement was reached with Germany.

Britain's reaction to Switzerland's economic accommodation with Germany was to tighten the blockade measures against her. After the fall of France Dr. Keller, head of the Swiss Ministry of Trade, visited London in order to negotiate a working agreement, as the war-trade agreement of April 1940 had been invalidated by events. The Swiss delegates argued that it would be advantageous to Britain to allow Switzerland to trade with other countries, otherwise she would inevitably be placed completely under German economic domination. The British, however, were understandably reluctant to allow the Swiss to import, through Axis-controlled territory, goods which might be taken by the Axis. They were also afraid that the Germans might bring pressure on the Swiss to disgorge goods imported for their own use. After prolonged discussion an agreement was reached on 15 October 1940 under which Britain agreed to relax the blockade in order to allow Switzerland to import certain essential commodities, when her existing stocks did not exceed two months' requirements. This concession, however, was to be cancelled if it became evident that the Swiss had been obliged to give way to German pressure for the re-export of imported goods, or if the goods were retained by the Italian and Vichy Governments on the way. The British also agreed to release some more of the ships which had been chartered by the Swiss Government and which had been detained by the British after the fall of France, and to allow them to be used for the shipment of coal, iron, and foodstuffs through Italian ports. As a result of the additional concessions made by Switzerland to Germany in 1941 the British blockade measures were more strictly enforced against her. . . .

(4) *Swiss Reactions to the Widening of the War*

Towards the end of 1941 there was a growing feeling of uneasiness and frustration in Switzerland. The attack on Russia in the summer and the concentration of Germany's forces on the eastern front had temporarily removed the danger of a military invasion. By the end of 1941 the number of men mobilized had decreased from over half a million in the summer of 1940 to about 71,000. No one could tell when or how the war would end. Meanwhile the Swiss had to put up with many of the discomforts of a state of war, including shortages of food and fuel, a nightly blackout, and governmental regulations and interference in their daily lives, without the compensatory excitement experienced by a belligerent. This feeling of frustration manifested itself in fairly widespread discontent and increasing criticism of the Government by the Socialist and Independent Parties. There were complaints of a lack of contact between the Government and people resulting in a mutual lack of confidence.

At the end of 1941 the balance between the opposing belligerent Powers was radically changed by the entry of the United States and Japan into the war. Although the tide of Germany's victories only began to ebb at the end of 1942, her failure to obtain a decisive victory over Russia and the immense, although as yet largely undeveloped, potentialities of her new adversary, America, made it clear that the war would be of long duration. Moreover, the odds had now turned against an eventual victory by Germany. Meanwhile, however, the entry of the United States into the war increased Switzerland's difficulties, particularly in the economic sphere. Switzerland's problem was to maintain her neutrality and her political independence until Hitler was forced to relax his grip on Europe. . . .

The need for constant vigilance and for arbitrary measures was shown by the result of a number of trials in 1942–3. Several of the accused, who included officers and other ranks in the Swiss army, were found guilty of betraying military secrets to Germany and were sentenced to death or imprisonment. The first death sentences were imposed in 1942.[1] . . .

(5) *New Threats from Germany and Difficulties with Great Britain and the United States*

It was, however, not yet possible to take radical action against the main source of treasonable acts, the German organizations and Consulates in Switzerland. The growing success of the Allies did not mean that there was any improvement in the immediate situation of the occupied and neutral countries in Europe. On the contrary, it merely increased Hitler's determination to tighten his grip on Europe. Renewed threats were directed against the remaining neutrals. Thus in 1942 Switzerland was officially reminded by the Nazi press that she was originally part of the Reich. Her attitude was likened to that of a nasty dog. Germany was too busy at the moment to attend to the matter but at a later date would deal with political and economic outsiders in Europe. Goebbels said that Switzerland and Sweden were lacking in the most elementary appreciation of the security of their nations and their future existence, and Hitler referred to bourgeois states that would not survive the war. Paul Schmidt, Press Chief at the German Foreign Ministry, threatened recalcitrant Swiss editors and journalists with deportation to Siberia or liquidation after the occupation of Switzerland. He also reminded the Swiss Government of Bismarck's words 'that Governments often have to pay for window panes smashed by their newspapermen'.

---

[1] [Original note.] The sentences imposed by military courts during the war included nineteen death sentences and thirty-three sentences to imprisonment for life.

In 1943 the Government had real grounds for fear that German threats might indeed be translated into action. Hitherto, also, although Hitler had been greatly irked by Switzerland's continued independence and neutrality, the advantages which would have accrued from the invasion and conquest of Switzerland had been clearly outweighed by the drawbacks. The Germans were aware that any attack would be strongly resisted by the Swiss, whose first defensive step would be to blow up the St. Gotthard and Simplon tunnels which provided the main transit route for German supplies and arms to Italy. Restoration of the tunnels would be a lengthy undertaking even in favourable conditions. Harassed by guerrilla warfare by the Swiss forces, unsubdued in their mountain redoubt, the task of rebuilding the tunnels would present the conquerors with almost insuperable difficulties. Moreover, Switzerland's main assets, which were economic and financial, would be wiped out. As there would be no compensatory booty in the shape of raw materials and surplus food supplies, a devastated and impoverished Switzerland would be a liability instead of an asset. Nevertheless, in the years 1942–3 new considerations arose to persuade the Germans that these disadvantages might be outweighed by the danger of an independent country in the *Festung Europa* which they were preparing to defend. The Germans were afraid that, if and when the Allies invaded Europe, the Swiss, whose sympathies were with their enemies, might allow them free passage through their territory. The Federal Government, apprised by the Swiss army information service that the German OKW were considering plans for a preventive occupation, repeated their assurances that Switzerland would defend her neutrality against all comers. At the same time a secret meeting took place between General Guisan and the German SS Commander, Schellenberg, in March 1943 in the Emmenthal. Apparently Guisan was successful in convincing Schellenberg that the Swiss were determined to defend their neutrality in all circumstances, for shortly after the meeting between the two Generals the Swiss learned that the OKW had decided to abandon the project.[1]

[1] Editor's note. While Himmler and the SS were anxious to carry out the operation against Switzerland, it was opposed by Hitler's economic advisers and by the German generals.

Although the main threat to Switzerland's neutrality came from Germany, relations with the opposing camp were also not without their difficulties. . . . The Allies' growing strength enabled them to intensify their economic war against Germany and they were less and less willing to tolerate Swiss economic aid to their enemy. . . . However, the Allies' demands on Switzerland were less harsh than those made on some other neutrals, owing to several factors. They appreciated the need for avoiding extreme demands which might have resulted in a diplomatic rupture or even encouraged a German attack on Switzerland. Swiss independence was extremely valuable to the Allies because Switzerland had undertaken the diplomatic representation of their interests in Axis countries, and also, through the International Red Cross in Geneva, responsibility for the welfare of thousands of prisoners of war in the Axis countries. Also Switzerland was the only remaining window open in the centre of the European continent, and the Allies, through their Legations in Berne, were able to obtain valuable information on Germany. . . .

(d) The Liberation of Europe and its Aftermath, 1944–6

(1) *Swiss Relations with the Western Powers*

When the Allies' long-anticipated attack in force on the European continent matured in the summer of 1944 a term was set to the duration of Switzerland's imprisonment in Hitler's Europe. At the same time immediate difficulties were not eased and new anxieties were added. With hostilities once more approaching their frontiers the Swiss feared that the retreating or advancing armies might violate their territory. Even before the arrival of Allied ground forces Switzerland had not been immune from the results of military operations. Ever since the fall of France there had been recurrent incidents when British, and later, American, airmen had missed their targets and dropped bombs on Swiss territory, inflicting damage and casualties. During 1944 these errors increased in frequency and magnitude. Among the most serious of these was the bombing of Schaffhausen by a formation of American Liberators on 1 April 1944, which destroyed a considerable part of the town. In

September Swiss fighter planes signalling to an American bomber to land were attacked in daylight and railway carriages were machine-gunned.

The Swiss were disturbed by the frequency of these incidents, which they felt were due not only to the American airmen's insufficient geographical knowledge and training, but were symptomatic of the Americans' impatience with, and disregard of, the rights of neutral states under international law. In order to decrease the danger of such incidents the Federal Council authorized the lifting of the blackout over Switzerland on 12 September 1944. Germany was no longer in a position to make effective objections to this measure. The governments of border cantons were instructed to arrange for public and private lighting to be kept on throughout the night. Swiss flags were prominently displayed on stations and on the roofs of outstanding buildings in order to make the Swiss borders more easily recognizable during the day. Notwithstanding these precautions and the vigilance of the Swiss air force incidents continued in which further damage was caused and additional Swiss lives were lost.

Fortunately the fears of the Swiss that their frontiers might be violated by ground forces proved unfounded. After D-Day General Guisan wished to call up big additional forces, but, after anxious discussions in the Federal Council on the effect which this mobilization would have on food production, it was decided to call up only a limited number of the frontier defence forces. After the Allies had landed in the South of France on 15 August further partial mobilization was decreed.

On 28 August advance guards of the American forces reached the Swiss frontier. Switzerland was able to resume contact with the outside world from which she had been almost completely isolated since the surrender of Italy had resulted in the closing of the German ring round her territory.

DOCUMENT 27. 'A Test of Neutrality: Sweden in the Second World War' by H. Gunnar Hägglöf, Swedish Ambassador to Britain (The Stevenson Memorial Lecture No. 9, delivered to the London School of Economics and the Royal Institute of International Affairs, and reprinted in *International Affairs*, April 1960).

Against the vast panorama of the second World War the destinies of the northern Kingdom of Sweden appear as not much more than a tiny detail, but it is perhaps a detail of some peculiar configuration and interest. In September 1939 twenty European States declared their neutrality. When the war came to an end in 1945, only five European neutrals remained, the other fifteen having been dragged into the war, mostly against their own will. Of the five European neutrals remaining at the end of the war, Ireland, Spain, and Portugal were on the western fringe of Europe. Switzerland was certainly in the centre of the turmoil, but it would appear nevertheless that Sweden was the State which saw its neutrality threatened in the most insistent and varied way.

This is the story which I shall try to tell, although I must point out that many points of importance remain obscure and unexplained at the present stage of historical research.

It was on 3 September 1939 that the European War broke out and the lights went out in Europe for the second time in a generation. But the foreign policy of a country is not formed from one day to another.

When the Finnish delegates met Stalin in the Kremlin at the beginning of those grim talks in October 1939, the master of All the Russias announced: 'I am sorry, gentlemen, we cannot do anything about geography.' Let us repeat this truism, that geography, geography in its strategic sense, is the basis of the foreign policy of a country, and perhaps especially of a country with limited means of action, a small country.

Then there is history. Nations are, as we all know, to a very large extent guided by what they consider to be their historical experience. I am not going to tell you the story of the rise and fall of the Swedish Empire in the seventeenth and eighteenth centuries. Nor will I go into the fascinating story of how a French Marshal was elected Crown Prince by a Swedish Assembly, who clamoured for the reconquest of Finland, and how this same Marshal, instead of making war on Russia, established his dynasty in Norway also, and, as the first King of the Bernadottes, led his two Scandinavian Kingdoms on the path of peace and retrenchment, the beginning of the policy of neutrality. All through the nineteenth century this policy gained strength. In the first World War all the three Scandinavian

States were able to pursue successfully a policy of neutrality, the underlying reason for this being, of course, that the balance of power between the two belligerent groups remained stable almost until the ultimate collapse of Austria and Germany.

In the new world after the first World War, Sweden, like other ex-neutrals, devoted all the energies of her foreign policy to the League of Nations. The building up of an international order within the framework of the League became the hope of successive Swedish Governments, and there is in my opinion little doubt that Sweden would have abandoned the policy of neutrality for good if Great Britain, the country which during the period between the two world wars had the greatest moral influence in Scandinavia, had given a strong lead to the movement for an effective international security organization. This was not to be. Instead, disappointment followed disappointment, and when at last the experiment of applying sanctions against Italy failed in 1936, Sweden, together with Belgium, Luxembourg, the Netherlands, Denmark, Finland, and Norway, declared in Geneva that for the future they denounced the obligation to participate in sanctions. They returned to neutrality.

But neutrality is not a magic formula by which you protect yourself from the pressures and problems of the outside world. As Stalin said: 'We cannot do anything about geography.' Switzerland is surrounded by three great Powers, whose rivalries and belligerencies have formed a background to Swiss neutrality. Sweden is surrounded by three small countries, which all belong to the Scandinavian family of nations. The old question, which had beset the Swedish policy of neutrality from its very beginning a century before, raised its head again in the 1930s: what did a policy of neutrality mean with regard to Sweden's relations with her Nordic neighbour countries? Finland pursued quite openly a policy aiming at a pact of mutual assistance with the other Scandinavian States and especially with Sweden. But Denmark and Norway insisted on the strictest neutrality, and refused out of hand the very idea of a Scandinavian pact. The Swedish Government also took a negative attitude, although it allowed its Foreign Minister to negotiate with Finland on common measures for the defence of the Aaland Islands.

The other great problem which pressed itself on the Swedish Government during those darkening years of the 1930s was the question of the Swedish iron ore exports. The German steel industry was based on imports of about 20 million tons of iron ore, nearly half of which came from Sweden, the rest mainly from countries like France, Spain, or North Africa, which would disappear as sources of delivery to Germany in the event of a world war. The Swedish Government knew, and was unhappy in the knowledge, that the country was in possession of a raw material of immense importance to Germany. When, in 1937, the British Government started conversations about the matter, great interest was shown on the Swedish side, but the British let the question lapse, and nothing came of these pre-war talks. On the other hand, Great Britain, by the naval agreement of 1935, had in fact renounced her naval influence in the Baltic. After the conclusion of this agreement, Hitler said, in a private conversation in November 1935, that the Baltic was now 'a bottle that we Germans can close. The English cannot exercise any control there. We are the masters of the Baltic.' It was noteworthy that all the iron ore needed by Germany could be shipped from the harbours on the Baltic.

With these and other worries on her mind Sweden, like the other twenty small States in Europe, glided towards the war, which appeared more and more unavoidable. Ever since Hitler had assumed power in Germany, Swedish public opinion had been markedly anti-Nazi, and it now turned more and more vehemently against the German policy of force. There did not exist in Sweden any pro-Nazi groups of any importance; the nation stood in practice 100 per cent united against Nazi Germany. The Swedish press was more unrestrained in its attacks against the Nazi regime than that of any other country, and this press campaign was continued when the war had started.

Although in most quarters of the North it was realized that Hitler and the Nazis stood for a brutal policy of violence, there were few people who gave any serious thought to the possibility that the Nordic States themselves could be drawn into the war. What was still remembered was that they had remained aloof from the first World War. During the years before the second War, the Nordic Governments seem more or less consciously to have based their policy on the assumption that, in a possible future European Great War, Germany and Italy, united in their Pact of Steel, would stand against the Western Powers, Great Britain and France, actively or passively assisted by the Soviet Union—a combination offering a close parallel to the grouping of Powers in the first World War.

The German–Russian pact of 23 August 1939 completely reversed all such comfortable calculations. The whole system of the balance of power, on which, ever since Napoleonic days, the neutrality of the Nordic States had been based, was upset at one blow. In the same way as Napoleon's pact with Alexander I at Tilsit had led to the loss of Finland and to other upheavals in the North, so the Moscow pact of August 1939 was to lead to another Northern catastrophe.

There may well have been some farsighted men who already in August could see the signs in the skies, but this did not influence the actual policy of the Governments concerned. After the outbreak of war on 3 September the Swedish Government, like a number of other neutrals, pursued as its first objective the establishment of an agreement with both the belligerent parties in regard to blockade and war trade. This had been the main problem in the first World War, and the general desire was to avoid the mistakes then committed. As far as Sweden was concerned, in any case, it was evident that the iron ore problem had to be discussed.

The Swedish Government was able, during the first two months of the war, to reach an agreement with Great Britain. It was assumed, on both the British and the Swedish side, that the iron ore shipments via Narvik would have to pass the Norwegian territorial limit into the Atlantic, and it would therefore be possible for the British Navy to intercept them. On the Swedish side, it was stated further that Sweden would do her best to limit her exports of iron ore to Germany on technical grounds. Following this war trade agreement with Great Britain, the Swedish Government was able, within its framework, to reach a settlement with Germany about trade with that country. Sweden had thus achieved one of the main aims of her policy of neutrality, by concluding two parallel war trade agreements. This small triumph was never to be celebrated, however. Other, more fateful, events intervened.

The German–Russian pact was beginning to show its effects. As early as September 1939 the Foreign Ministers of the three Baltic Republics were called to Moscow to sign agreements which established what virtually amounted to a Russian protectorate. On 5 October Moscow requested negotiations with Finland on 'concrete political questions', and the Russian demands proved to be very far-reaching. The negotiations reached an impasse, and on 30 November the Russians attacked Finland by force of arms.

Sweden is bound to Finland by the ties of seven hundred years of common life; to preserve an independent Finland is for Sweden a political interest of the first order. It was clear that Sweden would give Finland not only diplomatic but also extensive material support. Nevertheless, the Swedish Government felt it its duty, at an early stage of the Finnish–Russian negotiations, to make it clear to Finland that she could not count on Sweden's taking any active military part. There were many reasons for this, one of the most decisive being Germany's attitude. During a later period of the war, when the Russo-German friendship had been reversed, it was often said that Germany would in no way have opposed a Swedish military intervention in Finland. At the time of the Finnish–Russian Winter War, however, the German Government maintained an icy silence. It is known moreover that the German Navy was quite willing actively to assist the Russian submarines, who were engaged in attacks on Finnish and Swedish ships in the Northern Baltic. It is admittedly almost impossible to say what sort of attitude Germany would in fact have taken if Sweden had sent troops to Finland, but it is quite certain that Germany would have intervened if the Western Powers had interfered in Scandinavia. And how would it have been possible for Sweden, engaged in the Finnish–Russian war, to prevent, or by active measures to avert, military assistance from the West? The Swedish Government decided to give Finland every material assistance possible, foodstuffs, industrial equipment, arms, aeroplanes, etc., but not to send troops. This meant taking up a position, not of strict neutrality, but rather of non-belligerency.

The striking Finnish military successes in December 1939 and January 1940 aroused admiration all over the Western world. In the atmosphere of uncertainty, dejection, and listlessness which prevailed during the autumn and early winter of 1939–40, while the main armies were stationary behind the defences of the Western front, brave little Finland stood out as an example, and released a wave of enthusiasm. In France demands for active measures to aid Finland were given great publicity, and later the same thing happened in Great Britain. The Governments of M. Daladier in Paris and Mr Chamberlain in London did not wish to refuse these demands. As a matter of fact, the French General Staff had already previously pleaded for the opening up of new theatres of war in order to divert German troops from the Western front. During the autumn plans had been made for a possible intervention in the Balkans; now there seemed to be a chance of a military diversion in the North of Europe. In addition, the intervention now suggested offered a special, quite overwhelming interest—that it would render difficult, maybe even prohibit, the iron ore deliveries from Sweden to Germany.

In September 1939 Mr Churchill had put forward a proposal to send into the Baltic a force of old battleships, specially armoured for the purpose, in order to try to isolate Germany from Scandinavia and in particular to cut the Swedish iron ore shipments, and also another proposal to lay mines in Norwegian territorial waters in order to force the iron ore ships out into the open sea, where they might be intercepted by the British Navy. Mr Churchill did not succeed in getting full Cabinet support for these proposals; but he renewed his efforts at the end of December 1939. His opinion was—to quote the official British historian—

> that every effort should be made to cut off all Germany's supplies of Scandinavian ore by the end of 1940. Such an achievement would be equal to a first class victory in the field or from the air, and might indeed be immediately decisive. The Narvik source should accordingly be stopped at once by mines laid in Norwegian waters; the supply from the ice-free port of Oxelösund should be stopped by methods which would be 'neither diplomatic nor military'; the case of Luleå would not become urgent until April.[1]

[1] J. R. M. Butler, "Grand Strategy", Vol. II, p. 97; also Winston S. Churchill, *The Second World War: Vol. I. The Gathering Storm* (Cassell, 1948), pp. 490–2.

Mr Churchill was not deterred by the prospect of an extension of the war to Sweden and Norway; he believed that the Western Powers had more to gain than to lose by such a development, and he had no doubt that they could take and hold bases on the Norwegian coast. The official British historian of these events points out that at the allied military discussions at the end of December 'the idea was mooted of using the sympathies of the Swedish and Norwegian peoples for Finland as a means of securing the consent of their Governments for the entry of Allied troops. The troops would be able to occupy Narvik and the Swedish iron ore fields as part of the process of assisting Finland.'

The Allied deliberations on this rather tortuous plan dragged on for three months, and during this period they addressed from time to time rather threatening Notes to the Norwegian and Swedish Governments. The Swedish Government was surprised and dismayed by these Notes. The Swedish leaders felt that they had thoroughly discussed and settled the iron ore question in the negotiations for their war trade agreement with Great Britain, and they knew as a statistical fact that the iron ore exports through Narvik were quite insignificant. Moreover, they were convinced that an Allied intervention in Scandinavia would lead to immediate German counteraction, which would make Scandinavia a theatre of war and render Finland's position more difficult and probably hopeless. In these circumstances it was quite obvious that the Swedish Government would reject all the Allied overtures.

Meanwhile the Winter War dragged on, and the Russian overwhelming strength made itself felt more and more. In spite of all heroism the Finnish front began to give way.

The Soviet Ambassador in Stockholm, Madame Alexandra Kollontay, was a very remarkable diplomatist. During the whole of the Winter War she sought to keep in touch with the Swedish Foreign Minister, Günther, in order to find a way towards a peaceful settlement. These negotiations between the two belligerents, Soviet Russia and Finland, via Madame Kollontay and Mr Günther, constitute a most fascinating chapter. Now, looking back on the whole story, it is possible to see the historical importance for the world of the problems at stake. The Western Powers seemed to wish to throw themselves into a military adventure which might have brought them into open conflict with Soviet Russia. Finland, engaged in a struggle of life and death, must have been sorely tempted to accept the aid which the Western Powers were offering. If only for prestige reasons, Russia was unwilling to accept conditions less far-reaching than those announced before the war. Sweden could not and would not exert any pressure on Finland; the Swedish Government did not wish to become a mediator, but solely to provide a point of contact. What Sweden could promise was far-reaching economic aid after the war, and willingness to conclude a defence agreement.

The peace conditions were bitter enough for Finland, but, for the North as a whole, the general feeling was that the storm had passed. It was assumed that either the Great War on the Western front would now begin in earnest, or a military intervention in the Balkans would follow. Nevertheless, during March 1940, various warnings were received of preparations for German action in Scandinavia. Such information came from the Swedish Legation in Berlin, to the effect that military action was to be expected against Denmark and, at least, southern Norway.

We now know that German measures to occupy Norway had been under discussion within the German leadership since October 1939. These plans were developed further during the winter, and immediately after the 'Altmark' incident of 16 February 1940, Hitler seems to have taken a definite decision to attack Norway. The Germans appeared to have realized, as the Scandinavian Governments had not, that the Western Powers were actually planning a military intervention in Scandinavia. Hitler pushed on with his military preparations with remarkable speed, and by 10 March the Germans were in a position to launch an attack at only four days' notice.

The Russo-Finnish treaty, however, changed the atmosphere. The German Chief of Staff, General Jodl, noted in his diary:[1] 'The conclusion of peace deprives Britain, but us too, of any political basis for occupying Norway.' But this was only a temporary hesitation. On 26 March Admiral Raeder informed Hitler that sooner or later it would be necessary for Germany to

[1] Diary of General Jodl, 12 March 1940, published in W. Hubatsch, *Die deutsche Besetzung von Dänemark und Norwegen* (Göttingen, 1952), pp. 379–403.

occupy the Norwegian coast, and he urged that this should be done as soon as possible. Hitler agreed, and the date for the attack was ultimately fixed for 9 April.

What were Hitler's reasons for attacking Denmark and Norway? He has himself stated more than once that he felt the need to forestall an Allied occupation of Norway. In a conversation with General von Falkenhorst on 21 February, he said that the successes which Germany gained in the East and which were to come in France would be annihilated by a British occupation of Norway.[1] We shall see later that during subsequent periods of the war Hitler still kept his eye on the Norwegian coast.

It should be pointed out that the occupation of Norway was the main objective, while that of Denmark came as a supplementary measure. In his order of 1 March 1940, Hitler indicated his motives for the occupation of Norway as, in the first place, his wish to prevent British interventions in Scandinavia and the Baltic; secondly, his need to secure the supply of iron ore from Sweden; and thirdly, his desire to extend the sphere of operations of the German Navy and Air Force against Great Britain. That these were his real motives seems to be confirmed by all the documents so far available, those of the German Staffs, the evidence in the Nuremberg trials, and the diaries of Jodl and Halder.

During the preparatory staff discussions, the idea of an attack on Sweden seems at some time to have been put forward. As late as the end of March 1940, Admiral Fricke, one of the chiefs of the German Navy, suggested that it would be better to wait for an Allied action against Norway and then rely on the German Army to make a landing in Sweden in order to secure the iron ore fields and to open a counter-attack against the Allies in Norway. Fricke's suggestion was probably motivated by his fear of the terrible risks the German Navy would run during a direct attack on Norway across the North Sea. There exists also a memorandum, probably discussed among officers of the Supreme Staff but unlikely to have gone any further, according to which Luleå and the ore rail-line were to be occupied by German troops. These speculations, however, seem to have been dismissed by the German leadership without

[1] *International Military Tribunal: Nazi Conspiracy and Aggression* (10 vols.), Supplement B (Washington, U.S. Government Printing Office, 1948), p. 1537.

comment. An attack against Sweden would have stopped the iron ore deliveries, probably for a prolonged period. During the autumn of 1939, I had several times occasion to tell German delegates that, even if the iron ore mines, as such, could not be quickly destroyed, it would be the action of a moment to blow up the indispensable power stations. It was, I often reflected, a providential arrangement that the iron ore mines and the power stations were located in the northernmost, and not in the southernmost, part of Sweden.

If the German leaders had had any intention of invading Sweden, they must have been conscious of the fact that such an invasion would have demanded numerically considerably larger forces, owing to the size of the country and also to the state of Swedish defence which, though it certainly was not strong in April 1940, was still a good deal stronger than that of Denmark or Norway. It has always to be remembered that Hitler was planning the invasion of Scandinavia on the assumption that it was to be carried out with a number of divisions so limited that the attack on France, which had long been planned to come in the spring of 1940, would not be delayed or on the whole affected.

The events of 9 April were the hardest blow Scandinavia had suffered since Napoleonic days. Our two Scandinavian neighbour nations were attacked in the most brutal manner, and Sweden found herself completely isolated. The German troops in Denmark and Norway and the German Navy in the Skagerak cut us off from the Western world.

In the foregoing I have underlined repeatedly that small States can pursue a policy of neutrality with some chance of success only if there exists some sort of balance of power between the belligerents. This was so during the first World War. But even before the outbreak of the second World War, the underlying balance of power had been radically upset by the German–Russian pact. The ensuing war between Finland and Russia had brought the clouds of major war to Scandinavia. The thunderbolt came, the German attack on Denmark and Norway. The result from Sweden's point of view was that there was no balance of power between the belligerents on which to fall back.

But was there not, even after the German attack, a balance of power? In Moscow they seemed to think so. The Soviet Government greeted the German occupation of Denmark and Norway almost with enthusiasm. This was quite natural. The threat of an Allied intervention in Finland had meant a serious worry to Moscow, and had perhaps contributed to the Russian willingness to make peace. Now the Germans had bolted the door between the Baltic and the Western Powers; nobody could have been more pleased than the Moscow Government. But while Moscow accepted with great satisfaction an extension of the German sphere to cover Denmark and Norway, the Soviet Government after a few days' consideration made it clear that it did not want a German attack on Sweden. On 13 April Mr Molotov told the German Ambassador in Moscow that the Soviet Union was strongly interested in the maintenance of Sweden's neutrality. The German Foreign Minister confirmed, on 15 April, that Germany had no intention of undertaking any military action if Sweden did not support the Western Powers.

Consequently it can be said that in the spring of 1940 there did exist a certain counterweight to the German dominance; but it did not last long. After the fall of France, the German dominance weighed all the heavier in the Baltic region as well. Towards the end of the summer German troops began to pass through the north of Finland in transit from Norway. This was welcomed with relief by Finland. Then came the conversations between Molotov and Hitler in November 1940. Hitler stated clearly and decisively that he did not want another war in Finland. Molotov repeatedly referred to the fact that, in the Moscow agreement of August 1939, Finland was assigned to the Russian sphere. Hitler replied that he certainly did not wish to deny this, but that he had to point out that a war against Finland would mean a serious strain on the relations of the Soviet Union with Germany. The whole of this long Hitler–Molotov dialogue is one of the most dramatic documents to be found in the history of diplomacy.[1]

In fact, this conversation led to a more restrained Russian policy towards Finland. There had been a swing in the balance

---

[1] *Beziehungen zwischen Deutschland und der Sovjet Union 1939–41* (Tübingen, 1949), pp. 264–72. See also Gerhard L. Weinberg, *Germany and the Soviet Union 1939–41* (Leyden, 1954), p. 143.

of power in the North of Europe, and it continued during the winter of 1940–41. Sweden was left face to face with a Germany who dominated the European continent, and whose armies were stationed along the one thousand miles of frontier between Sweden and Norway. Soon German troops appeared in Northern Finland also. At the same time Germany possessed quite formidable means of exerting constant and immediate economic pressure. For her daily needs of coal, metal goods, and chemicals Sweden was dependent on imports. It is true that on her side Sweden had her iron ore, but after the capture of the French iron ore fields Germany did not depend on this in the same way as before.

Thus it may with every reason be said that the balance was uneven, and that Sweden was forced to make concessions which were not really consistent with neutrality. In June 1940, after hostilities in Norway had ceased, the Swedish Government accepted an arrangement by which German soldiers on leave were allowed to travel through Sweden to and from Norway in special trains, the numbers going each way being more or less equal; later this agreement was supplemented by others regarding transit on certain other lines. Sweden also agreed to the transit of war materials. On the other hand she consistently refused German demands for Swedish exports of war materials. The most considerable, and in my opinion the most serious, of these concessions was granted later, in the summer of 1941, when a whole German division with full equipment was allowed to travel from Norway through Sweden in order to reach the Finnish theatre of war in the campaign against Russia.

From the summer of 1940 to the middle of 1942, the policy of the Swedish Government may be said to have been simply to gain time. It was a matter of making as few concessions as possible, while trying to keep the country itself free from German influence and using the time to rearm. Throughout this period there were interminable economic negotiations with Germany, a sort of permanent tug of war. It was essential to prevent Sweden from being dragged into the German 'New Order' of Europe. It can be said that she maintained the economic front, and trade was kept within the limits of her own needs. Meanwhile Parliament gave steady support to the National Coalition Government, and a massive rearmament took place, industrial and manpower resources being fully mobilized for this essential purpose.

In conversations which I had the honour to have with Sir Winston Churchill after the war, he told me that on many evenings during these dark years he had stood looking at the map of Scandinavia which hung in a corner of the Cabinet room. 'I stood there and thought of isolated Sweden. My advice to Sweden was always: to keep quiet and to rearm.' This was in fact the policy which the Swedish Government came to pursue. It was a policy which imposed itself without any far-sighted planning, a policy of gaining time and of rearming, a policy of patience.

There were, however, important sections of Swedish public opinion which became increasingly impatient. The press had never stopped attacking Nazi Germany and her leaders, and these attacks became more and more insistent as conditions worsened in occupied Denmark and Norway. Gradually public opinion became increasingly critical of the Government and its concessions to Germany. By means of measures against the press the Government tried to tone down, or even to suppress, some expressions of opinion which they regarded as excessive. Passions rose even to bitterness. It is one of the most difficult problems in the practical application of neutrality to maintain and pursue, for reasons of political necessity, a policy of neutrality in the face of a free and democratic public opinion which has all its sympathies on the side of one group of belligerents. Looking back on all these divergencies, it nevertheless seems to me that this conflict between Government and public opinion was a healthy and even in many ways a useful feature. There is no doubt that public opinion exercised a great and increasing influence on the Government's foreign policy.

During this second period of the war, from the fall of France in the summer of 1940 to the middle of 1942, the basic position of Sweden was, of course, extremely precarious. At any time during this period it would have been possible for Germany to attack and conquer Sweden. The Swedes would have fought back, and nobody knows how long the fight would have lasted: some weeks or perhaps even months? The Greek Ambassador in London used to say: 'Nous avons tous notre petit quart d'heure.' The fact that Swedish neutrality was preserved during this period of the war was not due to Sweden's strength or to the inherent force of the idea of neutrality, but to the simple fact that Herr Hitler was otherwise occupied.

Even as late as February 1942 there were days of acute alarm. The well-informed Swedish Legation in Berlin received news of German staff discussions about an attack on Sweden, and all Swedish defence resources were immediately mobilized. At the time I used to say jokingly to the Swedish Minister in Berlin that never had so little information cost so much money. There is however reason to believe that plans regarding Sweden were in fact discussed in the German headquarters. We now know from the German Navy's records that in the autumn of 1941 Hitler became increasingly worried about Norway. When one would have expected him to be wholly concentrated on the situation on the Russian front, he spent hours pondering about the possibility of an Allied landing on the Norwegian coast. On 29 December 1941 'he was sure that if the British go about things properly they will attack Northern Norway; . . . this might be decisive for the war'.[1] To the despair of the German Naval Staff, he sent practically the whole fleet to Norwegian bases. He never ceased to worry about Northern Scandinavia. In November 1942 he declared: 'all available reports still lead me to fear that the enemy will attempt an invasion during the Arctic night and that Sweden's attitude cannot be depended on'.[2]

It is a remarkable fact that at about the same period the Allied Staffs also were sometimes diverted from their North African activities by dramatic ideas about Norway. Lord Alanbrooke tells how both in March 1942 and in September of the same year Mr Churchill suggested landings in Norway and that the Chiefs of Staff had some considerable difficulty in dissuading him from this idea.

The third period of the war, from the Swedish point of view, began towards the autumn of 1942, when the German Armies were fully engaged in Russia and in the Allied attack on North Africa. The terrible eruption of Nazi power all over the continent of Europe had forced Sweden to retreat from the principles of strict neutrality. But by the middle of the war Swedish

[1] F. H. Hinsley, *Hitler's Strategy* (Cambridge, 1951), p. 196.
[2] *Ibid.*, p. 198.

defences had acquired some not inconsiderable strength, and as the tide of war turned Sweden felt able to return to a policy of strict neutrality.

It should be pointed out that the Government had maintained full and friendly contact with Great Britain during the darkest days of the war. After the occupation of Norway and Denmark, the Swedish Government gave a spontaneous assurance that it had every intention of trying to fulfil its obligations under the war-trade agreement with Great Britain, in spite of the fact that imports from the West had ceased. In a Note to the British Government in the summer of 1940, after the German victory in France, the Swedish Government also emphasized its desire to maintain the traditional friendly relations with Great Britain. On the British side, it was made clear that Sweden's neutrality was an asset to the Allies, which they had some considerable interest in maintaining. This view was shared by the Norwegian Government, who, soon after the outbreak of the German–Norwegian war, declared that it wished Sweden to remain neutral. In a memorandum of 19 May 1940, the Norwegian Government declared that it was of vital interest for Norway that Sweden remained outside the war. Swedish participation in the war on the Allied side was not desirable from the Norwegian point of view.

This general attitude did not of course prevent the Western Allies from criticizing, and even from condemning, the concessions which Sweden made in 1940 with regard to the transit of German soldiers and war material through Sweden. Between Sweden and Norway there were also other bones of contention: Norwegian ships in Sweden, the situation of the Norwegian diplomatic mission in Sweden, and so on.

From the middle of 1942 onwards, the Swedish Government felt strong enough to reassert its position *vis-à-vis* Germany. In the following year the whole transit arrangement with Germany was cancelled, and, at the same time, Sweden accepted the requests of the Western Allies substantially to reduce Swedish trade with Germany. The British Ministry of Economic Warfare was in fact so pleased with Sweden's policy after the summer of 1943 that its chief spokesman declared that Sweden had gone further to meet the Allied requests than any other neutral State. He did not mention, of course, and in fact he could not have foreseen, that the Allied requests would increase far beyond what was agreed or planned, until at the end of 1944 all trade between Sweden and the continent was stopped by the Swedish Government.

From 1942 onwards it became possible gradually to assist the neighbouring Scandinavian countries in a more effective way. The Swedish Government intervened in Berlin, hoping to prevent some of the German excesses in Denmark and Norway. These interventions often met with a very sharp rebuff in Berlin, and in 1941 and 1942 there were sometimes doubts whether they were really useful. But they became gradually more effective. In the last phases of the war the Swedish Red Cross under the leadership of Count Folke Bernadotte, and with the help of many others, was able to assist in the evacuation of tens of thousands of prisoners from the concentration camps. Sweden also undertook to give facilities for the organization of Danish and Norwegian units on Swedish territory, such units being officially designated as police forces. That their training was remarkably thorough is proved by the fact that these policemen were given permission to receive training in artillery handling on the Swedish artillery fields.

At the same time Sweden prepared a sort of minor Marshall plan to help the neighbouring countries. In the summer of 1943, I had informal talks in London with U.N.R.R.A. and some other Allied authorities. After due consideration of the issues involved, the Swedish Government decided to set up an organization of its own to help the occupied countries after their liberation. It was of course difficult, indeed impossible, to send foodstuffs to the Norwegian and Finnish peoples during the war, as this was prohibited by our agreements with Great Britain. The Swedish assistance plan aimed therefore at massive deliveries of foodstuffs and other necessities after the liberation, and stocks of goods were accumulated for quick delivery.

Sweden had always deplored Finland's participation in the German war against Russia, and from 1943 onwards Swedish efforts to extricate Finland from the war became more and more insistent. But Finland was placed in a most difficult position, with Russian armies attacking from the east and German armies occupying the north of the country. It was not until the autumn of 1944 that a Finnish–Russian armistice was concluded and the Germans were driven from Finland.

During the last phase of the war and the first years of peace, Sweden tried to be a positive and a stabilizing factor in the North. This was of course no more than an obvious duty for a country which had been spared the devastation of war and occupation. But it nevertheless seems justifiable to ask how the post-war situation in the North of Europe would have developed if Sweden had in fact been devastated, impoverished, politically embittered, and left without means of helping the other countries on their road towards peace and stability.

This is really the end of my story and I should come to a full stop here. But there are perhaps some of you who would like to ask me: what is the meaning of the story, what are the conclusions? This is, I think, a fair question, and I would like to be able to give an answer. I think that there are some observations which can be made with the backing of 'historical experience'.

First, it seems obvious that neutrality has to be supported by a reasonably efficient defence system. If Norway had had a somewhat stronger defence, it is doubtful whether Germany would have taken the enormous risks of an attack across the North Sea and against a most difficult coastline.

Secondly, there are good reasons for assuming that a policy of neutrality requires steady support from all the important political groups of the country. This was the case in Switzerland and in Sweden, but not in all countries which declared themselves neutral at the beginning of the war.

Thirdly, and most important, there is the problem of the balance of power. This whole lecture has pointed to this clear and simple conclusion: *the basic condition of neutrality is the existence of a balance of power.*

The military strength of the neutral State is one factor in this balance of power; but, when the neutral State has relatively limited military means at its disposal, it is clear that the balance of power is to a larger extent determined by the attitudes and actions of the great Powers. This simple fact has seldom received full recognition, and least of all in the small neutral States themselves. During the nineteenth century, neutrality was seldom, if ever, put to the hard test. In the absence of such testing, neutrality was looked upon mainly as a juridical concept. During the first World War, the balance of power remained stable almost to the very end, which was, in the last analysis, the basic reason why neutrality was relatively successful. In the second World War, the balance of power was radically upset right from the beginning, and I have tried in the course of this lecture to describe how this lack of balance affected Scandinavia.

Sweden was the only Scandinavian country not to be attacked. The reasons for this have already been discussed, but it is necessary to point out once again the precariousness of the Swedish position. If, in the spring of 1940, the Western Allies had intervened in Norway *before* the Germans did so, it is more than likely that Germany would have countered the Allied intervention by an attack on Sweden, followed by an offensive against the Allies in Norway. The same could possibly have happened in the winter of 1942, if the Churchillian idea of a landing in Northern Norway had been realized.

What therefore is the conclusion? The precariousness of neutrality?

There is certainly nothing in the history of the second World War to support the belief, if this belief still exists, that neutrality is a magic prescription, or, if you prefer it, a juridical formula, banning the danger of war. On the contrary, the history of the second World War proves, if anything, the precariousness of neutrality. Since the war, a majority of the small States of Europe have abandoned the policy of neutrality and joined military alliances.

In politics, however, as in ordinary human life, one should never be dogmatic. In foreign policy, one has always to remember the words of Stalin: 'Gentlemen, we cannot do anything about geography.' The geography of this globe shows much diversity, and so do the effects of the global balance of power. It is in the light of this that some European countries, even after the second World War, have found that their special geographical and strategic position is such that it is better to base their foreign policy on neutrality.

The precariousness of neutrality? Yes, certainly. But let us consider the whole vast panorama of the second World War. Is there any State, however powerful, which did not run the risk of being either destroyed in the course of the war, or hopelessly isolated after its conclusion? Neutrality was precarious, no doubt, but even the greatest Powers in the world proved to be at some time in a most precarious position. The great and obvious lesson of the second World War, and a lesson which has been reinforced many times by the post-war development of nuclear weapons, is, of course, that the world cannot continue without a World Order.

PART V

Neutrality in the Atomic Age

The peculiar problems facing neutrals in the atomic age have been discussed in the Introduction. Nevertheless, all kinds of neutrals—traditional neutrals, neutralized states, nonaligned states, and states that adopt neutrality in a particular war, can be found in this period. Switzerland is an example of the first kind, Austria of the second, India of the third, and Cambodia, in relation to the Vietnamese war, of the fourth, although Cambodia also counts herself as one of the nonaligned states.

In the first extract, a Swiss politician and former President of the Swiss Confederation, Dr. Max Petitpierre, reviews his country's status in the changed conditions of postwar Europe. In the second, a British scholar, Dr. Peter Lyon, describes how neutralization was imposed on, and accepted by, Austria as a condition of ending the four-power occupation that had persisted for ten years after the end of the Second World War.

DOCUMENT 28. Extracts from 'Is Swiss Neutrality Still Justified?' by Max Petitpierre, from *Switzerland, Present and Future* (New Helvetic Society, 1963).

It is not the first time that circumstances have brought up or, more accurately, have forced us to reply to this question. Up to the present it has not arisen in time of war—that is to say, at a time when neutrality takes on its full significance and deploys all its effects—nor has it ever been purely academic but has always had relation to a dilemma which Switzerland was facing.

So it was in 1920, for example, when our country was able to join the League of Nations through an ingenious formula, which safeguarded the essential aspects of our neutrality but which was proved by experience to be so little satisfactory that it had to be abandoned for a return to traditional neutrality.

Again, in 1945, when the United Nations Organization was constituted by the San Francisco Charter, Switzerland, alone of all the countries which had the possibility of joining, did not put forward her candidature because this would have been against her concept of her neutral status. The debates of the Assembly, by which the Charter had been adopted, showed there was incompatibility between neutrality and the functions of a member of the Organization, and so a solution such as that accepted in 1920 was impossible. Faced with deciding between membership in the United Nations and neutrality, we chose the latter, while doing everything we could to establish the closest, most comprehensive relations possible with the new Organization. . . .

It is an armed neutrality. We have always believed that, if a foreign power threatened it by seeking to enter the Confederation's territory, Switzerland must be prepared to repel such attacks. Thus, the need for as strong a national defence system as possible. It was Machiavelli who said that "The Swiss are so free only because they are so well armed." And if, during these last centuries, they have seldom had to take up arms to defend their territory, they did fight until the 19th century on many battlefields in Europe and overseas in the service of other countries. The army, formed wholly of militia, is one with the people, who today are still ready to make any sacrifices needed for the country's defence. Switzerland's 1962 military budget represents 35·3 per cent of the Confederation's expenditure. If all Western Europe had the same proportion of armed forces, there would be 360 divisions at its disposal. Thus, Switzerland is no military vacuum in the centre of Europe. And her neutrality, proof of her will for peace, is not unarmed pacifism.

Moreover, Switzerland has never accepted that her neutrality should influence her citizens' freedom of thought and speech. Neutrality is a state concept, engaging the state only. There is no such thing as neutrality in ethics.

Finally, if neutrality is in itself fundamentally passive since it implies abstention, a refusal to commit oneself, Switzerland has, in recognition of the privilege of having escaped the horrors of war, done all she possibly could to help its victims and with no discrimination among nationalities. It was not by chance that Switzerland became the birthplace of the Red Cross. And the work of the International Committee of the Red Cross is bound up with the neutrality of Switzerland.

Neutrality is a principle of foreign policy, but for both the Confederation and the individual Swiss it is something much greater than that. Neutrality plus federalism have made Switzerland a nation. Neutrality and federalism arose from the same need: to ensure union amongst the Confederates and then the unity of the country, one of the essential components of this unity being respect for dissimilarities. . . .

While federalism and "direct" democracy relate to the country's home life, neutrality has been the signpost in the peripeteia of international affairs. It has not allowed our taking sides in controversies between other countries, but it has not prevented cooperation in all spheres where peaceful collaboration was possible. The reserve which we have set ourselves in politics, the fact that we have no territorial disputes with our neighbours, nor any pretensions towards other states, and that we are not the object of any vindications, have led to the Swiss Federal Capital, Berne, being chosen as the seat of the first international institutes of a particular type as well as to Swiss often being asked to lead them. A Swiss town, Geneva, was selected as the seat of the League of Nations. Even though Switzerland was not a member of the United Nations, its European headquarters, as well as those of affiliated organizations, were established at Geneva, where many international conferences are also organized.

Switzerland occupies a place in international affairs which she would never have had but for her neutrality.

The 1939–1945 war radically altered the political structure of Europe and the world. The Soviet Union took advantage of the Allied victory to subjugate East European countries freed from the Nazi yoke, forming satellite states on which Communist regimes were imposed. A divided Europe and the raising of an ideological barrier between the Communist countries and the Western democracies were the result. Communist leaders make no secret of their ambition to extend their system to the entire world. To them "peaceful coexistence" among nations signifies not joint efforts to resolve together the problems on which depend peace and the future of humanity, but ruthless strife by which they expect they will win. During the last few years and at an ever faster pace another world phenomenon has appeared, in that little by little Europe's colonies have become independent. Most of them are not in a position to deal satisfactorily with their own problems, and help from outside is necessary: this can only be given by the more industrialized countries. As a general rule the newly independent countries strive to remain apart from the conflict of ideologies and have chosen neutralism as their political line.

The Communist menace, plus consciousness—realized somewhat belatedly—of interdependence, incited the majority of West European countries to form a defensive military alliance with the United States and with Canada, and six of these countries set about reaching economic and political unity through integration with a view to making Europe into an entity comparable in size and influence to the two world powers, the Soviet Union and the United States, and associated with the latter in an Atlantic community. . . .

It is in the light of these different types of problems that the question of whether Switzerland's neutrality is still justified must be considered. Our country is now, in effect, in a very different situation from that which previously existed.

Neutrality used to mean that our foreign policy was essentially a matter of maintaining good relations with other countries, while standing aside from the problems between them, and of developing our trade with them. Political passivity was the main characteristic. Today we are directly involved in developments which will affect our future and which will also have their influence on our traditional institutions and the concepts behind them.

Because our neighbours seek unity through integration, neutrality no longer has the object of protecting us against them.

We are not placed, as we were amongst the four countries around us, between the Communist world and the Western world; we are part of the latter. Its civilization is ours.

Nevertheless, neutrality has kept its primary meaning in the sense that it constitutes refusal to revert to war or to participate voluntarily in armed conflict, or to take on obligations which could drag us into war. We would only take up arms in the event of our independence being attacked by military action against our territory.

The justifiability of neutrality could be questioned if it obliged our country to stand aloof, to withdraw within herself, if it condemned her to passiveness and inaction in a world where, and at a time when, there is general effervescence.

But it is not so.

The ideological conflict, in which we have taken part simply because we are opposed to Communism, in which we see not progress but a backward step for countries with a democratic regime such as ours, is outside the field covered by neutrality.

Neutrality does not prevent us, as an industrialized country, from doing our part to help those not so advanced to make good their deficiencies. It allows us to collaborate with other countries in giving assistance on both a global and a European scale. It also perhaps gives us—experience during recent years has proved it—special opportunities. We have not had colonial problems to settle. Our policy of neutrality inspires confidence in the countries which have chosen neutralism—non-commitment—as the guiding principle of their foreign policies. So do our democratic institutions. Our federalism can be used as an example by the new states, mostly in Africa, which have been formed on the basis of haphazard colonization, with heterogeneous populations insofar as race and religion are concerned. Up to the present we have not refused any opportunity given us to cooperate, and we belong to nearly all the organizations through which assistance is furnished to countries which ask for it. Nor does neutrality prevent us from joining with other countries in scientific and technical research. We are persuaded that Europe must not remain behind in this respect, and from the start we have participated in the agreements made between a number of European countries in regard to atomic and space research.

If neutrality constrains us to singularity in politics, it does not oblige us to isolate ourselves. . . .

The vindication of our neutrality on these historic grounds and because of our concern for our political independence, plus the fact that neutrality does not prevent us from participating with certain limitations in the formation of Europe, do not comprise a complete answer to the question.

The further problem arises as to whether our neutrality—twice recognized as being in the interests of peace and of Europe—has still its use in the world of today.

Of itself neutrality is negative since it ordains abstention and sets limits to a neutral state's activities in the international sphere. But our concept of neutrality has changed. We have striven to make it a basis for action. While Switzerland's neutrality may have lost its early historic significance from the European point of view, on a wider scale it still has its value because it alone allows the undertaking of certain activities and certain services.

For as long as there is no efficacious, collective security system to assure world peace, neutrality remains useful, even necessary. First, it is logical that in times of conflict only a neutral state can intervene to help war victims, open its doors to refugees, act as intermediary in the exchange of sick or wounded prisoners of war, or represent one belligerent's interests in another's country; and maintain at least a minimum contact between the warring parties and with a minimum of international relations, a minimum of international spirit.

If in times of peace it has but a very small part to play, the present period of neither war nor peace but of open or latent conflict, of increasing political and diplomatic strife, has given new importance to neutrality: there are many more opportunities for a neutral state to undertake often thankless and sometimes dangerous roles in the interest of peace.

Of old, wars ended in peace treaties which created a new order—often precarious and not enduring, but still order. Today, uncertain and equivocal situations are protracted indefinitely, as in Germany, Korea, Laos, Vietnam, the Congo, the Near East; independence has changed the relationships between the metropoles and their ex-colonies and there are tasks which the former can no longer undertake and which the new states, with their lack of trained people, cannot accomplish. Agreement on the choice of such an important man as the Secretary General of the United Nations was only possible through calling on statesmen from neutral countries: Dag Hammarskjöld and U Thant.

When the active intervention of the United Nations Organization is involved in a conflict, it may be of advantage to ask a country, which is not bound by the Organization's decisions and policy, to fulfill some task.

Or, a state's good offices may be required as a third party in helping to solve a conflict or to put an end to a war. This state will be all the more likely to accept such a charge if it has not taken a position or shared in decisions for or against one or the other of the parties. Concrete instances could be cited to illustrate these possible fields of action, but this is not the place to list all the mandates accepted by the neutral countries or the services they have been able to render since the end of the war. But Switzerland and Swiss citizens have had a role to play in most regions of the world, and in the main outside Europe, where conflict and difficulty have arisen. We have done as much as we could to put neutrality at the service of peace in accepting missions which could be accomplished only because of it. As a neutral country, Switzerland has responsibilities towards humanity which were bestowed indirectly by international law and by the ninety states parties to the 1949 Geneva Conventions for the improvement of the treatment of sick and wounded in armed forces, of prisoners of war, and for the protection of civil populations. All these conventions call for intervention by an impartial, humanitarian body and cite the International Red Cross Committee, which is entirely Swiss in composition and which works through all-Swiss delegations. Previously such intervention was needed only during a war; now it is continuous and can take many different forms— although invariably in relation to helping victims of armed conflict, civil war, acts of violence or other troubles. The International Red Cross Committee's present activities make an impressive list. If Switzerland abandoned her neutrality, the Committee would undoubtedly become extinct. No other body exists which could replace it. Is there not in this one fact a justification for neutrality? . . .

It can be argued that countries which, while not permanently neutral, are not involved in a particular conflict, could often be charged with a specific mission, deriving from that conflict, or that a special international commission could be set up. This is true. But here again—without wishing to exaggerate the value of the services Switzerland can render—there is no doubt but that the very diverse circumstances stemming both from her history and from her geographical position have given Switzerland a place of her own. In growing into a tradition which the Swiss themselves scrupulously respect and because of which they have always warded off, sometimes under dangerous conditions, all threats from more powerful neighbours, a certain conception of orthodox and somewhat rigid neutrality has become identified with Switzerland, has turned into a characteristic, and has defined her international position. We have no pretensions that this is a privileged position but, from a political point of view it is different from that of most other nations. It is not acknowledged by everyone, but it has fortunately often been recognized even by those governments which are today the hardest towards the neutral European countries. For example, in an aide-memoire which the United States' Government handed to the Federal Council on June 10, 1953, asking that Switzerland participate in two neutral Commissions to supervise and ensure the enforcement of the armistice at the end of the war in Korea, it is said: "The American Government has full understanding of the Swiss Government's desire to maintain its policy of neutrality and impartiality"; and further on, "The Government and the people of the United States, as well as many other Governments and peoples in the world, have for a long time considered Switzerland as the country which can be called on to render the impartial services often so essential to the settlement of wars or international controversies . . ." We would be happy if neutrality were always appreciated in this manner. . . .

In the final issue, neutrality's justification does not lie in foreign opinion, even though this is important to us and we must seek to inform it and influence it. Justification lies above all in our own conviction that in breaking away from neutrality we would lose our national character; that we would be playing false with ourselves without real benefit either for Europe or for the civilization to which we belong; that, in addition, we would be surrendering any possibilities such as those given us in the past and even today of playing a modest and limited, but still useful, role on the sidelines of big political controversies and military conflicts on which we can have no direct influence. But this conviction must go together with the will to be available for the tasks and missions which can only be accomplished, or can more easily be accomplished, by a neutral state. We must accept that Switzerland may be called into service whenever her neutrality can serve peace and humanity, and we must not flinch from the risks and material sacrifices which may follow.

Attachment to neutrality does not prevent us from joining in the setting up of Europe. In any move toward integration, two opposing tendencies come out: one towards unification and a central power as strong as possible; the other for respecting differences and for maintaining certain regional autonomies. History has formed Europe of very dissimilar elements and its unity lies in these two tendencies. It is the second which we must continue to uphold—not in order to keep the first in check, but to bring about a better equilibrium between them and to ensure that features essential to Europe are not distorted into something going far beyond that which is necessary for unity.

DOCUMENT 29. Extracts from 'Austria—A Neutralized State' from *Neutralism* by Peter Lyon (Leicester University Press, 1963).

AUSTRIA—A NEUTRALIZED STATE

Prior to 1955, neutralization—the institution of a status of permanent neutrality—had seemed to be an obsolete nineteenth century practice. The neutralization of Austria in that year revived public interest in the device of neutralization and led to much rather loose talk about "the Austrian example". Yet it is doubtful if the success of Austria in achieving some degree of immunization from the struggles of the Cold War can provide a truly heartening example for other states. After all, it took nine years of occupation and the cumbersome method of four-power control to restore the sovereignty of a small country with a population of only seven million people; and, even so, the progress of the negotiations for Austrian independence was extremely hazardous and influenced at all stages by the general climate of East-West relations. Austria's new status, which involved shouldering some onerous burdens, sprang almost entirely from her insignificance as a military factor; and, more specifically, from a coincidence of Russian strategic re-assessments and propaganda aims in the context of 1955. . . .

After 1945, with Russia determined to treat Austria as a defeated nation and to wring as much reparation as possible,

Austrian leaders could only turn to the Western Powers for the foreign aid necessary to economic recovery. It was their considerable achievement that Austria became a member of the Marshall Plan organization and of the European Payments Union without driving the Soviet authorities to believe that Austria was bound irretrievably to the Western camp.

Indeed, in many respects the period of four-power occupation now appears as a trying and extremely difficult training for the post-1955 role of permanent diplomatic neutrality. From 1945 until 1955 Austria, though divided into four occupation zones, had a government whose authority was recognized throughout the country and by all four occupying powers—by the Russians equally, despite the constant electoral resistance of the Austrians to Communism. If the evacuation of all foreign forces was to be achieved—for in the heyday of their co-operation the Allied Powers had stated, in the Moscow Declaration of 1st November 1943, that they wished "to see re-established a free and independent Austria"—Austrian *bona fides* had to be acceptable to both of the Cold War camps.

This *tour de force* was achieved, despite the ten years of occupation and the trials of several hundred great power meetings before the conclusion of the Austrian State Treaty. The end to the deadlock sprang entirely from a dramatic reversal of Soviet policy, though patient Austrian diplomacy had prepared the ground. (This included canvassing India's support and good offices to promote Austria's cause with the Soviet Union.) There were strategic as well as diplomatic advantages for the Soviets in conceding Austria's neutralization at this time. For as well as conforming with the post-Stalin 'new look'—a diplomacy which was seeking a *détente* with Tito and improved relations with Asian neutralists—there were strategic advantages for the Soviet Union in thus separating two N.A.T.O. powers (Italy and West Germany) and seeing the Swiss-Austrian wedge of neutral territory hindering the logistic consolidation of N.A.T.O. And Austria's neutralization entailed the transfer of 5,000 American troops from Salzburg to south of the Brenner.

The process which swiftly produced Austria's neutralization began with Mr Molotov's speech to the Supreme Soviet at the beginning of March 1955, when he declared that delay in concluding an Austrian State Treaty was unjustified but that guarantees must be found against another Anschluss and against Austria's participation in any alliance before the treaty could be signed. Later he amplified these remarks to Austria's ambassador in Moscow, making it clear that agreement between the powers about Germany was no longer regarded by the Soviet government as an indispensable prerequisite to any settlement of Austria's status. At the end of March the Austrian Federal Chancellor was invited to Moscow and an Austrian delegation duly arrived there on 12th April where, after two days' negotiations, a memorandum was signed on 15th April by which Austria: agreed to make a declaration "in a form imposing upon Austria an international obligation, that Austria will maintain permanent neutrality of the same type as that maintained by Switzerland";[1] agreed to delivery of goods to the U.S.S.R. in payment of the value of the Soviet enterprises in Austria to be transferred in accordance with the Austrian State Treaty; agreed that Austria should pay (one million tons of crude oil annually for ten years) for the transfer of oil properties belonging to the U.S.S.R. in Austria, and in United States dollars for the transfer of the assets of the Soviet-held Danube Shipping Company in eastern Austria; and, agreed that the two countries should conclude trade, barter and payments agreements to last, in the first instance, for five years. Exactly one month later the Foreign Ministers of the four occupying powers signed in Vienna the Austrian State Treaty providing for the establishment of a sovereign and democratic Austria within the frontiers of 1938. An Anschluss was forbidden and the rights of non-German minorities were guaranteed. Austria was allowed to keep an army of whatever size it wished, but atomic and other special weapons were forbidden. There were to be no reparations but the onerous terms of the Moscow Memorandum were to be fulfilled by Austria.

[1] Mr. Molotov's oft-repeated comparison of Austria's position with Switzerland was inexact. Switzerland suffers no constitutional or international limitation on the kind of armaments it can possess, as Austria does in Article 13 of the State Treaty. But such a limitation has not, traditionally, been regarded as incompatible with neutralization. In 1914 Luxembourg was forbidden to keep a standing army. It is interesting to note that two years later Mr. Mikoyan was recommending to Austrian leaders that they should follow the model of Finnish neutrality, stressing that whenever he referred to Austrian neutrality he meant 'a neutrality without any reservations whatever'. *Daily Telegraph*, 23 April 1957.

These two instruments, together with the Constitutional Law of Neutrality of 26th October 1955[1]—which came into force and was given international publicity on 5th November 1955—regulate Austria's new international status. General international recognition of this new status was soon forthcoming, and in December 1955 Austria was one of sixteen states admitted to the United Nations under the East-West package deal. On a strict reading of the Charter, and one that prevailed at the San Francisco Conference in 1945, neutrality and United Nations membership are incompatible; but a more flexible interpretation allows that the Charter admits neutrality by implication.[2] In line with this latter view a leading Austrian international lawyer has argued, plausibly, that by the time Austria was admitted to the United Nations her neutrality had already received almost universal recognition and that in consequence members are obliged to respect this status if sanctions are invoked. The then Austrian State Secretary for Foreign Affairs, Dr Bruno Kreisky, defined the official Austrian conception of neutrality in an article he wrote for a leading American journal:
‘ . . .

(1) A neutral country cannot join a military alliance in time of peace because in so doing it would destroy its ability to remain neutral in time of war.

(2) Similarly, a neutral country must bar foreign military bases from its territory, since they would diminish its former freedom of action—or rather non-action—in time of war.

(3) A neutral country must not accept any obligations—political, economic or other—which would tend to impair its neutrality in wartime'[3]

[1] The neutrality declaration which became an integral part of the Constitution on 5 November 1955 contained the following passage: 'For the purpose of the lasting maintenance of her independence externally, and for the purpose of the inviolability of her territory, Austria declares of her own free will her perpetual neutrality. Austria will maintain and defend this with all means at her disposal. For the securing of this purpose in all future times Austria will not join any military alliances and will not permit the establishment of any foreign military bases on her territory.'

[2] In Articles 43 (3) and 48 (1) where member states may be called upon to act for the maintenance of international peace and security as the Security Council may determine; it is arguable that in certain circumstances a state may be excluded from these provisions.

[3] Bruno Kreisky, 'Austria Draws the Balance' in *Foreign Affairs*, January 1959, pp. 269–81.

Dr Kreisky maintained that Austria's permanent neutrality was a question of Hobson's choice if Austria was to become independent: "To venture out into the open without having sought shelter with one of the blocs seemed fraught with grave consequences. Whatever the merit of this argument, it had the flaw of pre-supposing a choice between neutrality and the *status quo*. At no time could we choose between neutrality and alignment with a bloc. And in fact what did the *status quo* amount to? Was it not itself a form of passive neutralization—neutralization by occupation? Under the circumstances, what alternative was open to a nation which longed to be master once again of its own destiny?"

Nevertheless, the Austrians have shown great skill in making a friend of necessity and in evolving a form of diplomacy which is, perhaps surprisingly, more like that of Sweden than of their Western neighbour, Switzerland. By joining the Council of Europe, like Sweden and unlike Switzerland, Austria openly demonstrated its affinities with the West. However, as a vital condition of her continued independence, she has been scrupulous in the maintenance of her military and diplomatic neutrality between both blocs; providing a neutral stage for international conferences of all political complexions; performing neutral good offices during and after the Hungarian Revolution, despite strained relations with neighbouring Communist states; and protesting strongly at the violation of Austrian air space by American military transport planes *en route* southwards during the crisis in Jordan and Lebanon in the summer of 1958.

In dealing with these difficulties, Austrian leaders have shown considerable diplomatic skill, a skill which is equally evident in the way Austria manages to keep on generally favourable terms with both super-powers. Since 1945 relations with the United States have been consistently amicable. In addition to vital American economic aid, given during the nine years of occupation, subsequently the United States Export-Import Bank has advanced substantial loans for developing Austria's iron industry. Only two relatively minor, and related, issues have threatened to impair relations. These were the question of the settlement of the claims of American oil companies whose properties were confiscated by Hitler's Germany in 1938, and the question of the release of 2,000 million schillings

in counterpart funds held in a blocked account to the credit of
the United States. Both of these issues were settled, virtually, by
the end of 1959. Equally, and in sharp contrast to the pre-1955
period, there has been marked evidence since 1955 of official
Austro-Russian cordiality. The visit of Mr Mikoyan in April
1957 was an undoubted success and produced a Soviet promise
that Austrian deliveries of oil to Russia would be reduced,
provided trade in general between the two countries continued
to rise. In the following year the Russians agreed to reduce by
one half Austrian oil delivery obligations under the State
Treaty. The Russians, who had never had vital need of Austrian
crude oil, now seemed more interested in stimulating Danubian
trade and in underlining the power of 'the Austrian example'.
Mr Khrushchev's eight-day official visit to Austria in July 1960
produced some further, though small, economic concessions by
the Soviets. But the Austrians had to suffer Mr Khrushchev's
frequent sallies into the delicate field of defining Austria's international status. Their distinguished visitor insisted, *inter alia*,
that if Austria were to join the Common Market, or to suffer
the passage over her territory of American rockets from Italy,
her neutrality would be violated. These embarrassing remarks
elicited from the host government a reply to the effect that it
was Austria's sovereign right to decide for itself whether or not
its neutrality was threatened or violated, and what counter-
measures to take if this occurred. While it would welcome a joint
guarantee of its territorial integrity by all four powers, it could
not agree to such a guarantee by one power only. Even so, the
Austrians wisely realize that it is in their every interest to do all
they can to agree with Soviet claims that peaceful and profitable
relations can be maintained between a 'bourgeois' and a
'socialist' state. . . .

Undoubtedly, however, economic ties and sentiment, as well
as long intertwined histories, make Western Germany the most
important of Austria's neighbours. The Austrian State Treaty,
the chief 'charter' of neutralized Austria, expressly forbids "all
agreements having the effect, either directly or indirectly, of
promoting political or economic union with Germany". As the
majority of Austrian industries are *grossdeutsch* by tradition and
interest, and as Germany is the most important customer and
supplier in Austria's close overall links with the six European

Common Market countries,[1] it seems that the government's reason for joining the 'Outer Seven' of the European Free Trade Association was based not on economic considerations, but rather because of a strict regard for Austria's neutral status.

If non-Communist Europe is really to congeal into two separate economic blocs, then Austria, like Switzerland, will find herself separated from her main markets. And in terms of the Cold War as well as of Western European rivalries, the political and economic factors converge to emphasize that Austria, more than Switzerland, is at the blocked crossroads of Europe: "The eastern frontier of the Common Market, just like the western frontier of the Soviet bloc, cuts across the natural trade routes of central Europe. Since these are political as well as economic frontiers, they leave no room for a stable position for a country placed as Austria is. Austria's problem of association probably cannot be really settled until the relationships between western and eastern Europe changes, and what used to be central Europe can, in some form, come into existence again. Until then, the Austrians can only improvise." The task of working out an association with the Common Market without seriously impairing her permanently neutral status, especially in Soviet eyes, is a task to tax all the Austrian powers of improvisation.

Though analogies between Austria and Germany are often made, there are many reasons why 'the Austrian example' of neutralization is far from suggesting a clear precedent for Germany, despite the attractions of this idea for some Germans. The most compelling differences are that Austria has a population of seven million while there would be over seventy million in a neutral Germany, made up of the two Germanies of today; Austria's is an armed neutrality with no limit on the size of her army—a freedom hardly likely to be granted to a 'neutralized' Germany. Moreover, Germany cannot be compared to a small, unambitious state with no revisionist demands or ability to impose its will on others. Even if Germany stayed aloof from Cold War entanglements, its neighbours would be concerned over its foreign policy to an extent which would make neutraliza-

[1] In 1959 50% of Austria's exports went to Common Market countries; and between 50% and 60% of her imports came from these countries. 26% of her exports went to Western Germany.

tion an essentially unreal status. As long as Germany is divided, the fact of division is likely to deter increases in the strength of the old *Alldeutsch* impulses within Austria towards a new *Anschluss*—though Professor Wiskemann maintains that there are signs that such sentiments are still present in the Tyrol, Salzburg and in Styria. . . .

Few would now dispute the contention of Herr Raab, the Austrian Chancellor, who during his visit to Moscow in July 1958 said that "the overwhelming majority of Austrians today favour this neutrality, and it is increasingly realized that we took the right decision for our future." It may be that the old tag of Imperial days—"Felix Austria"—has again become appropriate. Less than eight years after the Austrian State Treaty the internal aspect seems as propitious as her external relations. But both are delicately poised. The example of Switzerland and Sweden suggests that a successful neutral needs, as well as restraint and care in her external relations, national unity and stability in internal politics, undoubted viability in economic life and military strength sufficient to deter a would-be aggressor from achieving easy conquest. To date, Austrian leaders have amply shown their diplomatic skills, but it is too early to be confident of the country's national unity or its economic strength, and its puny defences have already caused its military leaders much disquiet.[1]

*

The next two documents are concerned with nonalignment; its professed principles, and its embodiment in Indian foreign policy at the end of the Korean War. The Belgrade Conference of September 1961 was the first big gathering of specifically nonaligned states, although many of its members had taken part in the Conference of Afro-Asian states at Bandung in 1955. (The Bandung Conference, however, had contained a number of strongly anti-communist states like Japan and the Philippines,

---

[1] The strength of the Austrian army varies between 35,000 and 55,000 men, owing to the nine-month conscription period. By April 1961 some 110,000 trained reservists were available. It was reported in 1958 (though by September 1961 neither had been achieved) that in order to provide some effective protection of neutrality the Austrian government proposed 'to build up a strong protective fighter unit and also to obtain the revision of clause 13 of the Austrian Treaty, which prohibits the possession of anti-aircraft missiles'. Quoted from Lajos Lederer, 'Austria's Arms Talks with Russia' in the *Observer*, 12 October 1958.

and two communist states, North Vietnam and China.) Document 30 gives an abridged version of the Declaration that emerged from this Conference. There is a good deal of platitude in this Declaration, most of which has been omitted here, but it does convey something of the attitudes and reasoning that this large group of states is willing to subscribe to publicly. It is instructive to contrast the clear-cut stand on colonial issues such as Algeria or Angola with the innocuous statement on the representation of China. What does nonalignment mean in the cold war if it does not include support for the representation of communist as well as anti-communist states in the United Nations? Yet paragraph 26 of the second part of this Declaration refrains from committing the Conference as a whole to Chinese representation, and claims to speak only for those members of the Conference who recognize Peking, implying that there are others that do not.

DOCUMENT 30. Extracts from the Declaration of the Belgrade Conference of Heads of State and Government of Nonaligned Countries, 1–6 September 1961.

The Conference of Heads of State or Government of the following non-aligned countries:

1. Afghanistan	13. Indonesia
2. Algeria	14. Iraq
3. Burma	15. Lebanon
4. Cambodia	16. Mali
5. Ceylon	17. Morocco
6. Congo	18. Nepal
7. Cuba	19. Saudi Arabia
8. Cyprus	20. Somalia
9. Ethiopia	21. Sudan
10. Ghana	22. Tunisia
11. Guinea	23. United Arab Republic
12. India	24. Yemen

25. Yugoslavia

and of the following countries represented by observers:

1. Bolivia   2. Brazil   3. Ecuador

was held in Belgrade from September 1 to 6, 1961, for the purpose of exchanging views on international problems with a view to contributing more effectively to world peace and security and peaceful co-operation among peoples.

The Heads of State or Government of the aforementioned countries have met at a moment when international events have taken a turn for the worst and when world peace is seriously threatened. Deeply concerned for the future of peace, voicing the aspirations of the vast majority of people of the world, aware that, in our time, no people and no government can or should abandon its responsibilities in regard to the safeguarding of world peace, the participating countries—having examined in detail, in an atmosphere of equality, sincerity and mutual confidence, the current state of international relations and trends prevailing in the present-day world—make the following declaration: . . .

I

War has never threatened mankind with graver consequences than today. On the other hand, never before has mankind had at its disposal stronger forces for eliminating war as an instrument of policy in international relations.

Imperialism is weakening. Colonial empires and other forms of foreign oppression of peoples in Asia, Africa and Latin America are gradually disappearing from the stage of history. Great successes have been achieved in the struggle of many peoples for national independence and equality. . . .

Prompted by such developments in the world, the vast majority of people are becoming increasingly conscious of the fact that war between peoples constitutes not only an anachronism but also a crime against humanity. This awareness of peoples is becoming a great moral force, capable of exercising a vital influence on the development of international relations.

Relying on this and on the will of their peoples, the Governments of countries participating in the Conference resolutely reject the view that war, including the cold war, is inevitable, as this view reflects a sense both of helplessness and hopelessness and is contrary to the progress of the world. They affirm their unwavering faith that the international community is able to organize its life without resorting to means which actually belong to a past epoch of human history.

However, the existing military blocs, which are growing into more and more powerful military, economic and political groupings, which, by the logic and nature of their mutual relations, necessarily provoke periodical aggravations of international relations the cold war and the constant and acute danger of its being transformed into actual war have become a part of the situation prevailing in international relations. . . .

II

The present-day world is characterized by the existence of different social systems. The participating countries do not consider that these differences constitute an insurmountable obstacle for the stabilization of peace, provided attempts at domination and interference in the internal development of other peoples and nations are ruled out. . . .

Furthermore, any attempt at imposing upon peoples one social or political system or another by force and from outside is a direct threat to world peace.

The participating countries consider that under such conditions the principles of peaceful co-existence are the only alternative to the cold war and to a possible general nuclear catastrophe. Therefore, by these principles which include the right of peoples to self-determination, to independence and to the free determination of the forms and methods of economic, social and cultural development—must be the only basis of all international relations. . . .

III   . . .

The non-aligned countries represented at this Conference do not wish to form a new bloc and cannot be a bloc. They sincerely desire to co-operate with any Government which seeks to contribute to the strengthening of confidence and peace in the world. . . .

The participants in the Conference consider that, under present conditions, the existence and the activities of non-aligned countries in the interests of peace are one of the more important factors for safeguarding world peace.

The participants in the Conference consider it essential that the non-aligned countries should participate in solving outstanding international issues concerning peace and security in the world as none of them can remain unaffected by or indifferent to these issues.

They consider that the further extensions of the non-committed area of the world constitutes the only possible and indispensable alternative to the policy of total division of the world into blocs, and intensification of cold war policies. The non-aligned countries provide encouragement and support to all peoples fighting for their independence and equality.

The participants in the Conference are convinced that the emergence of newly-liberated countries will further assist in narrowing of the area of bloc antagonisms and thus encourage all tendencies aimed at strengthening peace and promoting peaceful co-operation among independent and equal nations.

1. The participants in the Conference solemnly reaffirm their support to the "Declaration on the Granting of Independence to Colonial Countries and Peoples", adopted at the 15th Session of the General Assembly of the United Nations and recommend the immediate unconditional, total and final abolition of colonialism and resolved to make a concerted effort to put an end to all types of new colonialism and imperialist domination in all its forms and manifestations. . . .

3. The participating countries consider the struggle of the people of Algeria for freedom, self-determination and independence, and for the integrity of its national territory including the Sahara, to be just and necessary and are, therefore, determined to extend to the people of Algeria all the possible support and aid. The Heads of State or Government are particularly gratified that Algeria is represented at this Conference by its rightful representative, the Prime Minister of the Provisional Government of Algeria.

4. The participating countries draw attention with great concern to the developments in Angola and to the intolerable measures of repression taken by the Portuguese colonial authorities against the people of Angola and demand that an immediate end should be put to any further shedding of blood of the Angolan people, and the people of Angola should be assisted by all peace-loving countries, particularly member

states of the United Nations, to establish their free and independent state without delay. . . .

6. The participating countries demand the immediate evacuation of French armed forces from the whole of the Tunisian territory in accordance with the legitimate right of Tunisia to the exercise of its full national sovereignty. . . .

8. The participants in the Conference resolutely condemn the policy of apartheid practised by the Union of South Africa and demand the immediate abandonment of this policy. They further state that the policy of racial discrimination anywhere in the world constitutes a grave violation of the Charter of the United Nations and the Universal Declaration of Human Rights. . . .

10. The participants in the Conference condemn the imperialist policies pursued in the Middle East, and declare their support for the full restoration of all the rights of the Arab people of Palestine in conformity with the Charter and resolutions of the United Nations.

11. The participating countries consider the establishment and maintenance of foreign military bases in the territories of other countries, particularly against their express will, a gross violation of the sovereignty of such States. They declare their full support to countries who are endeavouring to secure the vacation of these bases. They call upon those countries maintaining foreign bases to consider seriously their abolition as a contribution to world peace.

12. They also acknowledge that the North American military base at Guantanamo, Cuba, to the permanence of which the Government and people of Cuba have expressed their opposition, affects the sovereignty and territorial integrity of that country. . . .

18. The participants in the Conference urge the Great Powers to sign without further delay a treaty for general and complete disarmament in order to save mankind from the scourge of war and to release energy and resources now being spent on armaments to be used for the peaceful economic and social development of all mankind. The participating countries also consider that:

(a) The non-aligned Nations should be represented at all further world conferences on disarmament;

(b) All discussions on disarmament should be held under the auspices of the United Nations;

(c) General and complete disarmament should be guaranteed by an effective system of inspection and control, the teams of which should include members of non-aligned Nations.

19. The participants in the Conference consider it essential that an agreement on the prohibition of all nuclear and thermo-nuclear tests should be urgently concluded. With this aim in view, it is necessary that negotiations be immediately resumed, separately or as part of negotiations on general disarmament. Meanwhile, the moratorium on the testing of all nuclear weapons should be resumed and observed by all countries. . . .

26. Those of the countries participating in the Conference who recognize the Government of the People's Republic of China recommend that the General Assembly in its forth-coming Session should accept the representatives of the Government of the People's Republic of China as the only legitimate representatives of that country in the United Nations.

*

India had been practising nonalignment long before the Belgrade Conference, in fact before even Bandung. Indian mediation played an important part in both the Korean armistice arrangements of 1953 and the Geneva accords which concluded the first Indo-Chinese war in 1954. The importance of India lay in the fact that it was one of the few states which both sides in the cold war were prepared to regard as genuinely neutral. The communists regarded Sweden and Switzerland as pro-Western neutrals—with some justification, at any rate in the case of the latter (see Document 28); the Western powers likewise, and perhaps with greater justification, were not prepared to regard Poland and Czechoslovakia as impartial arbiters simply because they had abstained from taking an active part in the war; since they were clearly communist states. Thus to avoid deadlock, an Indian chairman was appointed to the Neutral Nations Repatriation Commission, of which the two Western neutrals and the two communist neutrals were made members. In the next document, a dis-tinguished student of Asian affairs generally and Indian foreign policy in particular, Michael Brecher, describes India's role as chairman of this Commission. Its job was to ensure that prisoners of war on both sides should be given an opportunity to decide whether or not to return to their countries of origin after hearing representations from their own governments. This arrangement solved a bitter dispute in the Korean armistice talks, arising out of the claim that communist prisoners held in South Korea did not want to go back to North Korea, or China, as the case may be.

DOCUMENT 31. Extracts from 'Neutralism: An Analysis' from *The New States of Asia* by Michael Brecher (Oxford University Press, 1963).

The most striking feature of India's role in the Korean truce-making settlement from 1950 onwards is the extent to which its support alternated between one side and the other. On the four major issues that arose in the Neutral Nations Repatriation Commission (NNRC), India's chairman agreed in letter with the Polish and Czech delegates to the Commission but sided with the Swiss and Swedes in action. These four examples were on: (1) the use of force at the time of repatriation of prisoners; (2) the dismantling of prisoner-of-war organizations during that period; (3) the extension of the explanation period when prisoners were being persuaded as to whether they ought to return to their homelands; and finally, (4) the ultimate disposition of the prisoners of war.

From the very outset, in June 1950, India voted for United Nations condemnation of North Korea, but it insisted throughout that North Korea ought to be heard in the Security Council. India opposed the crossing of the 38th parallel, but after all efforts to bring North and South Koreans together at the conference table seemed to be exhausted, India agreed to the crossing. India refused to condemn China as an aggressor in 1951 yet she maintained her ambulance unit in South Korea throughout the war. On the prisoner repatriation question, she drafted a resolution which favoured the Western position for the most part but with enough modifying clauses to make it palatable to the Chinese and North Koreans. As for India's role in the Neutral Nations Repatriation Commission, one finds this curious, perhaps unique, capacity to satisfy both sides on all the major issues—the positive contributions of neutralism in that case.

On the breaking-up of the prisoner-of-war organizations, India agreed that this was undesirable; on the other hand, it agreed with the Poles and Czechs that it would be desirable to segregate the leaders of these prisoner-of-war concentrations because of the trouble they were causing; then it proceeded to turn round once more and say that this would be very difficult because it would involve the use of force, and the Commission did not have enough power to do this. On the question of the right to use force, India agreed with the Polish and Czech delegates that there was nothing to prevent it in the terms of reference of the NNRC but added that the use of force was a major, substantive step and should not be taken without unanimity in the Commission. Since this was lacking, force was not used.

Another example concerns the extension of the explanation period, which was to be ninety days. The Polish and Czech members of the Commission pointed out that of the ninety days about fifty days or more were wasted because the United Nations and South Korean Commands were not acting in a way to facilitate explanations. According to the Communist delegates, 'ninety days means ninety days for explanations, and therefore, the ninety-day period ought to be extended until there were ninety full days of explanations'. The Indian chairman agreed 'because the prisoners had in reality only forty days'. 'On the other hand,' said the Swiss and Swedish delegates in effect, 'the terms of reference provide specifically for ninety days from the beginning of the explanation period; therefore, explanations must cease exactly ninety days thereafter; according to the letter of the NNRC, the ninety-day period has ended, so there must be no extension.' India agreed.

Finally, the Korean settlement provided for a return of prisoners only after a political conference took place. 'Well,' said the Polish and Czech delegates, 'the prisoners must remain in the compounds until a political conference meets [the proposed 14-power conference].' The political conference never took place. India agreed and so it could not officially transfer them to civilian status. But, unilaterally, it did restore the prisoners to the detaining sides without violating the letter of the NNRC.

Is this not a curious type of policy? Not at all. The Indian motive was clear, and I think consistent with neutralism. It was mainly to keep the Commission alive and to achieve the important objective of a Korean settlement. The phrase 'to judge every issue on its merits' does not mean to judge it, in the narrowest sense, on the merits of each tactical issue as it arises; rather, on the larger merits of reducing the level of international tension. By this unusual capacity to satisfy the four delegates to the Left and Right, India did bring off a Korean settlement. Not everybody was satisfied. But the record demonstrates that on the whole the NNRC was a major success in mediation in difficult circumstances.

The significance of the Korean episode in terms of neutralism is something else again. In so far as anyone in the Western world knew what neutralism was, and not many people did—not that many know even now—it seemed rather peculiar. To most people it was neutrality, and neutrality was isolationist. As a result of the NNRC the stigma of isolationism attaching to neutralism was terminated. People began to ask themselves the question, 'What kind of neutrality is this, when the neutral state actively intervenes in the settlement of disputes? This is not classical neutrality.' Of course it wasn't, but since neutrality and neutralism are almost identical words it was assumed that they were the same policy or status.

*

Cambodia was one of the three states that came into existence as a result of the Geneva Conference on Indo-China in 1954. The others were Laos and Vietnam. Vietnam was to be temporarily partitioned until a government for the whole country had been elected, under international supervision, which was to be not later than 1956. In fact South Vietnam, supported by the U.S.A., refused to discuss the holding of such elections, and the two segments of the country emerged as separate sovereign states. Laos and Cambodia were sovereign states from the start, and were admitted to the United Nations in 1955; but Laos was rent by three rival factions, two of them supported by the North Vietnamese and the Americans respectively, and the country was precariously neutralized, under a coalition government, in July 1962, after a protracted international conference at Geneva.

In Cambodia itself, however, Prince Sihanouk was able to establish an effective and popular régime; and his problems have been largely external. Cambodia borders on South Vietnam, Laos and Thailand. Sihanouk suspects both Thailand and South Vietnam of designs on his state; and he has found it particularly difficult to maintain his country's integrity since the outbreak of the war in Vietnam in 1960 and its escalation in the middle 'sixties. The next two documents are taken from a full-length study of Cambodia's foreign policy under Sihanouk by Michael Leifer. The first extract describes a tense incident in 1965, when Cambodia was being accused of offering sanctuary to the National Liberation Front guerrillas, and the United States was being pressed heavily to extend the war into Cambodian territory; indeed South Vietnam was already doing this on a considerable scale. Sihanouk's appeal to the American government on this occasion was successful.

The second extract is concerned with Sihanouk's long-term policy. He expects the communists to win the war, and realizes that his troubles will not be over then; indeed they may well have grown, since a united Vietnam under communist rule may be equally hostile as, and more powerful than, South Vietnam in its present form. His strategy, again, seems to be to appeal to Vietnam's more powerful ally, China. This makes Cambodia's brand of neutrality, which was originally deliberately modelled on Nehru's nonalignment policy for India, something quite different from that of any other state studied in this book.

DOCUMENT 32. Extracts from *Cambodia* by Michael Leifer (Pall Mall and Praeger, 1967).

(i) *Cambodia and the War in Viet-Nam*

On October 22, 1965, the International Control Commission in Cambodia reported to the co-chairmen on its investigations of incidents along the border of South Viet-Nam and Cambodia. It stated that Cambodia had reported 206 such incidents in 1963, 275 in 1964, and 385 up to May 31, 1965 (the date the report ended). Regarding eight major incidents between May, 1964, and May, 1965, the Commission "found conclusive evidence in these incidents that the armed forces of the Republic of South Viet-Nam were responsible for these violations. The Commission is also convinced that none of these incidents was provoked by the Royal Government of Cambodia."

These border clashes arose from the South Vietnamese conviction that Cambodian territory was being used by the Viet-Cong, either as a sanctuary or as a means of communication, through which reinforcements could be introduced into South Viet-Nam from North Viet-Nam. The Cambodian Government has periodically invited correspondents of leading American newspapers to test for themselves the validity of such charges. While they cannot establish or deny the truth about the presence of mobile Viet-Cong bands that are believed to retreat, when pressed, into the difficult terrain of the border provinces, they have been able to check map references quoted by South Vietnamese and American sources indicating major bases. *The New York Times* correspondent Seymour Topping reported in October, 1965:

> ... There are some remote jungle areas of the Cambodian-Viet-Nam border that are impossible to check for Viet-Cong activity and it is doubtful that even the Phnom Penh Government knows what transpires there. ... Viet-Cong guerrillas are known to slip occasionally into Cambodian frontier areas to evade pursuit or to outflank some Vietnamese position. It would be impossible for an army 20 times the size of the Cambodian force of 30,000 men to close the border to such forays.

While Topping was prepared to admit this degree of infiltration, he found no evidence to substantiate the charge that Cambodia served as a base for major Viet-Cong activity. Indeed, he confidently asserted: "It is the consensus of Western diplomats and independent observers stationed in Cambodia that the country is not a major sanctuary or a major route for the delivery of military equipment and supplies to the Viet-Cong. This was also the prevailing view among American officials posted in Phnom Penh prior to the severance of diplomatic relations."

The following month, however, there was increasing evidence that the Viet-Cong was using Cambodian territory in the manner that Topping admitted. After a major clash in the Ia Drang Valley, between Viet-Cong and troops of the United States First Cavalry, it was suggested that the remnants of the defeated Viet-Cong force had retreated over the Cambodian border. At the end of November, U.S. Under-Secretary of State U. Alexis Johnson revealed that part of Cambodian territory was being watched by United States aircraft and that they were authorized to return fire if attacked. This announcement coincided with renewed charges by the governments of Thailand and South Viet-Nam that North Vietnamese lines of infiltration passed through Cambodia. To the hypersensitive Cambodians, these were alarming developments. They had no desire to see a reunited Communist Viet-Nam; nor were they willing to become the victims of attempts by those opposing the Communists to seal off their frontiers.

The Cambodian Government demonstrated its nervousness time and time again in reaction to what it considered pointers to action by its neighbors with possible American backing. At the end of November, 1965, for example, Joseph Alsop claimed in the *New York Herald Tribune* that Cambodia was supplying the Viet-Cong with Chinese arms through the port of Sihanoukville. Cambodia vehemently denied this charge and proposed to the president of the International Control Commission that his organization ensure strict control of landings at Sihanoukville and make public its findings. In May, 1966, *New York Times* correspondent C. L. Sulzberger aroused Cambodian ire by claiming that a Viet-Cong supply route called the "Sihanouk Road" passed from Laos through the province of Stung Treng.[1]

Cambodian fears had been intensified following a State Department announcement that military commanders had the authority to take action to protect their forces. This announcement was interpreted in Cambodia as a green light to "violate our frontiers and exercise on our territory the alleged right of hot pursuit under the fallacious pretext of self-defense." The United States Government, itself anxious to prevent Cambodia from becoming involved in the Viet-Nam War, accordingly began to realize that its announcement of the right to pursue Viet-Cong units across the Cambodian border had only aggravated the situation. Calmer counsel prevailed, and the United States officially recognized that Cambodia was not conniving with the Viet-Cong, but that it had a difficult task in

[1] [Original note.] The *New York Times*, 2 May 1966. This charge was refuted by Harrison Salisbury, another correspondent of the same newspaper, 10 June 1966.

seeking to patrol a long inhospitable frontier region. At the same time, it clarified its announced policy of hot pursuit: A government spokesman said that American troops would not trespass across the frontier, but "only return fire in tactical situations."

(ii) *Sihanouk's view of the future* encompasses a Communist success in Viet-Nam and Chinese political dominance in Southeast Asia. His ultimate hopes for the future viability of Cambodia are founded on two premises: (1) that historic differences, rather than ideological affinity, will determine the relationship to be established between China and a reunited Viet-Nam; and (2) that China, conscious of the contagion of polycentrism and the subordination of Marxism-Leninism to national interests, will not wish to see a powerful Viet-Nam develop at the expense of the other Indochinese nations. Sihanouk expects that China, in its own interests, will seek to interpose its power and political presence between Cambodia and Viet-Nam. Only a direct quotation can convey the intensity with which this hope is expressed:

> La Chine, c'est en effet le synonyme de la survie du Cambodge (et pour l'instant même de la monarchie Khmer) dans l'indépendence, la paix, l'intégrité territoriale. Si nous éloignons de la Chine, nous sommes devôrés par les vauteurs que sont les eternels avaleurs de terre Khmère.

For Cambodia, a close and harmonious association with China is absolutely vital, but such an association must be based on mutual convenience, not sentiment. Sihanouk has never deluded himself on this point. For Cambodia, the value of the association will depend on the unwillingness of China to sacrifice the smaller state's vital interests for some gain. As long as China is prepared and able to exercise restraint over the Vietnamese and, of course, the Thais, Cambodian policy toward China will be based on reciprocity. Indeed, such would appear to be the essence of policy toward a number of smaller states that have no direct national interest in Cambodia. Reciprocation toward China will continue to involve support for Chinese diplomatic positions, which is of some value coming from a non-Communist state. If China begins to treat Cambodia like a dispensable piece of real estate, mutual relations can be expected to alter. It is, however, questionable that, in such a case, Cambodia will be able to exercise any control over the situation. Without the ability to invoke countervailing power, Cambodia is dependent on Chinese good will.

One indication of Cambodia's apprehension over its future relationship with China concerns its northern and western frontiers. Cambodia is genuinely afraid that China, which now sponsors the Thailand Patriotic Front, will seek increasingly to persuade the Thais of the virtues of a neutral or pro-Communist posture. Cambodia would like to see a genuinely neutral Thailand, free of American military bases and free of the pernicious and troublesome Khmer Serai. Yet it is alarmed by the prospect of a Thailand associated with China, a prospect more likely if ever the United States feels obliged to remove its military establishment from South Viet-Nam. The Thai Government would then, according to Sihanouk, adopt a so-called traditional policy of accommodation to the prevailing wind. In such circumstances, Thailand may be accorded a more benign regard by Peking than is Cambodia. Cambodians still fear that Thailand will eventually seek to retrieve those provinces the French restored to Cambodia in 1946. Cambodia is thus of two minds about Thailand. For cultural and political reasons, Sihanouk would like to establish a *modus vivendi* with the Thais, since Cambodians do not regard Thais with the same racial animosity as they do the Vietnamese. . . . On the other hand, if Cambodian leaders were to choose between having Thailand as a neighbor aligned with China or with the United States, they would probably opt for the latter. In this way, Thailand's irredentist designs may be checked by continuing Chinese support for Cambodian territorial integrity against a mutual enemy.

For the time being, Cambodia remains perched in precarious fashion on the sidelines of a war that still threatens to engulf it, and the outcome of which may give Cambodians no satisfaction. It also has to face the periodic harassment of neighbors aligned with the West who distrust Cambodia for past and present associations. Through determined, if unconventional, leadership, it has been able to avoid the cauldron of conflict. Through a policy that combines long-term priorities and pragmatic, day-to-day decisions, it has preserved an independent existence—no mean achievement in the environment of Indochina. This existence is still tenuous, and the danger is far from removed that the modern Khmer State will suffer the same unfortunate fate as its illustrious forebear.

Postscript

The documents that appear in this book can amount to no more than an introduction to the history of neutrality in the twentieth century. Of necessity, only a few of the countries that remained neutral, or tried to, in the two world wars, have been represented. The cases of Greece, the Netherlands and Turkey in the First World War, and of Eire, Iran, the Low Countries, Portugal, Spain and Turkey, in the Second, would all have provided interesting material; so would the policies of the Latin-American states in both wars, and in the Bolivia-Paraguay conflict in the middle years of the League, which for some of them, at any rate, was more comparable to the examples found here because of the proximity of the fighting. Again, out of the vast array of states which have professed nonalignment in the last twenty years, only two cases are documented in this book. Moreover, any one of the historical cases examined here will look different in the eyes of another writer, or of one of the statesmen concerned; and only the theme of Belgian neutralization up to 1914, and to a lesser extent the policies of the United States between 1914 and 1940, have been illustrated from a variety of viewpoints.

Any general conclusions drawn from this material must then be tentative. If they fit the cases examined here, and as presented here, they should stimulate the reader to explore and test them against the many other cases that have had to be omitted, and against different versions of the same events.

Perhaps the most interesting question for debate is how far President Wilson's prophecy of 1917, that 'Neutrality is no longer feasible or desirable where the peace of the world is involved' (see Document 12(b)) has been borne out by the history of the last fifty years. The Second World War seemed to prove its truth; would-be neutrals with one or two exceptions were swept into the war. The cold war and the invention of nuclear weapons transformed the setting of world politics, and it is difficult to see whether they have made the neutral more or less vulnerable than the committed. The only sensible thing to do about a third world war is to avert it. The controversy is over whether it is best averted by detachment or deterrence.

Happily, another world war now looks highly unlikely for the foreseeable future. But as the cold war recedes, local wars will persist, and in those local wars the outside world, including the states neighbouring on the belligerents, must either intervene on one side or other or remain neutral. So long as China is excluded from the United Nations, any intervention by the latter body could not be genuinely collective, at least in any area of interest to the Chinese; and a less than collective intervention might simply increase the risk of extending the war.

There remains neutrality, in one of its forms. There are signs that neutralization as a technique for handling indirect conflicts between major powers may be coming back into vogue again; it has already been tried in Austria (1955) and, less successfully, in Laos (1962); it could be the way out in Vietnam. Apart from this, voluntary neutrality of third states in local wars can obviously be salutary if it leads to mediation, or the participation of the neutral in a United Nations peacekeeping force. Even if the third state cannot make its neutrality positive, being neutral may well be the least unsatisfactory course of action open to it, both for itself, and for the world as a whole.

My tentative conclusion then is that neutrality, far from being an anachronism, is a condition that states are likely to find themselves in, by accident or design, with increasing frequency in the last third of this century. This will not, I think, be a status governed very meticulously by the international law of neutrality; that law is out of date and not in very high repute among many of the new states that are likely to be among the belligerents; and the documents presented in this book show that it was never strictly respected even by the parties to the Hague Conventions that defined its rules. The neutrality that we are likely to see will, then, be a somewhat messy neutrality; its rules may be improvised, and the powerful may be able to disregard them. But there will persist, if I am right, a reluctance of third parties to involve themselves in others' conflicts, which may well lead to a dampening down of those conflicts; and that, even at the cost of some injustice, may be no bad thing.

Select Bibliography

Much useful material about neutrality can be found scattered among the leading journals devoted to international relations, e.g. *International Affairs* and *International Relations* in Britain, and *Foreign Affairs* and *International Organization* in the United States. In addition, the publications of the Campaign for Nuclear Disarmament, and of its offshoot CUCAND, although they tend to be partisan, often make valuable contributions to the subject. Relevant books on the subject include:

BLACK, C. E., FALK, R. A., KNORR, K. and YOUNG, O. R., *Neutralization and World Politics*, Princeton University Press, 1968. A study of the system of neutralization.

BORCHARD, E. and LAGE, W. P., *Neutrality for the United States*, New Haven: Yale University Press, 1937, 1940. Useful as a study of the period before 1940.

BRECHER, MICHAEL, *India in World Politics*, London: Oxford University Press, 1968. A study which concentrates heavily on Krishna Menon's views.

BULL, HEDLEY, *The Control of the Arms Race*, London: Weidenfeld & Nicolson for the Institute of Strategic Studies, 1961. Chapter IV sets out the case against British neutrality.

CAMMAERTS, EMILE, *Albert of Belgium*, London: Ivor Nicholson & Watson, 1935. Valuable account of Belgium's unusual status as a neutralized state.

CRABB, CECIL VAN, *The Elephants and the Grass*, New York: Praeger, 1965; London: Pall Mall, 1965.

FOX, ANNETTE BAKER, *The Power of Small States*, University of Chicago Press, 1959. Outstanding source on the Second World War.

GARNER, J. W., *International Law and the World War*, London, Longmans, 1920. Difficult to obtain, but worth while.

JANSEN, G. H., *Afro-Asia and Nonalignment*, London, Faber, 1966. An attack on nonalignment by an Indian, following the Sino-Indian conflict of 1962.

JESSUP, PHILIP S. (ed.), *Neutrality: Its History, Economics and Law*, New York: Columbia University Press, 1935, Oxford University Press, 1936. Account of the more general aspects of neutrality.

LEIFER, MICHAEL, *Cambodia*, New York: Praeger, 1967; London, Pall

Mall, 1967. Illuminating account of the foreign policy of a non-aligned state. (Compare this with the views put forward in Michael Brecher's book.)

LYON, PETER, *Neutralism*, Leicester University Press, 1963. Useful general study of neutralism since 1945.

MARTIN, L. W. (ed.), *Neutralism and Nonalignment*, New York: Praeger, 1962; London: Pall Mall, 1963. General account of neutrality from the American point of view.

OAKES, SIR AUGUSTUS and MOWAT, R. B., *The Great European Treaties of the Nineteenth Century*, Oxford: Clarendon Press, 1918. Survey of the heyday of neutrality.

OGLEY, R., 'Bell, Bull and Canon' in *International Relations*, April 1965. The case for British neutrality.

ØRVIK, NILS, *The Decline of Neutrality, 1914–41*, Oslo: Grundt Tanum, 1953. The best book about neutrality in the earlier part of this century. (This work is being reprinted by Frank Cass and will be available in 1970.)

SIMS, NICHOLAS A., *Neutralism and International Conflict*, London: Colleges and Universities Campaign for Nuclear Disarmament (CUCAND), July 1966. The case for mediation.

TOYNBEE, ARNOLD and VERONICA M. (eds.), *A Volume of the Survey of International Affairs, 1939–46: The War and the Neutrals*, London: Oxford University Press for the R.I.I.A., 1956; and *A Volume of the Survey of International Affairs, 1939–46: The Initial Triumph of the Axis*, London: Oxford University Press for the R.I.I.A., 1958. The first mentioned book contains detailed case studies of almost all European neutrals in the Second World War. The latter work gives detailed accounts of the failure of many European states in their attempts to remain neutral.

WALTERS, F. P., *A History of the League of Nations*, London: Oxford University Press for the R.I.I.A., 1952. Account of the tension between collective security and neutrality at the time of the League of Nations.

YOUNG, O. R., *The Intermediaries*, Princeton University Press, 1967. An account of the processes of mediation.

Subject Index

For Product Safety Concerns and Information please contact our EU
representative GPSR@taylorandfrancis.com
Taylor & Francis Verlag GmbH, Kaufingerstraße 24, 80331 München, Germany